YAMAHA

XT125-250 • 1980-1984
SERVICE • REPAIR • MAINTENANCE

By

RON WRIGHT

ALAN AHLSTRAND

Editor

CLYMER PUBLICATIONS

*World's largest publisher of books devoted exclusively
to automobiles and motorcycles*

A division of INTERTEC PUBLISHING CORPORATION
P.O. Box 12901, Overland Park, Kansas 66212

FIRST EDITION
First Printing December, 1984
Second Printing July, 1985

SECOND EDITION
Revised by Ron Wright to include 1984 models
First Printing August, 1987
Second Printing May, 1989

Printed in U.S.A.

ISBN: 0-89287-370-1

MOTORCYCLE INDUSTRY COUNCIL

Technical Assistance from Richard Eanes.
Technical illustrations by Steve Amos.
Technical and photographic assistance by Brian Slark and Curt Jordan.

COVER: Photographed by Michael Brown Photographic Productions, Los Angeles, California. Motorcycle ridden by Tim Lunde. Helmet courtesy of Simpson Sports, Torrance, California. Esprit boots courtesy of Wheelsport, Inc. Motorcycle courtesy of Bill Krause Sportcycles, Inglewood, California.

CONTENTS

CHAPTER TEN
BRAKES 225

CHAPTER ELEVEN
FRAME AND REPAINTING 231

SUPPLEMENT
1984 SERVICE INFORMATION 233

QUICK REFERENCE DATA

MAINTENANCE SCHEDULE*

Every 300 miles (500 km) or as needed	Lubricate and adjust drive chain
First 600 miles (1,000 km) and first 2,500 miles (4,000 km); then every 2,000 miles (3,000 km) or 6 months	Check and adjust cam chain tension Check and adjust valve clearance Check and adjust decompression cable free play (XT250 only) Change engine oil and replace filter Clean oil strainer Clean and re-oil air filter Adjust brake free play Adjust clutch free play Check cables for fraying and lubricate
First 2,500 miles (4,000 km); then every 2,000 miles (3,000 km) or 6 months	Check exhaust system for leakage; repair as necessary Check and adjust engine idle speed
Adjust throttle cable free play if necessary	Lubricate the brake pedal shaft Lubricate clutch and brake lever pivot shafts Lubricate kick crank boss and sidestand pivot shaft Check steering for looseness Check wheel bearings for proper operation; replace if necessary Check battery specific gravity; fill as necessary
First 2,500 miles (4,000 km); then every 4,000 miles (6,000 km) or 1 year	Check crankcase ventilation hose for cracks or damage; replace hose if necessary Check emission control system (1983 California models) Check fuel line for damage; replace if necessary
Every 9,500 miles (15,000 km) or 2 years	Replace spark plug Change fork oil Lubricate rear swing arm pivot shaft Replace steering bearings

* This Yamaha factory maintenance schedule should be considered as a guide to general maintenance and lubrication intervals. Harder than normal use and exposure to mud, water, sand, high humidity, etc. will naturally dictate more frequent attention to most maintenance items.

TIRE INFLATION PRESSURE

Tire size	Air pressure
1980-1983	
Front tire	
2.75×21 (4 PR)	
Cold	18 psi (1.3 kg/cm²)
Maximum load limit[1]	18 psi (1.3 kg/cm²)
Off-road	14 psi (1.0 kg/cm²)
3.00×21 (4PR)	
Cold	18 psi (1.3 kg/cm²)
Maximum load limit[2]	22 psi (1.5 kg/cm²)
High-speed riding	22 psi (1.5 kg/cm²)
Rear tire	
100/80×17 (52P)	
Cold	22 psi (1.5 kg/cm²)
Maximum load limit[1]	26 psi (1.8 kg/cm²)
Off-road	14 psi (1.0 kg/cm²)
4.60×17 (4PR)	
Cold	22 psi (1.5 kg/cm²)
Maximum load limit[2]	26 psi (1.8 kg/cm²)
High-speed riding	26 psi (1.8 kg/cm²)
1984	
Front tire	
3.00×21 (4PR)	
Cold	18 psi (1.3 kg/cm²)
Maximum load limit[3]	22 psi (1.5 kg/cm²)
High-speed riding	22 psi (1.5 kg/cm²)
Rear tire	
4.10×18 (4PR)	
Cold	22 psi (1.5 kg/cm²)
Maximum load limit[3]	26 psi (1.8 kg/cm²)
High speed riding	26 psi (1.8 kg/cm²)

1. Maximum load limit: 201-351 lb. (91-159 kg).
2. Maximum load limit: 198-353 lb. (90-160 kg).
3. Maximum load limit: 201 lb. (91 kg).

APPROXIMATE REFILL CAPACITIES

Engine oil	
XT250	
Oil change*	1.4 qt. (1,300 cc)
Engine overhaul	1.7 qt. (1,600 cc)
XT125, XT200	
Oil change*	1.1 qt. (1,000 cc)
Engine overhaul	1.4 qt. (1,300 cc)
Front forks**	
XT125	6.50 oz. (192 cc)
XT200	8.42 oz. (250 cc)
XT250	
1980-1983	9.10 oz. (270 cc)
1984	10.9 oz. (323 cc)

* With filter change.
** Capacity for each fork leg.

TUNE-UP SPECIFICATIONS

Valve clearances
  Intake
    XT125, XT200   0.0028 in. (0.07 mm)
    XT250
      1980-1983   0.0020-0.0039 in. (0.05-0.10 mm)
      1984   0.003-0.005 in. (0.08-0.12 mm)
  Exhaust
    XT125, XT200   0.0051 in. (0.13 mm)
    XT250
      1980-1983   0.0047-0.0067 in. (0.12-0.17 mm)
      1984   0.005-0.007 in. (0.12-0.17 mm)
Compression pressure
  XT125, XT200   128-149 psi (9-10.5 kg/cm^2)
  XT250
    1980-1983   142-185 psi (10-13 kg/cm^2)
    1984   128-171 psi (9-12 kg/cm^2)
Spark plug
  Type
    XT125, XT200   NGK D8EA
                                      ND X24ES-U
    XT250
      1980-1983   NGK BP-7ES
                                      ND W22EP
      1984   NGK D8EA
                                      ND X24ES-U
  Gap
    XT125, XT200   0.024-0.028 in. (0.6-0.8 mm)
    XT250
      1980-1983   0.027-0.032 in. (0.7-0.9 mm)
      1984   0.024-0.028 in. (0.6-0.8 mm)
Torque specification   14 ft.-lb. (20 N•m)
Ignition timing   Fixed
Idle speed
  XT125   1,300 ±50 rpm
  XT200   1,250 ±50 rpm
  XT250
    1980-1983   1,200 rpm
    1984   1,350 ±50 rpm
Cylinder head fastener torque
  XT125, XT250   16 ft.-lb. (22 N•m)
  XT250 (1980-1983)
    M10   27 ft.-lb. (37 N•m)
    M8   14 ft.-lb. (20 N•m)
    M6   7 ft.-lb. (10 N•m)
  XT250 (1984)
    Flange bolt (M10)   29 ft.-lb. (40 N•m)
    Nut (M8)   14 ft.-lb. (20 N•m)
    Bolt (M6)   7 ft.-lb. (10 N•m)

RECOMMENDED LUBRICANTS

Engine oil
  Temperatures 40° and up   SAE 20W-40 SE/SF
  Temperatures below 40°   SAE 10W-30 SE/SF
Battery refilling   Distilled water
Fork oil   SAE 10 or equivalent
Cables and pivot points   Yamaha chain and cable
                                      lube or SAE 10W-30 motor oil
Air filter   Special air filter oil

Table 5 GENERAL TORQUE SPECIFICATIONS*

Item	ft.-lb.	N•m
Bolt		
6 mm	4.5	6
8 mm	11	15
10 mm	22	30
12 mm	40	55
14 mm	61	85
16 mm	94	130
Nut		
10 mm	4.5	6
12 mm	11	15
14 mm	22	30
17 mm	40	55
19 mm	61	85
22 mm	94	130

* Use these torque figures for all fasteners not individually listed.

BATTERY STATE OF CHARGE

Specific gravity	State of charge
1.110-1.130	Discharged
1.140-1.160	Almost discharged
1.170-1.190	One-quarter charged
1.200-1.220	One-half charged
1.230-1.250	Three-quarters charged
1.260-1.280	Fully charged

QUICK INDEX

YAMAHA

XT125-250 · 1980-1984
SERVICE · REPAIR · MAINTENANCE

INTRODUCTION

This detailed comprehensive manual covers all 1980-1984 Yamaha XT125-250 singles. The expert text gives complete information on maintenance, repair and overhaul. Hundreds of photos and drawings guide you through every step. This book includes all you need to know to keep your Yamaha running right.

General information on all models and specific information for 1980-1983 models is contained in Chapters One through Eleven. Specific information on 1984 models is contained in the Supplement at the end of the book

Where repairs are practical for the owner/mechanic, complete procedures are given. Equally important, difficult jobs are pointed out. Such operations are usually more economically performed by a dealer or independent garage.

A shop manual is a reference. You want to be able to find information fast. As in all Clymer books, this one is designed with this in mind. All chapters are thumb tabbed. Important items are indexed at the rear of the book. Finally, all the most frequently used specifications and capacities are summarized on the *Quick Reference* pages at the front of the book.

Keep the book handy. It will help you to better understand your Yamaha, lower repair and maintenance costs and generally improve your satisfaction with your bike.

CHAPTER ONE

GENERAL INFORMATION

The troubleshooting, maintenance, tune-up, and step-by-step repair procedures in this book are written specifically for the owner and home mechanic. The text is accompanied by helpful photos and diagrams to make the job as clear and correct as possible.

Troubleshooting, maintenance, tune-up, and repair are not difficult if you know what to do and what tools and equipment to use. Anyone of average intelligence, with some mechanical ability, and not afraid to get their hands dirty can perform most of the procedures in this book.

In some cases, a repair job may require tools or skills not reasonably expected of the home mechanic. These procedures are noted in each chapter and it is recommended that you take the job to your dealer, a competent mechanic, or a machine shop.

MANUAL ORGANIZATION

This chapter provides general information, safety and service hints. Also included are lists of recommended shop and emergency tools as well as a brief description of troubleshooting and tune-up equipment.

Chapter Two provides methods and suggestions for quick and accurate diagnosis and repair of problems. Troubleshooting procedures discuss typical symptoms and logical methods to pinpoint the trouble.

Chapter Three explains all periodic lubrication and routine maintenance necessary to keep your motorcycle running well. Chapter Three also includes recommended tune-up procedures, eliminating the need to constantly consult chapters on the various subassemblies.

Subsequent chapters cover specific systems such as the engine, transmission, and electrical system. Each of these chapters provides disassembly, inspection, repair, and assembly procedures in a simple step-by-step format. If a repair is impractical for the home mechanic it is indicated. In these cases it is usually faster and less expensive to have the repairs made by a dealer or competent repair shop. Essential specifications are included in the appropriate chapters.

When special tools are required to perform a task included in this manual, the tools are illustrated. It may be possible to borrow or rent these tools. The inventive mechanic may also be able to find a suitable substitute in his tool box, or to fabricate one.

The terms NOTE, CAUTION, and WARNING have specific meanings in this manual. A NOTE provides additional or explanatory information. A

CAUTION is used to emphasize areas where equipment damage could result if proper precautions are not taken. A WARNING is used to stress those areas where personal injury or death could result from negligence, in addition to possible mechanical damage.

SERVICE HINTS

Time, effort, and frustration will be saved and possible injury will be prevented if you observe the following practices.

Most of the service procedures covered are straightforward and can be performed by anyone reasonably handy with tools. It is suggested, however, that you consider your own capabilities carefully before attempting any operation involving major disassembly of the engine.

Some operations, for example, require the use of a press. It would be wiser to have these performed by a shop equipped for such work, rather than to try to do the job yourself with makeshift equipment. Other procedures require precision measurements. Unless you have the skills and equipment required, it would be better to have a qualified repair shop make the measurements for you.

Repairs go much faster and easier if the parts that will be worked on are clean before you begin. There are special cleaners for washing the engine and related parts. Brush or spray on the cleaning solution, let stand, then rinse it away with a garden hose. Clean all oily or greasy parts with cleaning solvent as you remove them.

WARNING
Never use gasoline as a cleaning agent. It presents an extreme fire hazard. Be sure to work in a well-ventilated area when using cleaning solvent. Keep a fire extinguisher, rated for gasoline fires, handy in any case.

Much of the labor charge for repairs made by dealers is for the removal and disassembly of other parts to reach the defective unit. It is frequently possible to perform the preliminary operations yourself and then take the defective unit in to the dealer for repair, at considerable savings.

Once you have decided to tackle the job yourself, make sure you locate the appropriate section in this manual, and read it entirely. Study the illustrations and text until you have a good idea of what is involved in completing the job satisfactorily. If special tools are required, make arrangements to get them before you start. Also, purchase any known defective parts prior to starting on the procedure. It is frustrating and time-consuming to get partially into a job and then be unable to complete it.

Simple wiring checks can be easily made at home, but knowledge of electronics is almost a necessity for performing tests with complicated electronic testing gear.

During disassembly of parts keep a few general cautions in mind. Force is rarely needed to get things apart. If parts are a tight fit, like a bearing in a case, there is usually a tool designed to separate them. Never use a screwdriver to pry apart parts with machined surfaces such as cylinder head or crankcase halves. You will mar the surfaces and end up with leaks.

Make diagrams wherever similar-appearing parts are found. You may think you can remember where everything came from — but mistakes are costly. There is also the possibility you may get sidetracked and not return to work for days or even weeks — in which interval, carefully laid out parts may have become disturbed.

Tag all similar internal parts for location, and mark all mating parts for position. Record number and thickness of any shims as they are removed. Small parts such as bolts can be identified by placing them in plastic sandwich bags that are sealed and labeled with masking tape.

Wiring should be tagged with masking tape and marked as each wire is removed. Again, do not rely on memory alone.

Disconnect battery ground cable before working near electrical connections and before disconnecting wires. Never run the engine with the battery disconnected; the alternator could be seriously damaged.

Protect finished surfaces from physical damage or corrosion. Keep gasoline and brake fluid off painted surfaces.

Frozen or very tight bolts and screws can often be loosened by soaking with penetrating oil like Liquid Wrench or WD-40, then sharply striking the bolt head a few times with a hammer and punch (or screwdriver for screws). Avoid heat unless absolutely necessary, since it may melt, warp, or remove the temper from many parts.

Avoid flames or sparks when working near a charging battery or flammable liquids, such as gasoline.

No parts, except those assembled with a press fit, require unusual force during assembly. If a part is hard to remove or install, find out why before proceeding.

Cover all openings after removing parts to keep dirt, small tools, etc., from falling in.

When assembling two parts, start all fasteners, then tighten evenly.

Wiring connections and brake shoes, drums, pads, and discs and contact surfaces in dry clutches should be kept clean and free of grease and oil.

When assembling parts, be sure all shims and washers are replaced exactly as they came out.

Whenever a rotating part butts against a stationary part, look for a shim or washer. Use new gaskets if there is any doubt about the condition of old ones. Generally, you should apply gasket cement to one mating surface only, so the parts may be easily disassembled in the future. A thin coat of oil on gaskets helps them seal effectively.

Heavy grease can be used to hold small parts in place if they tend to fall out during assembly. However, keep grease and oil away from electrical, clutch, and brake components.

High spots may be sanded off a piston with sandpaper, but emery cloth and oil do a much more professional job.

Carburetors are best cleaned by disassembling them and soaking the parts in a commercial carburetor cleaner. Never soak gaskets and rubber parts in these cleaners. Never use wire to clean out jets and air passages; they are easily damaged. Use compressed air to blow out the carburetor, but only if the float has been removed first.

Take your time and do the job right. Do not forget that a newly rebuilt engine must be broken in the same as a new one. Refer to your owner's manual for the proper break-in procedures.

SAFETY FIRST

Professional mechanics can work for years and never sustain a serious injury. If you observe a few rules of common sense and safety, you can enjoy many safe hours servicing your motorcycle. You could hurt yourself or damage the motorcycle if you ignore these rules.

1. Never use gasoline as a cleaning solvent.

2. Never smoke or use a torch in the vicinity of flammable liquids such as cleaning solvent in open containers.

3. Never smoke or use a torch in an area where batteries are being charged. Highly explosive hydrogen gas is formed during the charging process.

4. Use the proper sized wrenches to avoid damage to nuts and injury to yourself.

5. When loosening a tight or stuck nut, be guided by what would happen if the wrench should slip. Protect yourself accordingly.

6. Keep your work area clean and uncluttered.

7. Wear safety goggles during all operations involving drilling, grinding, or use of a cold chisel.

8. Never use worn tools.

9. Keep a fire extinguisher handy and be sure it is rated for gasoline (Class B) and electrical (Class C) fires.

EXPENDABLE SUPPLIES

Certain expendable supplies are necessary. These include grease, oil, gasket cement, wiping rags, cleaning solvent, and distilled water. Also, special locking compounds, silicone lubricants, and engine and carburetor cleaners may be useful. Cleaning solvent is available at most service stations and distilled water for the battery is available at supermarkets.

SHOP TOOLS

For complete servicing and repair you will need an assortment of ordinary hand tools **(Figure 1)**.

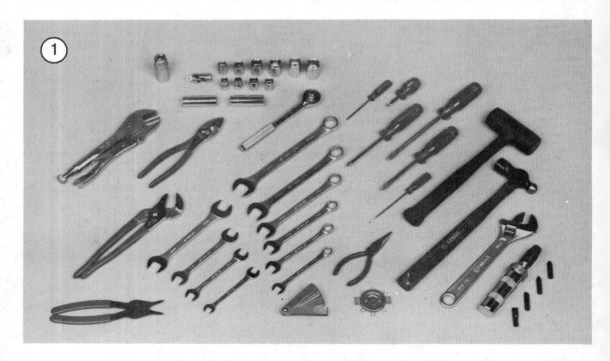

As a minimum, these include:

a. Combination wrenches
b. Sockets
c. Plastic mallet
d. Small hammer
e. Impact driver
f. Snap ring pliers
g. Gas pliers
h. Phillips screwdrivers
i. Slot (common) screwdrivers
j. Feeler gauges
k. Spark plug gauge
l. Spark plug wrench

Special tools required are shown in the chapters covering the particular repair in which they are used.

Engine tune-up and troubleshooting procedures require other special tools and equipment. These are described in detail in the following sections.

EMERGENCY TOOL KITS

Highway

A small emergency tool kit kept on the bike is handy for road emergencies which otherwise could leave you stranded. The tools and spares listed below and shown in **Figure 2** will let you handle most roadside repairs.

a. Motorcycle tool kit (original equipment)
b. Impact driver
c. Silver waterproof sealing tape (duct tape)
d. Hose-clamps (3 sizes)
e. Silicone sealer
f. Lock 'N' Seal
g. Flashlight
h. Tire patch kit
i. Tire irons
j. Plastic pint bottle (for oil)
k. Waterless hand cleaner
l. Rags for clean up

Off-Road

A few simple tools and aids carried on the motorcycle can mean the difference between walking or riding back to camp or to where repairs can be made. See **Figure 3**.

A few essential spare parts carried in your truck or van can prevent a day or weekend of trail riding from being spoiled. See **Figure 4**.

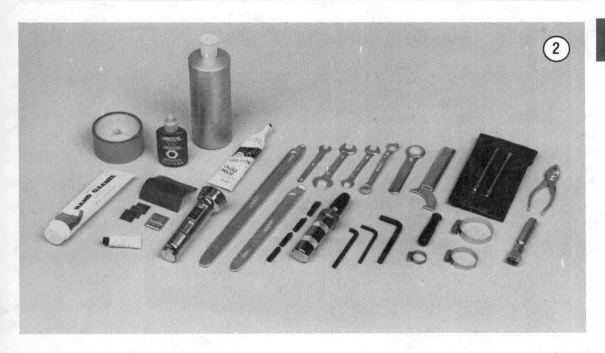

On the Motorcycle

  a. Motorcycle tool kit (original equipment)
  b. Drive chain master link
  c. Tow line
  d. Spark plug
  e. Spark plug wrench
  f. Shifter lever
  g. Clutch/brake lever
  h. Silver waterproof sealing tape (duct tape)
  i. Loctite Lock 'N' Seal

In the Truck

  a. Control cables (throttle, clutch, brake)
  b. Silicone sealer
  c. Tire patch kit
  d. Tire irons
  e. Tire pump
  f. Impact driver
  g. Oil

WARNING
Tools and spares should be carried on the motorcycle — not in clothing where a simple fall could result in serious injury from a sharp tool.

TROUBLESHOOTING AND TUNE-UP EQUIPMENT

Voltmeter, Ohmmeter, and Ammeter

For testing the ignition or electrical system, a good voltmeter is required. For motorcycle use, an instrument covering 0-20 volts is satisfactory. One which also has a 0-2 volt scale is necessary for testing relays, points, or individual contacts where voltage drops are much smaller. Accuracy should be ± ½ volt.

An ohmmeter measures electrical resistance. This instrument is useful for checking continuity (open and short circuits), and testing fuses and lights.

The ammeter measures electrical current. Ammeters for motorcycle use should cover 0-50 amperes and 0-250 amperes. These are useful for checking battery charging and starting current.

Several inexpensive VOM's (volt-ohm-milli-ammeter) combine all three instruments into one which fits easily in any tool box. See **Figure 5**. However, the ammeter ranges are usually too small for motorcycle work.

Hydrometer

The hydrometer gives a useful indication of battery condition and charge by measuring the

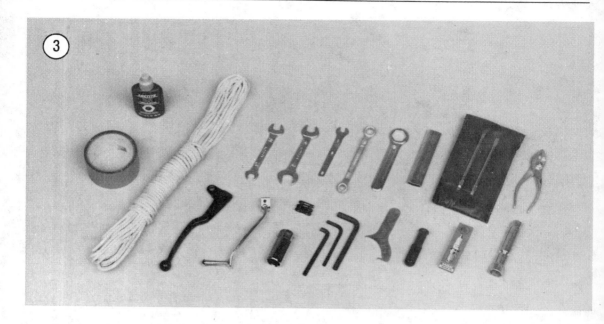

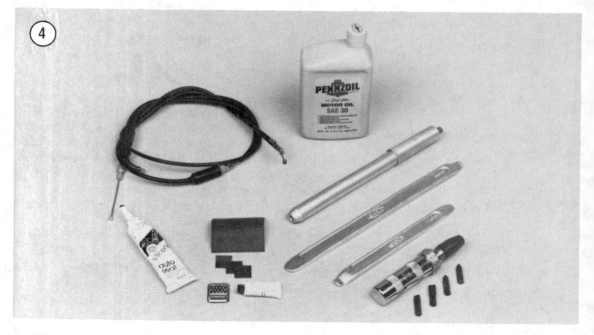

specific gravity of the electrolyte in each cell. See **Figure 6**. Complete details on use and interpretation of readings are provided in the electrical chapter.

Compression Tester

The compression tester measures the compression pressure built up in each cylinder. The results, when properly interpreted, can indicate general cylinder, ring, and valve condition. See **Figure 7**. Extension lines are available for hard-to-reach cylinders.

Dwell Meter (Contact Breaker Point Ignition Only)

A dwell meter measures the distance in degrees of cam rotation that the breaker points remain closed while the engine is running. Since

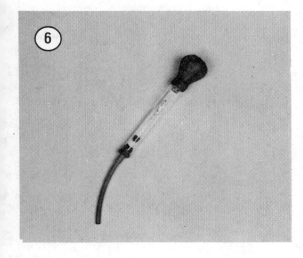

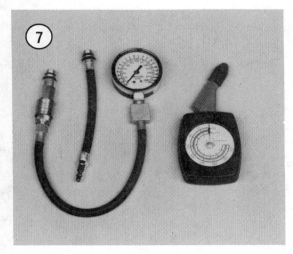

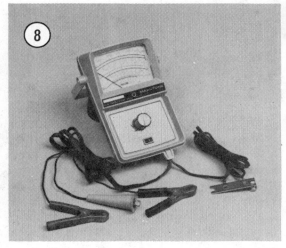

this angle is determined by breaker point gap, dwell angle is an accurate indication of breaker point gap.

Many tachometers intended for tuning and testing incorporate a dwell meter as well. See **Figure 8**. Follow the manufacturer's instructions to measure dwell.

Tachometer

A tachometer is necessary for tuning. See **Figure 8**. Ignition timing and carburetor adjustments must be performed at the specified idle speed. The best instrument for this purpose is one with a low range of 0-1,000 or 0-2,000 rpm for setting idle, and a high range of 0-4,000 or more for setting ignition timing at 3,000 rpm. Extended range (0-6,000 or 0-8,000 rpm) instruments lack accuracy at lower speeds. The instrument should be capable of detecting changes of 25 rpm on the low range.

> NOTE: *The motorcycle's tachometer is not accurate enough for correct idle adjustment.*

Strobe Timing Light

This instrument is necessary for tuning, as it permits very accurate ignition timing. The light flashes at precisely the same instant that No. 1 cylinder fires, at which time the timing marks on the engine should align. Refer to Chapter Three for exact location of the timing marks for your engine.

Suitable lights range from inexpensive neon bulb types ($2-3) to powerful xenon strobe lights ($20-40). See **Figure 9**. Neon timing lights are difficult to see and must be used in dimly lit areas. Xenon strobe timing lights can be used outside in bright sunlight.

Tune-up Kits

Many manufacturers offer kits that combine several useful instruments. Some come in a convenient carry case and are usually less expensive than purchasing one instrument at a time. **Figure 10** shows one of the kits that is available. The prices vary with the number of instruments included in the kit.

Manometer (Carburetor Synchronizer)

A manometer is essential for accurately synchronizing carburetors on multi-cylinder engines. The instrument detects intake pressure differences between carburetors and permits them to be adjusted equally. A suitable manometer costs about $25 and comes with detailed instructions for use. See **Figure 11**.

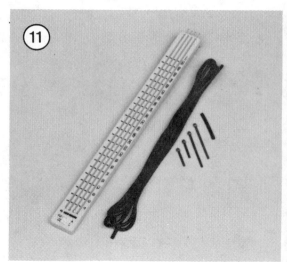

Fire Extinguisher

A fire extinguisher is a necessity when working on a vehicle. It should be rated for both *Class B* (flammable liquids — gasoline, oil, paint, etc.) and *Class C* (electrical — wiring, etc.) type fires. It should always be kept within reach. See **Figure 12**.

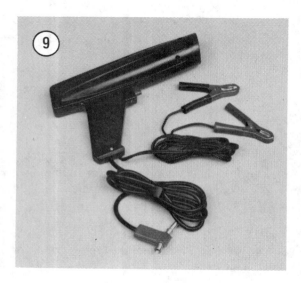

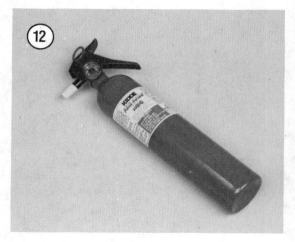

CHAPTER TWO

TROUBLESHOOTING

Troubleshooting motorcycle problems is relatively simple. To be effective and efficient, however, it must be done in a logical step-by-step manner. If it is not, a great deal of time may be wasted, good parts may be replaced unnecessarily, and the true problem may never be uncovered.

Always begin by defining the symptoms as closely as possible. Then, analyze the symptoms carefully so that you can make an intelligent guess at the probable cause. Next, test the probable cause and attempt to verify it; if it's not at fault, analyze the symptoms once again, this time eliminating the first probable cause. Continue on in this manner, a step at a time, until the problem is solved.

At first, this approach may seem to be time consuming, but you will soon discover that it's not nearly so wasteful as a hit-or-miss method that may never solve the problem. And just as important, the methodical approach to troubleshooting ensures that only those parts that are defective will be replaced.

The troubleshooting procedures in this chapter analyze typical symptoms and show logical methods for isolating and correcting trouble. They are not, however, the only methods; there may be several approaches to a given problem, but all good troubleshooting methods have one thing in common — a logical, systematic approach.

ENGINE

The entire engine must be considered when trouble arises that is experienced as poor performance or failure to start. The engine is more than a combustion chamber, piston, and crankshaft; it also includes a fuel delivery system, an ignition system, and an exhaust system.

Before beginning to troubleshoot any engine problems, it's important to understand an engine's operating requirements. First, it must have a correctly metered mixture of gasoline and air (**Figure 1**). Second, it must have an airtight combustion chamber in which the mixture can be compressed. And finally, it requires a precisely timed spark to ignite the compressed mixture. If one or more is missing, the engine won't run, and if just one is deficient, the engine will run poorly at best.

Of the three requirements, the precisely timed spark — provided by the ignition system — is most likely to be the culprit, with gas/air mixture (carburetion) second, and poor compression the least likely.

STARTING DIFFICULTIES

Hard starting is probably the most common motorcycle ailment, with a wide range of problems likely. Before delving into a reluctant or non-starter, first determine what has changed

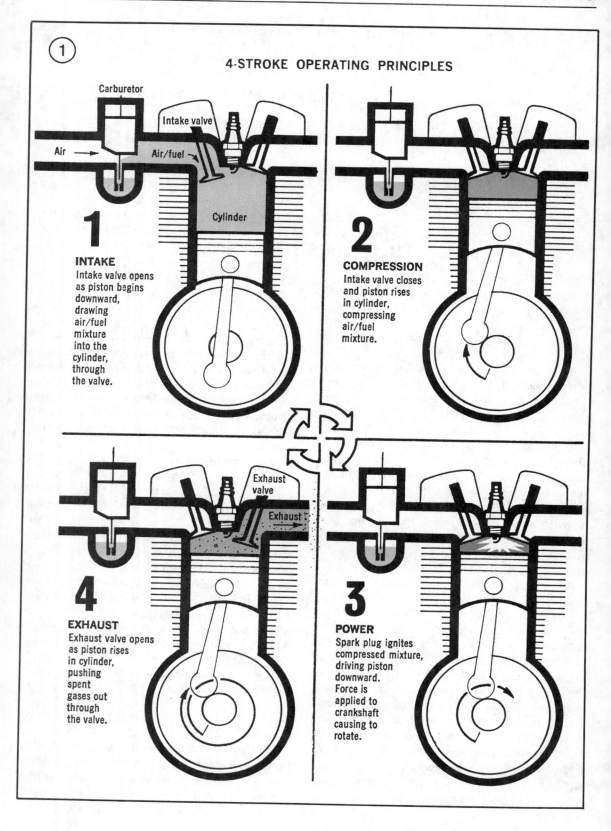

since the motorcycle last started easily. For instance, was the weather dry then and is it wet now? Has the motorcycle been sitting in the garage for a long time? Has it been ridden many miles since it was last fueled?

Has starting become increasingly more difficult? This alone could indicate a number of things that may be wrong but is usually associated with normal wear of ignition and engine components.

While it's not always possible to diagnose trouble simply from a change of conditions, this information can be helpful and at some future time may uncover a recurring problem.

Fuel Delivery

Although it is the second most likely cause of trouble, fuel delivery should be checked first simply because it is the easiest.

First, check the tank to make sure there is fuel in it. Then, disconnect the fuel hose at the carburetor, open the valve and check for flow (**Figure 2**). If fuel does not flow freely make sure the tank vent is clear. Next, check for blockage in the line or valve. Remove the valve and clean it as described in the fuel system chapter.

If fuel flows from the hose, reconnect it and remove the float bowl from the carburetor, open the valve and check for flow through the float needle valve. If it does not flow freely when the float is extended and then shut off when the flow is gently raised, clean the carburetor as described in the fuel system chapter.

When fuel delivery is satisfactory, go on to the ignition system.

Ignition

Remove the spark plug from the cylinder and check its condition. The appearance of the plug is a good indication of what's happening in the combustion chamber; for instance, if the plug is wet with gas, it's likely that engine is flooded. Compare the spark plug to **Figure 3**. Make certain the spark plug heat range is correct. A "cold" plug makes starting difficult.

After checking the spark plug, reconnect it to the high-tension lead and lay it on the cylinder head so it makes good contact (**Figure 4**). Then,

with the ignition switched on, crank the engine several times and watch for a spark across the plug electrodes. A fat, blue spark should be visible. If there is no spark, or if the spark is weak, substitute a good plug for the old one and check again. If the spark has improved, the old plug is faulty. If there was no change, keep looking.

Make sure the ignition switch is not shorted to ground. Remove the spark plug cap from the end of the high-tension lead and hold the exposed end of the lead about ⅛ inch from the cylinder head. Crank the engine and watch for a spark arcing from the lead to the head. If it's satisfactory, the connection between the lead and the cap was faulty. If the spark hasn't improved, check the coil wire connections.

If the spark is still weak, remove the ignition cover and remove any dirt or moisture from the points or sensor. Check the point or air gap against the specifications in the *Quick Reference Data* at the beginning of the book.

If spark is still not satisfactory, a more serious problem exists than can be corrected with simple adjustments. Refer to the electrical system chapter for detailed information for correcting major ignition problems.

Compression

Compression — or the lack of it — is the least likely cause of starting trouble. However, if compression is unsatisfactory, more than a simple adjustment is required to correct it (see the engine chapter).

An accurate compression check reveals a lot about the condition of the engine. To perform this test you need a compression gauge (see Chapter One). The engine should be at operating temperature for a fully accurate test, but even a cold test will reveal if the starting problem is compression.

Remove the spark plug and screw in a compression gauge (**Figure 5**). With assistance, hold the throttle wide open and crank the engine several times, until the gauge ceases to rise. Normal compression should be 130-160 psi, but a reading as low as 100 psi is usually sufficient for the engine to start. If the reading is much lower than normal, remove the gauge and pour about a tablespoon of oil into the cylinder.

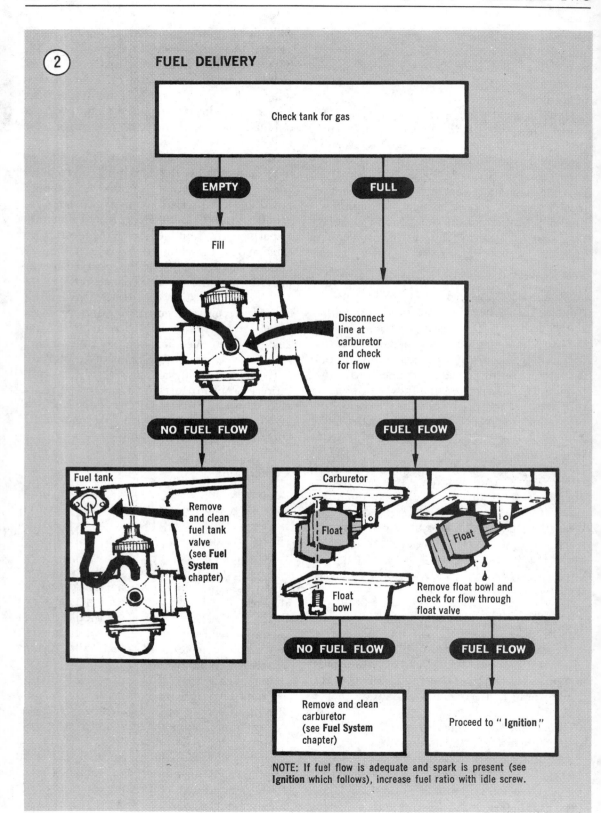

FUEL DELIVERY

Check tank for gas

EMPTY

FULL

Fill

Disconnect line at carburetor and check for flow

NO FUEL FLOW

FUEL FLOW

Fuel tank

Remove and clean fuel tank valve (see **Fuel System** chapter)

Carburetor

Float

Float

Float bowl

Remove float bowl and check for flow through float valve

NO FUEL FLOW

FUEL FLOW

Remove and clean carburetor (see **Fuel System** chapter)

Proceed to " **Ignition** "

NOTE: If fuel flow is adequate and spark is present (see **Ignition** which follows), increase fuel ratio with idle screw.

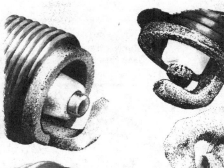

NORMAL
- Appearance—Firing tip has deposits of light gray to light tan.
- Can be cleaned, regapped and reused.

CARBON FOULED
- Appearance—Dull, dry black with fluffy carbon deposits on the insulator tip, electrode and exposed shell.
- Caused by—Fuel/air mixture too rich, plug heat range too cold, weak ignition system, dirty air cleaner, faulty automatic choke or excessive idling.
- Can be cleaned, regapped and reused.

OIL FOULED
- Appearance—Wet black deposits on insulator and exposed shell.
- Caused by—Excessive oil entering the combustion chamber through worn rings, pistons, valve guides or bearings.
- Replace with new plugs (use a hotter plug if engine is not repaired).

LEAD FOULED
- Appearance — Yellow insulator deposits (may sometimes be dark gray, black or tan in color) on the insulator tip.
- Caused by—Highly leaded gasoline.
- Replace with new plugs.

LEAD FOULED
- Appearance—Yellow glazed deposits indicating melted lead deposits due to hard acceleration.
- Caused by—Highly leaded gasoline.
- Replace with new plugs.

OIL AND LEAD FOULED
- Appearance—Glazed yellow deposits with a slight brownish tint on the insulator tip and ground electrode.
- Replace with new plugs.

FUEL ADDITIVE RESIDUE
- Appearance — Brown colored hardened ash deposits on the insulator tip and ground electrode.
- Caused by—Fuel and/or oil additives.
- Replace with new plugs.

WORN
- Appearance — Severely worn or eroded electrodes.
- Caused by—Normal wear or unusual oil and/or fuel additives.
- Replace with new plugs.

PREIGNITION
- Appearance — Melted ground electrode.
- Caused by—Overadvanced ignition timing, inoperative ignition advance mechanism, too low of a fuel octane rating, lean fuel/air mixture or carbon deposits in combustion chamber.

PREIGNITION
- Appearance—Melted center electrode.
- Caused by—Abnormal combustion due to overadvanced ignition timing or incorrect advance, too low of a fuel octane rating, lean fuel/air mixture, or carbon deposits in combustion chamber.
- Correct engine problem and replace with new plugs.

INCORRECT HEAT RANGE
- Appearance—Melted center electrode and white blistered insulator tip.
- Caused by—Incorrect plug heat range selection.
- Replace with new plugs.

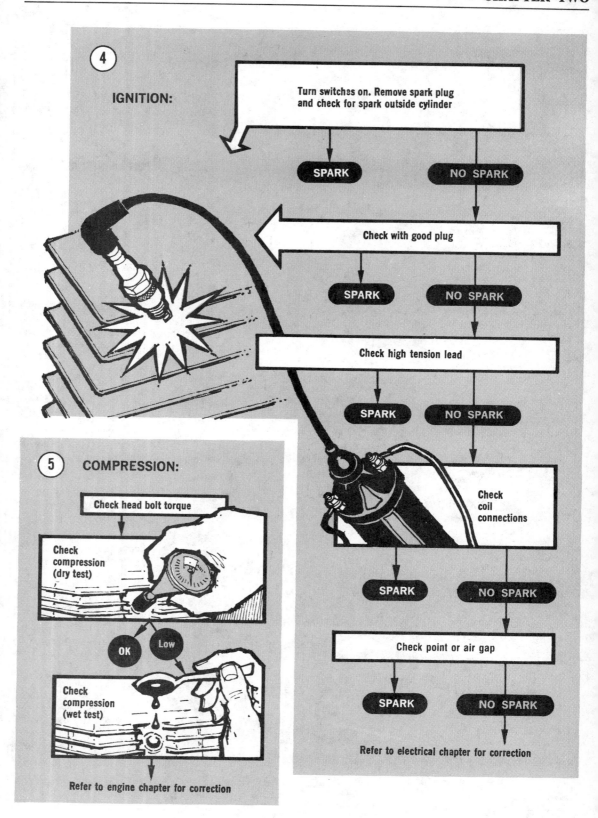

④ IGNITION:

Turn switches on. Remove spark plug
and check for spark outside cylinder

SPARK   NO SPARK

Check with good plug

SPARK   NO SPARK

Check high tension lead

SPARK   NO SPARK

Check
coil
connections

SPARK   NO SPARK

Check point or air gap

SPARK   NO SPARK

Refer to electrical chapter for correction

⑤ COMPRESSION:

Check head bolt torque

Check
compression
(dry test)

OK   Low

Check
compression
(wet test)

Refer to engine chapter for correction

2

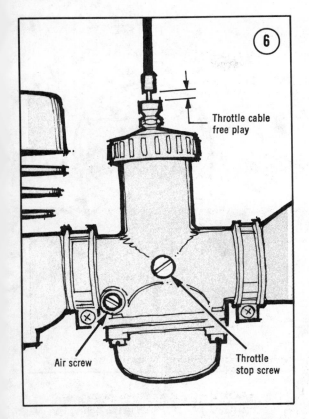

Throttle cable free play

Air screw

Throttle stop screw

Crank the engine several times to distribute the oil and test the compression once again. If it is now significantly higher, the rings and bore are worn. If the compression did not change, the valves are not seating correctly. Adjust the valves and check again. If the compression is still low, refer to the engine chapter.

> NOTE: *Low compression indicates a developing problem. The condition causing it should be corrected as soon as possible.*

POOR PERFORMANCE

Poor engine performance can be caused by any of a number of things related to carburetion, ignition, and the condition of the sliding and rotating components in the engine. In addition, components such as brakes, clutch, and transmission can cause problems that seem to be related to engine performance, even when the engine is in top running condition.

Poor Idling

Idling that is erratic, too high, or too low is most often caused by incorrect adjustment of the carburetor idle circuit. Also, a dirty air filter or an obstructed fuel tank vent can affect idle speed. Incorrect ignition timing or worn or faulty ignition components are also good possibilities.

First, make sure the air filter is clean and correctly installed. Then, adjust the throttle cable free play, the throttle stop screw, and the idle mixture air screw **(Figure 6)** as described in the routine maintenance chapter.

If idling is still poor, check the carburetor and manifold mounts for leaks; with the engine warmed up and running, spray WD-40 or a similar light lube around the flanges and joints of the carburetor and manifold **(Figure 7)**. Listen for changes in engine speed. If a leak is present, the idle speed will drop as the lube "plugs" the leak and then pick up again as it is drawn into the engine. Tighten the nuts and clamps and test again. If a leak persists, check for a damaged gasket or a pinhole in the manifold. Minor leaks in manifold hoses can be repaired with silicone sealer, but if cracks or holes are extensive, the manifold should be replaced.

A worn throttle slide may cause erratic running and idling, but this is likely only after many thousands of miles of use. To check, remove the carburetor top and feel for back and forth movement of the slide in the bore; it should be barely perceptible. Inspect the slide for large worn areas and replace it if it is less than perfect (**Figure 8**).

If the fuel system is satisfactory, check ignition timing and breaker point gap (air gap in electronic ignition). Check the condition of the system components as well. Ignition-caused idling problems such as erratic running can be the fault of marginal components. See the electrical system chapter for appropriate tests.

Rough Running or Misfiring

Misfiring (see **Figure 9**) is usually caused by an ignition problem. First, check all ignition connections (**Figure 10**). They should be clean, dry, and tight. Don't forget the kill switch; a loose connection can create an intermittent short.

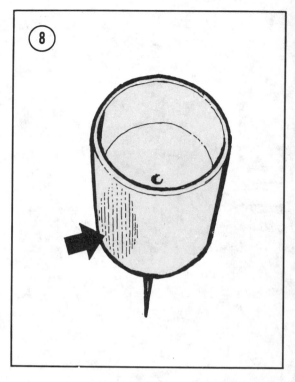

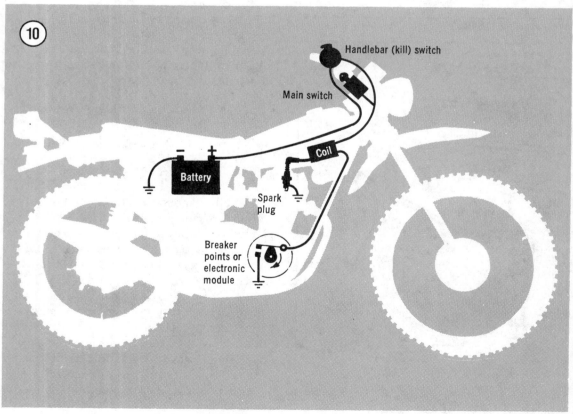

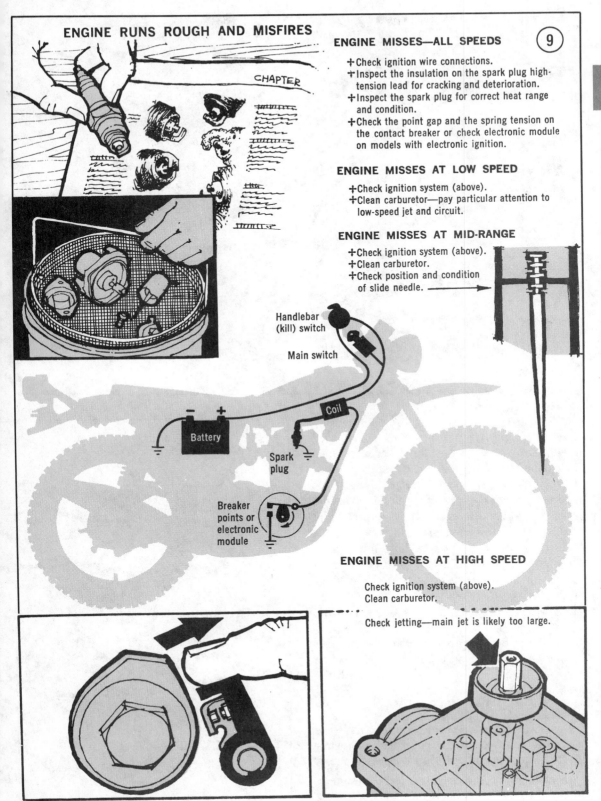

ENGINE RUNS ROUGH AND MISFIRES

CHAPTER

ENGINE MISSES—ALL SPEEDS ⑨

✝Check ignition wire connections.
✝Inspect the insulation on the spark plug high-tension lead for cracking and deterioration.
✝Inspect the spark plug for correct heat range and condition.
✝Check the point gap and the spring tension on the contact breaker or check electronic module on models with electronic ignition.

ENGINE MISSES AT LOW SPEED

✝Check ignition system (above).
✝Clean carburetor—pay particular attention to low-speed jet and circuit.

ENGINE MISSES AT MID-RANGE

✝Check ignition system (above).
✝Clean carburetor.
✝Check position and condition of slide needle. ➜

Handlebar (kill) switch

Main switch

Coil

Battery

Spark plug

Breaker points or electronic module

ENGINE MISSES AT HIGH SPEED

Check ignition system (above).
Clean carburetor.

Check jetting—main jet is likely too large.

2

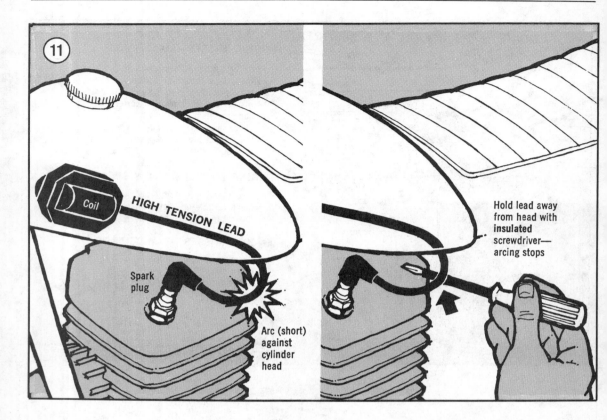

Check the insulation on the high-tension spark plug lead. If it is cracked or deteriorated it will allow the spark to short to ground when the engine is revved. This is easily seen at night. If arcing occurs, hold the affected area of the wire away from the metal to which it is arcing, using an insulated screwdriver (**Figure 11**), and see if the misfiring ceases. If it does, replace the high-tension lead. Also check the connection of the spark plug cap to the lead. If it is poor, the spark will break down at this point when the engine speed is increased.

The spark plug could also be poor. Test the system with a new plug.

Incorrect point gap or a weak contact breaker spring can cause misfiring. Check the gap and the alignment of the points. Push the moveable arm back and check for spring tension (**Figure 12**). It should feel stiff.

On models with electronic ignition, have the electronic module tested by a dealer or substitute a known good unit for a suspected one.

If misfiring occurs only at a certain point in engine speed, the problem may very likely be

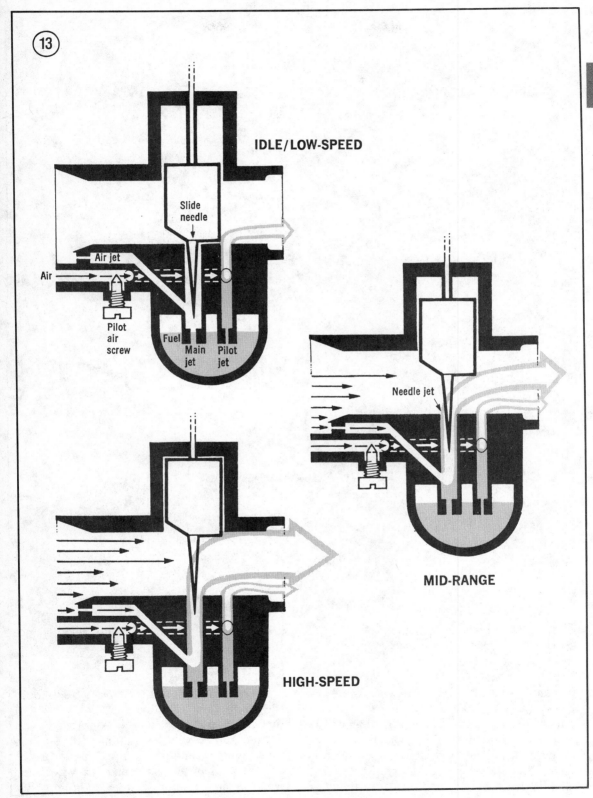

IDLE/LOW-SPEED

Slide needle

Air jet

Air

Pilot air screw

Fuel

Main jet

Pilot jet

Needle jet

MID-RANGE

HIGH-SPEED

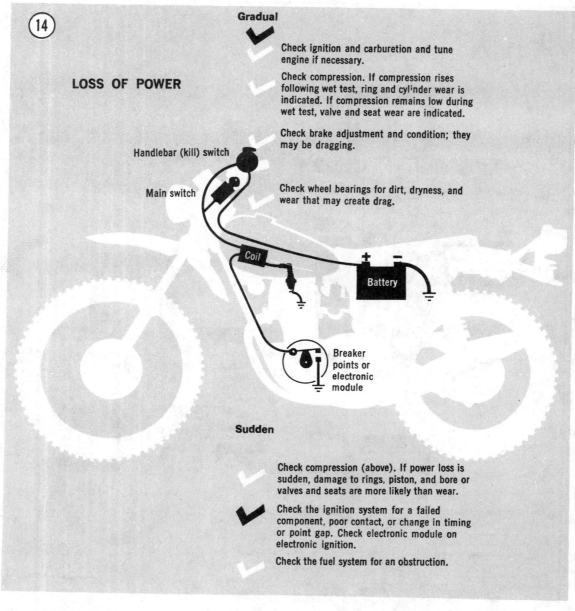

Gradual

Check ignition and carburetion and tune engine if necessary.

Check compression. If compression rises following wet test, ring and cylinder wear is indicated. If compression remains low during wet test, valve and seat wear are indicated.

Check brake adjustment and condition; they may be dragging.

Check wheel bearings for dirt, dryness, and wear that may create drag.

LOSS OF POWER

Handlebar (kill) switch

Main switch

Coil

Battery

Breaker points or electronic module

Sudden

Check compression (above). If power loss is sudden, damage to rings, piston, and bore or valves and seats are more likely than wear.

Check the ignition system for a failed component, poor contact, or change in timing or point gap. Check electronic module on electronic ignition.

Check the fuel system for an obstruction.

carburetion. Poor performance at idle is described earlier. Misfiring at low speed (just above idle) can be caused by a dirty low-speed circuit or jet (**Figure 13**). Poor midrange performance is attributable to a worn or incorrectly adjusted needle and needle jet. Misfiring at high speed (if not ignition related) is usually caused by a too-large main jet which causes the engine to run rich. Any of these carburetor-related conditions can be corrected by first cleaning the carburetor and then adjusting it as described in the tune-up and maintenance chapter.

Loss of Power

First determine how the power loss developed (**Figure 14**). Did it decline over a long period of time or did it drop abruptly? A gradual loss is normal, caused by deterioration of the engine's state of tune and the normal wear of the cylinder and piston rings and the valves and seats. In such case, check the condition of the

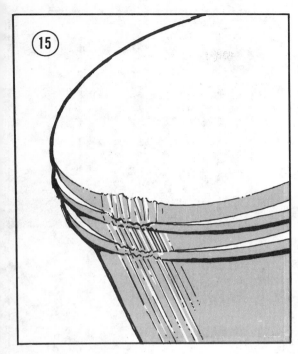

ignition and carburetion and measure the compression as described earlier.

A sudden power loss may be caused by a failed ignition component, obstruction in the fuel system, damaged valve or seat, or a broken piston ring or damaged piston (**Figure 15**).

If the engine is in good shape and tune, check the brake adjustment. If the brakes are dragging, they will consume considerable power. Also check the wheel bearings. If they are dry, extremely dirty, or badly worn they can create considerable drag.

Engine Runs Hot

A modern motorcycle engine, in good mechanical condition, correctly tuned, and operated as it was intended, will rarely experience overheating problems. However, out-of-spec conditions can create severe overheating that may result in serious engine damage. Refer to **Figure 16**.

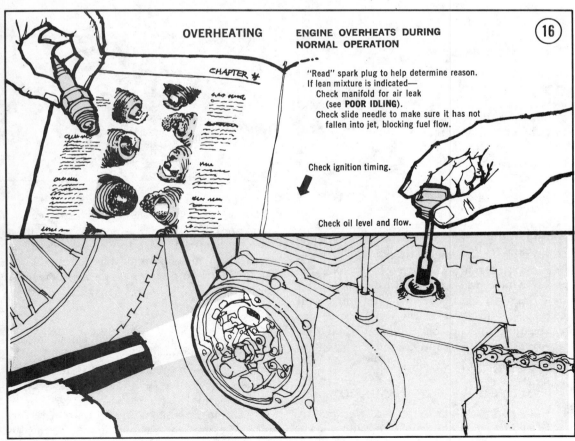

OVERHEATING

ENGINE OVERHEATS DURING NORMAL OPERATION

"Read" spark plug to help determine reason.
If lean mixture is indicated—
 Check manifold for air leak
  (see **POOR IDLING**).
 Check slide needle to make sure it has not
  fallen into jet, blocking fuel flow.

Check ignition timing.

Check oil level and flow.

Overheating is difficult to detect unless it is extreme, in which case it will usually be apparent as excessive heat radiating from the engine, accompanied by the smell of hot oil and sharp, snapping noises when the engine is first shut off and begins to cool.

Unless the motorcycle is operated under sustained high load or is allowed to idle for long periods of time, overheating is usually the result of an internal problem. Most often it's caused by a too-lean fuel mixture.

Remove the spark plug and compare it to **Figure 3**. If a too-lean condition is indicated, check for leaks in the intake manifold (see *Poor Idling*). The carburetor jetting may be incorrect but this is unlikely if the overheating problem has just developed (unless, of course, the engine was jetted for high altitude and is now being run near sea level). Check the slide needle in the carburetor to make sure it hasn't come loose and is restricting the flow of gas through the main jet and needle jet (**Figure 17**).

Check the ignition timing; extremes of either advance or retard can cause overheating.

Piston Seizure and Damage

Piston seizure is a common result of overheating (see above) because an aluminum piston expands at a greater rate than a steel cylinder. Seizure can also be caused by piston-to-cylinder clearance that is too small; ring end gap that is too small; insufficient oil; spark plug heat range too hot; and broken piston ring or ring land.

A major piston seizure can cause severe engine damage. A minor seizure — which usually subsides after the engine has cooled a few minutes — rarely does more than scuff the piston skirt the first time it occurs. Fortunately, this condition can be corrected by dressing the piston with crocus cloth, refitting the piston and rings to the bore with recommended clearances, and checking the timing to ensure overheating does not occur. Regard that first seizure as a warning and correct the problem before continuing to run the engine.

CLUTCH AND TRANSMISSION

1. *Clutch slips*—Make sure lever free play is sufficient to allow the clutch to fully engage

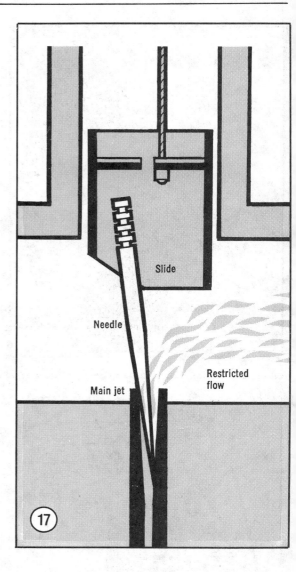

(**Figure 18**). Check the contact surfaces for wear and glazing. Transmission oil additives also can cause slippage in wet clutches. If slip occurs only under extreme load, check the condition of the springs or diaphragm and make sure the clutch bolts are snug and uniformly tightened.

2. *Clutch drags*—Make sure lever free play isn't so great that it fails to disengage the clutch. Check for warped plates or disc. If the transmission oil (in wet clutch systems) is extremely dirty or heavy, it may inhibit the clutch from releasing.

3. *Transmission shifts hard*—Extremely dirty oil can cause the transmission to shift hard.

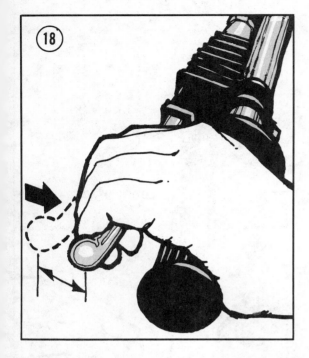

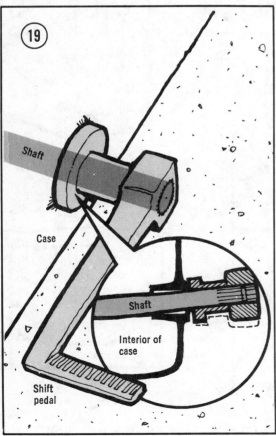

Check the selector shaft for bending (**Figure 19**). Inspect the shifter and gearsets for wear and damage.

4. *Transmission slips out of gear*—This can be caused by worn engagement dogs or a worn or damaged shifter (**Figure 20**). The overshift travel on the selector may be misadjusted.

5. *Transmission is noisy*—Noises usually indicate the absence of lubrication or wear and damage to gears, bearings, or shims. It's a good idea to disassemble the transmission and carefully inspect it when noise first occurs.

DRIVE TRAIN

Drive train problems (outlined in **Figure 21**) arise from normal wear and incorrect maintenance.

CHASSIS

Chassis problems are outlined in **Figure 22**.

1. *Motorcycle pulls to one side*—Check for loose suspension components, axles, steering

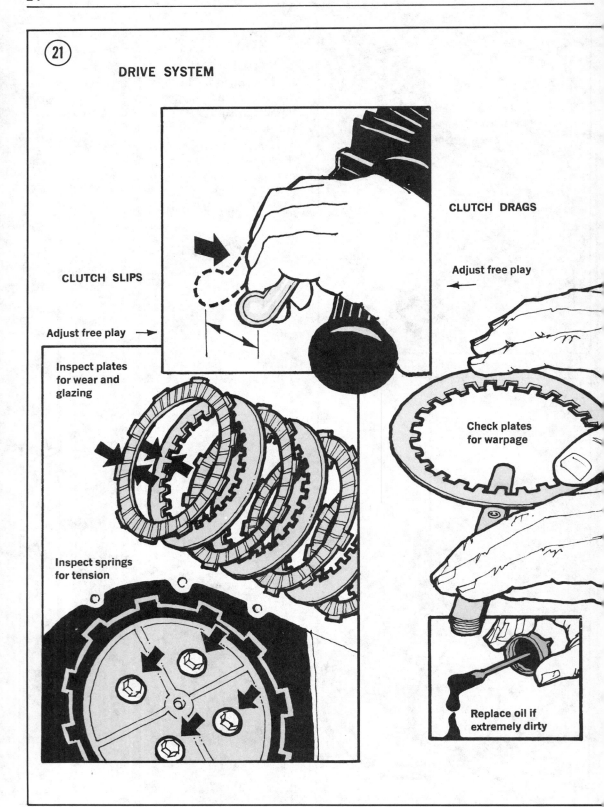

㉑ DRIVE SYSTEM

CLUTCH DRAGS

CLUTCH SLIPS

Adjust free play →

Adjust free play →

Inspect plates
for wear and
glazing

Check plates
for warpage

Inspect springs
for tension

Replace oil if
extremely dirty

TRANSMISSION SLIPS OUT OF GEAR

TRANSMISSION SHIFTS HARD

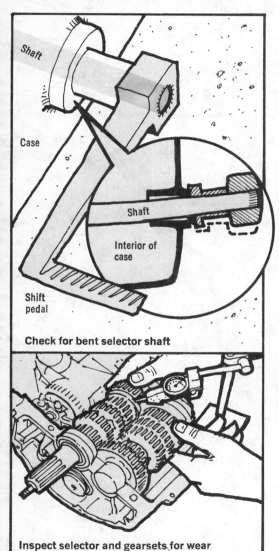

Check for bent selector shaft

Inspect selector and gearsets for wear

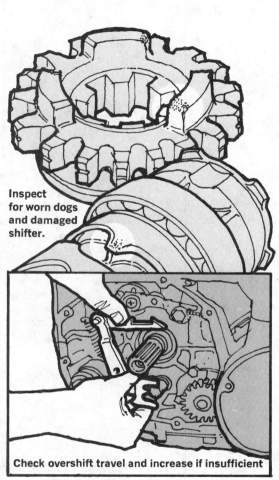

Inspect
for worn dogs
and damaged
shifter.

Check overshift travel and increase if insufficient

TRANSMISSION IS NOISY

Check oil level

Disassemble and inspect (see Transmission chapter)

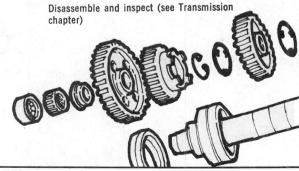

㉒

SUSPENSION AND HANDLING

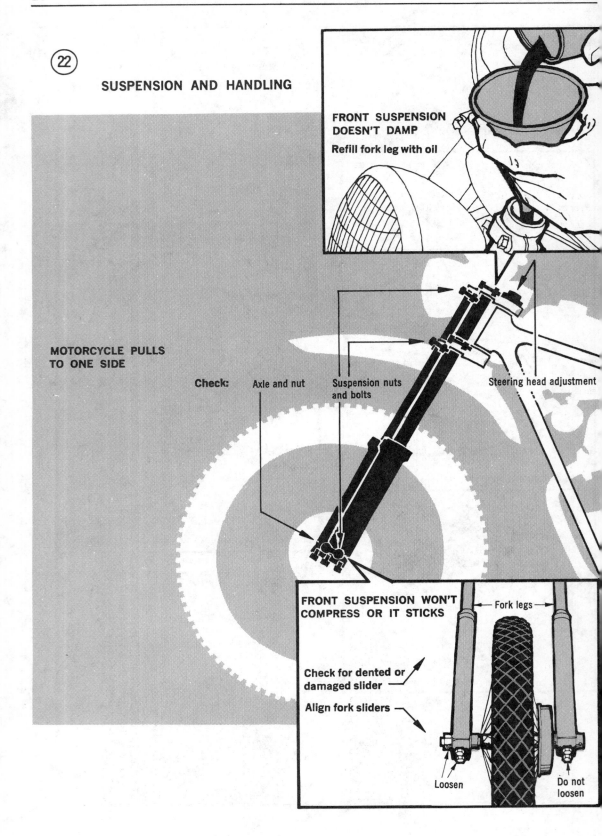

FRONT SUSPENSION
DOESN'T DAMP

Refill fork leg with oil

MOTORCYCLE PULLS
TO ONE SIDE

Check: Axle and nut   Suspension nuts   Steering head adjustment
                          and bolts

FRONT SUSPENSION WON'T
COMPRESS OR IT STICKS

Fork legs

Check for dented or
damaged slider

Align fork sliders

Loosen   Do not
                          loosen

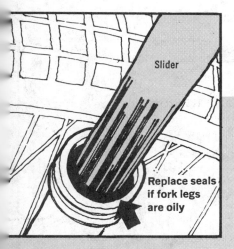

Slider

Replace seals if fork legs are oily

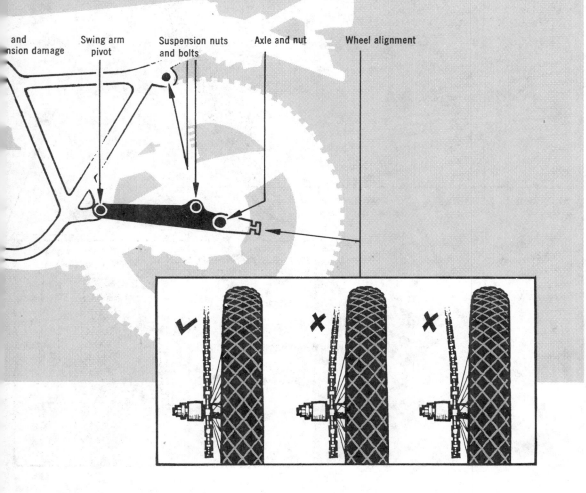

...and
...nsion damage

Swing arm pivot

Suspension nuts and bolts

Axle and nut

Wheel alignment

SUSPENSION AND HANDLING CONTINUED

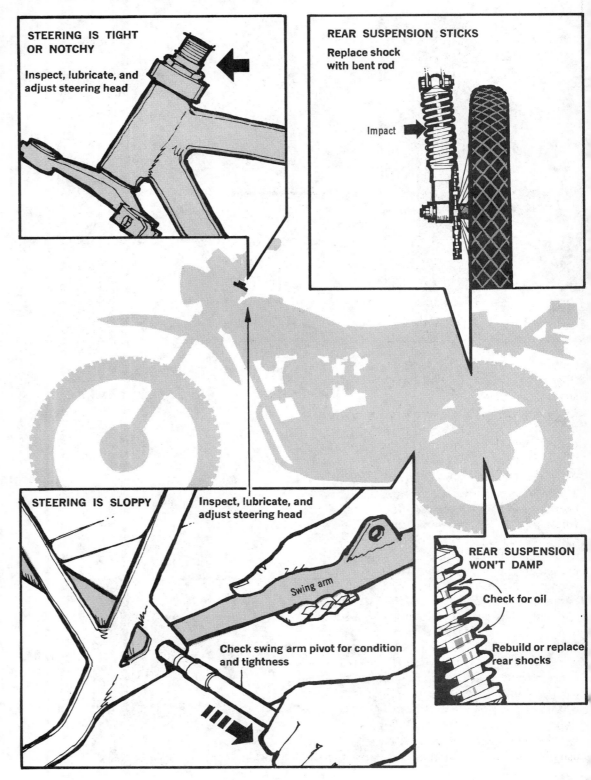

STEERING IS TIGHT OR NOTCHY

Inspect, lubricate, and adjust steering head

REAR SUSPENSION STICKS

Replace shock with bent rod

Impact

STEERING IS SLOPPY

Inspect, lubricate, and adjust steering head

Swing arm

Check swing arm pivot for condition and tightness

REAR SUSPENSION WON'T DAMP

Check for oil

Rebuild or replace rear shocks

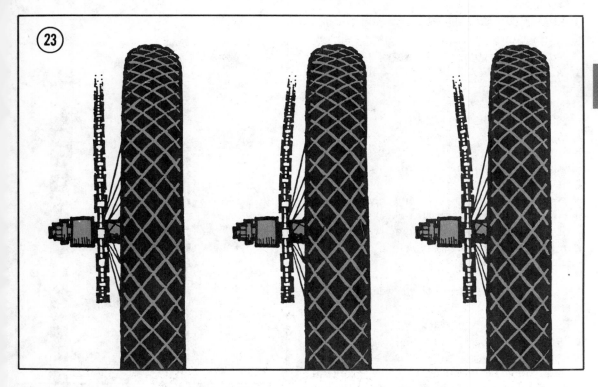

head, swing arm pivot. Check wheel alignment **(Figure 23)**. Check for damage to the frame and suspension components.

2. *Front suspension doesn't damp*—This is most often caused by a lack of damping oil in the fork legs. If the upper fork tubes are exceptionally oily, it's likely that the seals are worn out and should be replaced.

3. *Front suspension sticks or won't fully compress*—Misalignment of the forks when the wheel is installed can cause this. Loosen the axle nut and the pinch bolt on the nut end of the axle **(Figure 24)**. Lock the front wheel with the brake and compress the front suspension several times to align the fork legs. Then, tighten the pinch bolt and then the axle nut.

The trouble may also be caused by a bent or dented fork slider **(Figure 25)**. The distortion required to lock up a fork tube is so slight that it is often impossible to visually detect. If this type of damage is suspected, remove the fork leg and remove the spring from it. Attempt to operate the fork leg. If it still binds, replace the slider; it's not practical to repair it.

4. *Rear suspension does not damp*—This is usually caused by damping oil leaking past

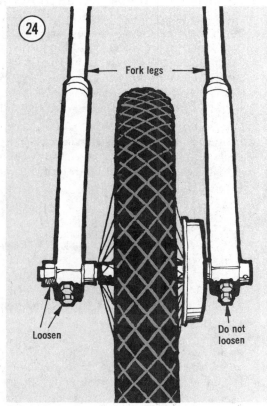

worn seals. Rebuildable shocks should be refitted with complete service kits and fresh oil. Non-rebuildable units should be replaced.

5. *Rear suspension sticks*—This is commonly caused by a bent shock absorber piston rod (**Figure 26**). Replace the shock; the rod can't be satisfactorily straightened.

6. *Steering is tight or "notchy"*—Steering head bearings may be dry, dirty, or worn. Adjustment of the steering head bearing pre-load may be too tight.

7. *Steering is sloppy*—Steering head adjustment may be too loose. Also check the swing arm pivot; looseness or extreme wear at this point translate to the steering.

BRAKES

Brake problems arise from wear, lack of maintenance, and from sustained or repeated exposure to dirt and water.

1. *Brakes are ineffective*—Ineffective brakes are most likely caused by incorrect adjustment. If adjustment will not correct the problem, remove the wheels and check for worn or glazed linings. If the linings are worn beyond the service limit, replace them. If they are simply glazed, rough them up with light sandpaper.

In hydraulic brake systems, low fluid levels can cause a loss of braking effectiveness, as can worn brake cylinder pistons and bores. Also check the pads to see if they are worn beyond the service limit.

2. *Brakes lock or drag*—This may be caused by incorrect adjustment. Check also for foreign matter embedded in the lining and for dirty and dry wheel bearings.

ELECTRICAL SYSTEM

Many electrical system problems can be easily solved by ensuring that the affected connections are clean, dry, and tight. In battery equipped motorcycles, a neglected battery is the source of a great number of difficulties that could be prevented by simple, regular service to the battery.

A multimeter, like the volt/ohm/milliammeter described in Chapter One, is invaluable for efficient electrical system troubleshooting.

See **Figures 27 and 28** for schematics showing

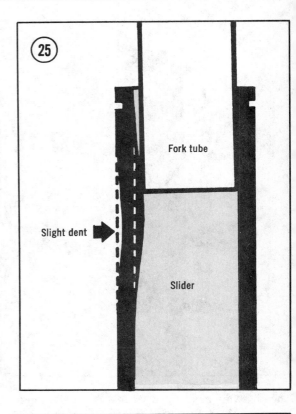

(25)

Fork tube

Slight dent

Slider

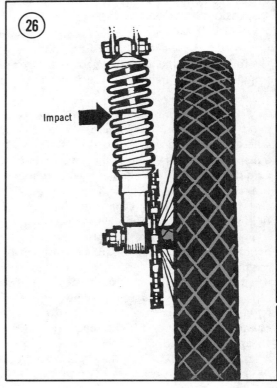

(26)

Impact

BASIC IGNITION CIRCUITS

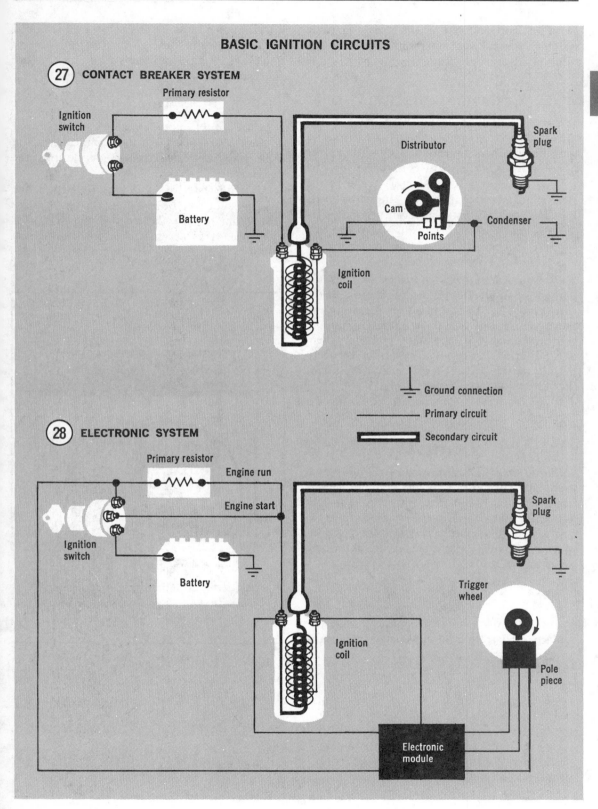

27 CONTACT BREAKER SYSTEM

Primary resistor

Ignition switch

Battery

Distributor

Spark plug

Cam

Points

Condenser

Ignition coil

Ground connection

Primary circuit

Secondary circuit

28 ELECTRONIC SYSTEM

Primary resistor

Engine run

Engine start

Ignition switch

Battery

Spark plug

Ignition coil

Trigger wheel

Pole piece

Electronic module

simplified conventional and electronic ignition systems. Typical and most common electrical troubles are also described.

CHARGING SYSTEM

1. *Battery will not accept a charge*—Make sure the electrolyte level in the battery is correct and that the terminal connections are tight and free of corrosion. Check for fuses in the battery circuit. If the battery is satisfactory, refer to the electrical system chapter for alternator tests. Finally, keep in mind that even a good alternator is not capable of restoring the charge to a severely discharged battery; it must first be charged by an external source.

2. *Battery will not hold a charge*—Check the battery for sulfate deposits in the bottom of the case (**Figure 29**). Sulfation occurs naturally and the deposits will accumulate and eventually come in contact with the plates and short them out. Sulfation can be greatly retarded by keeping the battery well charged at all times. Test the battery to assess its condition.

If the battery is satisfactory, look for excessive draw, such as a short.

LIGHTING

Bulbs burn out frequently—All bulbs will eventually burn out, but if the bulb in one particular light burns out frequently check the light assembly for looseness that may permit excessive vibration; check for loose connections that could cause current surges; check also to make sure the bulb is of the correct rating.

FUSES

Fuse blows—When a fuse blows, don't just replace it; try to find the cause. Consider a fuse

a warning device as well as a safety device. And never replace a fuse with one of greater amperage rating. It probably won't melt before the insulation on the wiring does.

WIRING

Wiring problems should be corrected as soon as they arise — before a short can cause a fire that may seriously damage or destroy the motorcycle.

A circuit tester of some type is essential for locating shorts and opens. Use the appropriate wiring diagram at the end of the book for reference. If a wire must be replaced make a notation on the wiring diagram of any changes in color coding.

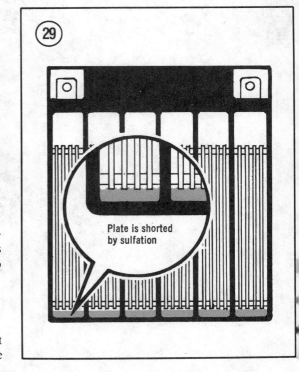

(29)

Plate is shorted
by sulfation

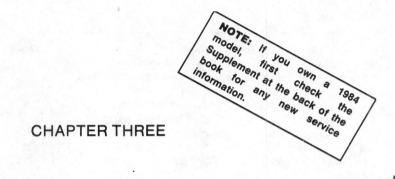
NOTE: If you own a 1984 model, first check the Supplement at the back of the book for any new service information.

CHAPTER THREE

LUBRICATION, MAINTENANCE
AND TUNE-UP

Your bike can be cared for by two methods: preventive or corrective maintenance. Because a motorcycle is subjected to tremendous heat, stress and vibration—even in normal use—preventive maintenance prevents costly and untimely corrective maintenance. When neglected, any bike becomes unreliable and dangerous to ride. When properly maintained, the Yamaha XT is one of the most reliable bikes available and will give many miles and years of dependable, fast and safe riding. By maintaining a routine service schedule as described in this chapter, costly mechanical problems and unexpected breakdowns can be prevented.

This chapter explains lubrication, maintenance and tune-up procedures required for the Yamaha XT125, XT200 and XT250 models. **Table 1** is a suggested factory maintenance schedule (**Tables 1-7** are located at the end of this chapter).

ROUTINE CHECKS

The following checks should be performed prior to the first ride of the day.

Engine Oil Level

Refer to *Checking Engine Oil Level* under *Periodic Lubrication* in this chapter.

General Inspection

1. Quickly inspect the engine for signs of oil or fuel leakage.

2. Check the tires for embedded stones. Pry them out with your ignition key.
3. Make sure all lights work.

> *NOTE*
> *At least check the brake light. Motorists cannot stop as quickly as you and need all the warning you can give.*

4. Check the throttle and brake levers. Make sure they operate properly with no binding.

Tire Pressure

Tire pressure must be checked with the tires cold. Correct tire pressure depends on the load you are carrying. See **Table 2**.

Battery

On XT250 models, remove the side cover and check the battery electrolyte level. On XT125 and XT200 models, the battery must first be removed. The level must be between the upper and lower level marks on the case (**Figure 1**).

For complete details see *Battery Removal/ Installation* and *Electrolyte Level Check* in this chapter.

Check the level more frequently in hot weather as the electrolyte will evaporate more quickly.

Lights and Horn

With the engine running, check the following.
1. Pull the front brake lever and check that the brake light comes on.

2. Push the rear brake pedal down and check that the brake light comes on after you have just begun depressing the pedal.

3. Move the headlight dimmer switch up and down between the HI and LO positions and check to see that both headlight elements are working.

4. Turn the turn signal switch to the left and right positions and check that all 4 turn signals are working.

5. Push the horn button and make sure that the horn blows loudly.

6. During these tests, if the rear brake pedal traveled too far before the brake light came on, adjust the rear brake light switch as described in Chapter Seven. If the horn or any of the lights failed to operate properly, refer to Chapter Seven.

PRE-CHECKS

The following checks should be performed prior to the first ride of the day.

1. Inspect all fuel lines (**Figure 2**) and fittings for wetness.

2. Make sure the fuel tank is full of fresh gasoline.

3. Make sure the engine oil level is correct.

4. Check the operation of the clutch and adjust the free play in the cable if necessary.

5. Check the throttle and the brake lever. Make sure they operate properly with no binding.

6. Make sure the engine kill switch works properly.

7. Check the wheel spokes and rim locks (if so equipped) for tightness; adjust if necessary.

8. Inspect the front and rear suspension; make sure they have a good solid feel with no looseness.

9. Check the drive chain for wear and correct tension.

10. Check tire pressure. Refer to **Table 2**.

11. Check the exhaust system for leakage or damage.

12. Check the tightness of all fasteners, especially engine mounting hardware.

SERVICE INTERVALS

The services and intervals shown in **Table 1** are recommended by the factory. Strict adherence to these recommendations will ensure long service from your Yamaha. If the vehicle is run in an area of high humidity the lubrication and services must be done more frequently to prevent possible rust damage.

For convenience when maintaining your vehicle, most of the services shown in **Table 1** are described in this chapter. Some procedures which require more than minor disassembly or adjustment are covered elsewhere in the appropriate chapter.

TIRES AND WHEELS

Tire pressure should be checked and adjusted to maintain good traction and handling and to get the maximum life out of the tire. A simple, accurate gauge can be purchased for a few dollars and should be carried in your motorcycle tool box. The appropriate pressures are listed in **Table 2**.

Tire Inspection

The tires take a lot of punishment, so inspect them periodically for excessive wear, cuts, abrasions, etc. If you find a nail or other object in the tire, mark its location with a light crayon prior to removing it. This will help locate the hole for repair. Refer to Chapter Eight for tire changing and repair information.

Check local traffic regulations concerning minimum tread depth. Measure the tread depth at the center of the tire tread using a tread depth gauge or small ruler. Yamaha recommends tire replacement when the front or rear tread depth is 1/8 in. (8 mm) or less. Replace the tire(s) at this point.

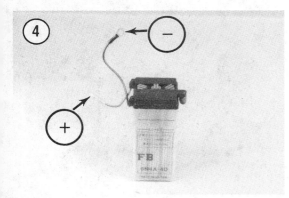

Rim Inspection

Frequently inspect the wheel rims. If a rim has been damaged it might be out of alignment. Improper wheel alignment can cause severe vibration and result in an unsafe riding condition.

CRANKCASE BREATHER HOSE

A crankcase breather system is used on all 1980-1982 models and 1983 non-California models.

Inspect the breather hoses for cracks and deterioration and make sure that the hose clamps are tight (**Figure 3**).

> *NOTE*
> *All 1983 models sold in California are equipped with special emission control components. Refer to Chapter Six for inspection and service procedures.*

BATTERY

> *CAUTION*
> *If it becomes necessary to remove the battery breather tube when performing any of the following procedures, make sure to route the tube correctly during installation to prevent acid spillage that would cause permanent damage to parts.*

Checking Electrolyte Level

The battery is the heart of the electrical system. It should be checked and serviced as indicated. The majority of electrical system troubles can be attributed to neglect of this vital component.

In order to correctly service the electrolyte level it is necessary to remove the battery from the frame. The electrolyte level should be maintained between the two marks on the battery case (**Figure 1**). If the electrolyte level is low, it's a good idea to completely remove the battery so that it can be thoroughly cleaned, serviced and checked.

Removal/Installation (XT125 and XT200)

1. Remove the right-hand side cover.
2. Unscrew the negative battery terminal and disconnect the positive battery terminal (in that order). The terminals are shown in **Figure 4**.
3. Remove the bolt holding the battery case (**Figure 5**) and remove the battery case and battery.
4. Remove the top battery case cover screw (**Figure 6**). Remove the cover and the battery (**Figure 7**).

Wheel Spoke Tension

Tap each spoke with a wrench. The higher the pitch of sound it makes, the tighter the spoke. The lower the pitch the looser the spoke. A "ping" is good; a "klunk" says the spoke is too loose.

If one or more spokes are loose, tighten them as described in Chapter Eight.

5. Service the battery as described in this chapter.

6. Installation is the reverse of these steps. Connect the positive cable first, then the negative cable.

Removal/Installation (XT250)

1. Remove the right-hand side cover.

2. Disconnect the battery negative cable from the battery.

3. Disconnect the battery positive cable from the battery.

4. Remove the battery hold-down strap. Pull the battery out slightly to provide access to the vent tube and disconnect it. See **Figure 8**.

5. Slide the battery out of the box.

6. Service the battery as described in this chapter.

7. Installation is the reverse of these steps. Connect the positive cable first, then the negative cable.

Cleaning

After the battery has been removed from the bike, check it for corrosion or excessive dirt. The top of the battery in particular should be kept clean. Acid film and dirt will permit current to flow between the terminals, causing the battery to slowly discharge.

For best results when cleaning, first rinse off the top of the battery with plenty of clean water (avoid letting water enter the cells). Then carefully wash the case, both terminals and the battery box with a solution of baking soda and tap water. Keep the cells sealed tightly with the filler plugs so that none of the cleaning solution enters a cell (this would neutralize the cell's electrolyte and seriously damage the battery). Brush the solution on liberally with a stiff bristle parts cleaning brush. Using a strong spray from a garden hose, clean all the residue from the solution off the battery and all painted surfaces.

Service

> *CAUTION*
> *Be careful not to spill battery electrolyte on painted or polished surfaces. The liquid is highly corrosive and will damage the finish. If it is spilled, wash it off immediately with soapy water and thoroughly rinse with clean water.*

1. Remove the caps from the battery cells and add distilled water to correct the level. Never add tap water or electrolyte (acid) to correct the level.

> *NOTE*
> *Distilled water is available at most supermarkets.*

2. After the level has been corrected and the battery allowed to stand for a few minutes, check the specific gravity of the electrolyte in each cell with a hydrometer (**Figure 9**). See *Testing* in this chapter.

Testing

Hydrometer testing is the best way to check battery condition. Use a hydrometer with

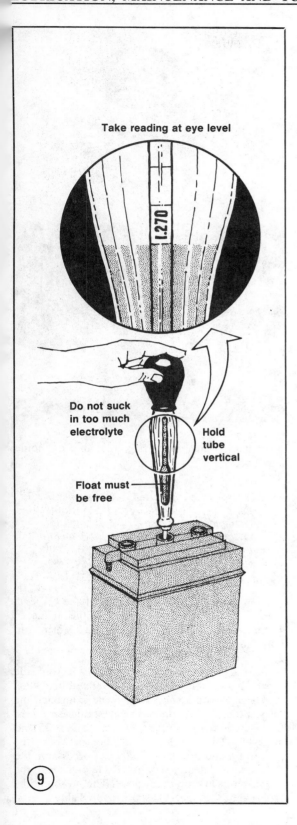

Take reading at eye level

1.270

Do not suck
in too much
electrolyte

Hold
tube
vertical

Float must
be free

⑨

numbered graduations from 1.100 to 1.300 rather than one with color-coded bands. To use the hydrometer, squeeze the rubber ball, insert the tip into the cell and release the ball. Draw enough electrolyte to float the weighted float inside the hydrometer. Note the number in line with the electrolyte surface; this is the specific gravity for this cell. Return the electrolyte to the cell from which it came. The specific gravity of the electrolyte in each battery cell is an excellent indication of that cell's condition. A fully charged cell will read from 1.275-1.280. A cell in good condition reads from 1.225-1.250 and anything below 1.225 is practically dead.

NOTE
Specific gravity varies with temperature. For each 10° that electrolyte temperature exceeds 80° F, add 0.004 to reading indicated on hydrometer. Subtract 0.004 for each 10° below 80° F.

If the cells test in the poor range, the battery requires recharging. The hydrometer is useful for checking the progress of the charging operation. **Table 3** shows approximate state of charge.

Charging

CAUTION
Always remove the battery from the motorcycle before connecting charging equipment. Never recharge a battery in the bike's frame due to the corrosive mist that is emitted during the charging process. If this mist settles on the bike's frame it will corrode the surface.

WARNING
During charging, highly explosive hydrogen gas is released from the battery. The battery should be charged only in a well-ventilated area and open flames and cigarettes should be kept away. Remember that the gas appliances in your home garage may have pilot lights. Never check the charge of the battery by arcing across the terminals; the resulting spark can ignite the hydrogen gas.

1. Connect the positive charger lead to the positive battery terminal and the negative charger lead to the negative battery terminal.
2. Remove all vent caps from the battery, set the charger at 6 volts and switch it on. If the output of the charger is variable, it is best to select a low setting—1 1/2 to 2 amps.

3

3. After battery has been charged for about 8 hours, turn the charger off, disconnect the leads and check the specific gravity. It should be within the limits specified in **Table 3**. If it is, and remains stable for one hour, the battery is charged.

4. To ensure good electrical contact, cables must be clean and tight on the battery's terminals. If the cable terminals are badly corroded, even after performing the cleaning procedures in this chapter, the cables should be disconnected, removed from the bike and cleaned separately with a wire brush and a baking soda solution. After cleaning, apply a very thin coating of petroleum jelly (Vaseline) to the battery terminals before reattaching the cables. After connecting the cables, apply a light coating to the connections also—this will delay future corrosion.

New Battery Installation

When replacing the old battery with a new one, be sure to charge it completely (specific gravity of 1.260-1.280) before installing it in the bike.

Failure to do so, or using the battery with a low electrolyte level, will permanently damage the battery.

PERIODIC LUBRICATION

Oil

Oil is graded according to its viscosity, which is an indication of how thick it is. The Society of Automotive Engineers (SAE) system distinguishes oil viscosity by numbers. Thick oils have higher viscosity numbers than thin oils. For example, an SAE 5 oil is a thin oil while an SAE 90 oil is relatively thick. Oil ratings are found on the top of oil cans (**Figure 10**).

Grease

A good quality grease (preferably waterproof) should be used. Water does not wash grease off parts as easily as it washes oil off. In addition, grease maintains its lubricating qualities better than oil on long and strenuous rides.

Cleaning Solvent

A number of solvents can be used to remove old dirt, grease and oil. Kerosene is readily available and comparatively inexpensive. Another inexpensive solvent similar to kerosene is ordinary diesel fuel. Both of these solvents have a very high temperature flash point (they have to be very hot in order to ignite and catch fire) and can be used safely in any adequately ventilated area away from

open flames (this includes pilot lights on home appliances).

> *WARNING*
> ***Never use gasoline***. *Gasoline is extremely volatile and contains tremendously destructive potential energy. The slightest spark from metal parts accidently hitting or a tool slipping could cause a fatal explosion.*

Engine Oil Check

The engine oil level is checked at the oil level check bolt on the right-hand side of the engine.

1. Start the engine and let it warm up approximately 2-3 minutes.
2. Shut off the engine.
3. Set the bike so that it is level; any tilt from side to side will produce a false oil level reading.
4. Check the oil level by observing it through the inspection window on the right crankcase cover. See **Figure 11** (XT250) or **Figure 12** (XT125 and XT200). The level should be between the maximum and minimum marks. If necessary, add the recommended type of oil (**Table 4**) through the oil filler cap to correct the level. The oil should be replaced at the intervals specified in **Table 1**.

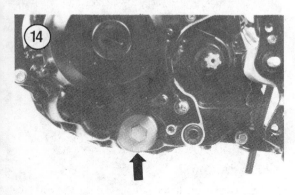

Engine Oil and Filter Change

Regular oil changes will contribute more to engine longevity than almost any other maintenance operation performed. The factory recommended oil change interval and the interval for cleaning the oil filter screen and changing the oil filter are found in **Table 1**.

These intervals assume that the bike is operated in moderate climates. If it is operated under dusty conditions, the oil will get dirty more quickly and should be changed more frequently than recommended.

Use only a high quality detergent motor oil with an API rating of SE or SF. The quality rating is stamped or printed on top of the can (**Figure 10**). Try to use the same brand of oil at each oil change. Refer to **Table 4** for correct oil viscosity to use under anticipated ambient temperatures (not engine oil temperature).

> *CAUTION*
> *The use of additional friction reducing additives in the oil will cause clutch slippage. In addition, the use of graphite oils will void any applicable Yamaha warranty. It is not established at this time if graphite will build up on the clutch friction plates, causing clutch problems. Until further testing is done by the oil and motorcycle industries, do not use this type of oil.*

To drain the oil you will need the following:
a. Drain pan.
b. Funnel.
c. Can opener or pour spout.
d. 2 quarts of oil.

There are a number of ways to discard the old oil safely. The easiest way is to pour it from the drain pan into a half-gallon plastic bleach or milk container. Some service stations and oil retailers will accept your used oil for recycling. Check local regulations before discarding the oil in your household trash.

1. Start the engine and let it reach operating temperature.
2. Shut it off and place a drip pan under the engine.
3. Remove the oil filler cap (**Figure 13**), drain plug and oil strainer. See **Figure 14** and **Figure 15** (XT125 and XT200) or **Figure 16** and **Figure 17** (XT250).

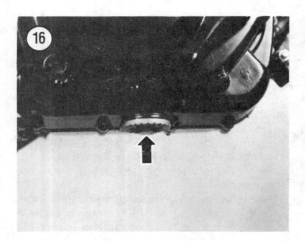

4. Remove the oil filter cover (**Figure 18**) and oil filter. See **Figure 19** (XT125 and XT200) or **Figure 20** (XT250).

> *NOTE*
> *If it is not necessary to replace the oil filter, remove only the lower oil filter cover bolt. This will allow complete draining of the oil filter cavity.*

5. Remove the air bleed screw. See **Figure 21** (XT125 and XT200) or **Figure 22** (XT250).

6. Let the oil drain for at least 15-20 minutes.

7. Inspect the sealing washers on all plugs and bolts. Replace if damaged.

8. Clean the oil strainer screen, spring (**Figure 23**) and plug in solvent and thoroughly dry with compressed air. Inspect the filter screen for holes or defects; replace as necessary. Thoroughly clean out the drain plug area in the crankcase with a shop rag and solvent.

9. Reinstall the oil bleed screw.

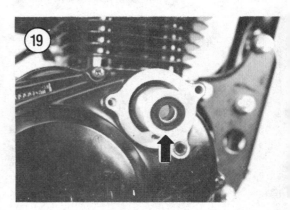

10. Install the filter screen, spring and drain plug. Tighten the drain plug as follows:
   a. XT125 and XT200 models: 31 ft.-lb. (43 N•m).
   b. XT250 models: 23 ft.-lb. (32 N•m).

11. Install a new oil filter. Install the oil filter cover and tighten the bolts securely.

12. Insert a funnel into the oil fill hole and fill the engine with the correct type (**Table 4**) and quantity (**Table 5**) of oil.

13. Screw in the oil filler cap securely.

14. Start the engine, let it run at moderate speed and check for leaks.

15. Turn the engine off and check for correct oil level; adjust as necessary.

16. Check the engine oil pressure as follows:

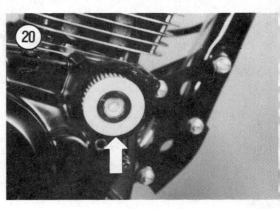

3

a. *XT125 and XT200*: Remove the oil check bolt in the cylinder head (**Figure 21**). Start the engine and allow it to idle. Do not increase engine rpm. Oil should flow out of the hole within one minute. If not, immediately stop the engine and find and correct the cause.

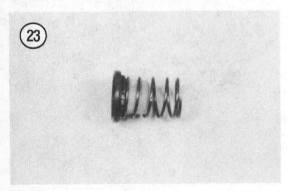

b. *XT250:* Remove the oil check bolt in the cylinder head (**Figure 22**) and the air bleed screw from the oil filter cover (**Figure 24**). Start the engine and allow it to idle. Do not increase engine rpm. Oil should flow out of both holes within one minute. If not, immediately stop the engine and find and correct the cause.

17. Reinstall all parts.

Front Fork Oil Change

The following procedure describes how to change the fork oil with the forks installed in the frame. The forks can be removed and disassembled if additional service is required. Refer to Chapter Eight.

The fork oil should be changed at the intervals described in **Table 1**. If it becomes contaminated with dirt or water, change it immediately.

1. Place a milk crate or wood block(s) under the bike's frame to raise the front wheel off the ground.
2. On XT125 and XT200 models, loosen the upper fork bridge bolts (**Figure 25**).
3A. *XT250*: Remove the fork cap by pushing the cap in and prying out the circlip (**Figure 26**).
3B. *XT125 and XT200*: Using a 17 mm Allen wrench or a 17 mm bolt and Vice Grips as shown in **Figure 27**, loosen and remove the fork cap.

4. Place a drain pan under the front fork and remove the drain bolt (**Figure 28**). Let the oil drain for a few minutes.

> *CAUTION*
> *Do not allow the fork oil to come in contact with any of the brake components.*

5. Inspect the gasket on the drain screw; replace it if necessary. Install the drain screw.
6. Repeat for the other fork.
7. Fill each fork with the specified type and quantity of fork oil. Refer to **Table 4** and **Table 5**.

> *NOTE*
> *The viscosity of the oil can vary according to your own preference and to the type of riding terrain (lighter viscosity for less damping and heavier for more damping action). The amount of oil should not be varied.*

> *NOTE*
> *In order to measure the correct amount of fluid, use a plastic baby bottle. These have measurements in fluid ounces (oz.) and cubic centimeters (cc) on the side. Many fork oil containers have a semi-transparent strip on the side of the bottle to aid in measuring.*

8. Inspect the O-ring seal on the upper fork cap (**Figure 29**) and replace if necessary.
9. Install the fork cap as follows:
   a. *XT250*: Insert the fork cap in the top of the fork tube. Push it down and hold it in place while installing the circlip. Make sure the circlip is fully seated in the fork tube.
   b. *XT125 and XT200*: Install the fork cap. Tighten to 17 ft.-lb. (20 N•m).

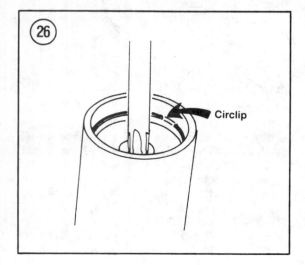

10. On XT125 and XT200 models, tighten the upper fork bridge bolts to 14 ft.-lb. (20 N•m).
11. After assembling each fork tube, slowly pump the forks several times to distribute the oil.
12. Road test the bike and check for leaks.

Drive Chain Lubrication

Lubricate the drive chain at the intervals specified in **Table 1** or more frequently if required.

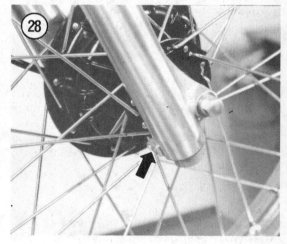

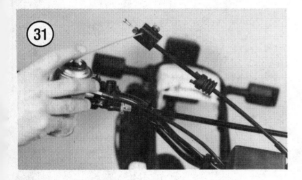

A properly maintained chain will provide maximum service life and reliability.

1. Place a milk crate or wood block(s) under the engine to support the bike securely.

2. Shift the transmission to NEUTRAL.

3. Oil the bottom run of the chain with a commercial chain lubricant (**Figure 30**). Concentrate on getting the lubricant down between the side plates, pins, bushings and rollers of each chain link.

4. Rotate the wheel to bring the unoiled portion of the chain within reach. Continue until all of the chain is lubricated.

Control Cables

The control cables should be lubricated at the intervals specified in **Table 1**. They should also be inspected at this time for fraying and the cable sheath should be checked for chafing. The cables are relatively inexpensive and should be replaced when found to be faulty.

The control cables can be lubricated either with any of the popular cable lubricants and a cable lubricator or with thin oil. The second method requires more time and the complete lubrication of the entire cable is less certain.

NOTE
Cable stiffness and breakage is normally caused by inadequate cable

lubrication. As the cable becomes dry, the hand lever must be pulled harder than normal to operate the cable. The tension increases at the end of the cable, eventually breaking it. Maintaining the cables as described will assure long service.

Lubricator method

1. Disconnect the cables from the front brake lever, the clutch lever and the throttle grip assembly.

NOTE
On the throttle cable it is necessary to remove the screws that clamp the housing together to gain access to the cable end.

2. Attach a lubricator to the end of the cable(s) following the manufacturer's instructions.

3. Insert the nozzle of the lubricant can in the lubricator, press the button on the can and hold it down until the lubricant begins to flow out of the other end of the cable. See **Figure 31**.

NOTE
Place a shop cloth at the end of the cable(s) to catch all excess lubricant that will flow out.

4. Remove the lubricator, reconnect the cable(s) and adjust the cable(s) as described in this chapter.

Oil method

1. Disconnect the cables from both the front and rear brake levers and the throttle housing.

NOTE
On the throttle cable it is necessary to remove the screws that clamp the housing together to gain access to the cable end.

2. Make a cone of stiff paper and tape it to the end of the cable sheath (**Figure 32**).

3. Hold the cable upright and pour a small amount of thin oil (SAE 10W-30) into the cone. Work the cable in and out of the sheath for several minutes to help the oil work its way down to the end of the cable.

NOTE
To avoid a mess, place a shop cloth at the end of the cable to catch the oil as it runs out.

4. Remove the cone, reconnect the cable and adjust the cable(s) as described in this chapter.

Swing Arm Bushing Lubrication

Lubricate the swing arm bushings at the intervals specified in **Table 1**. The swing arm must be removed on all models to perform this procedure. See Chapter Nine.

Brake Cam Lubrication

Lubricate the front and rear brake cam at the specified intervals (**Table 1**), or whenever the wheel is removed.

1. Remove the wheel as described in Chapter Eight or Chapter Nine.
2. Remove the brake panel assembly from the wheel hub.
3. Remove the brake shoes from the backing plate by pulling upon the center of each shoe.

NOTE
Place a clean shop rag on the linings to protect them from oil and grease during removal.

4. Wipe away old grease from the camshaft and pivot pins on the backing plate. Also clean the pivot hole and camshaft contact area of each shoe. Be careful not to get any grease on the linings.
5. Sparingly apply a high-temperature grease to all pivot and rubbing surfaces of the backing plate and the camshaft, to the brake shoe pivot points and to the spring ends.
6. Reassemble the brake assembly.
7. Reinstall the brake panel assembly into the wheel hub and reinstall the wheel. See Chapter Eight or Chapter Nine.
8. On rear wheels, adjust the drive chain and rear brake as described in this chapter.

Speedometer Cable Lubrication

Lubricate the cable every year or whenever needle operation is erratic.

1. Unscrew the retaining collar and remove the cable from the instrument (**Figure 33**).
2. Pull the cable from the cable sheath.
3. If the grease on the cable is contaminated, thoroughly clean off all old grease.
4. Thoroughly coat the cable with a good grade of multipurpose grease and reinstall into the sheath.
5. Make sure the cable is correctly seated into the drive unit. If the cable is hard to seat, disconnect the cable at the wheel (**Figure 34**), reassemble and reinstall.

Miscellaneous Lubrication Points

Lubricate the clutch lever, front brake lever, sidestand pivot point and footpeg pivot points. Use 10W-30 motor oil.

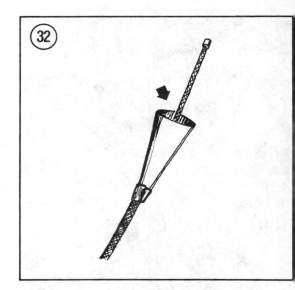

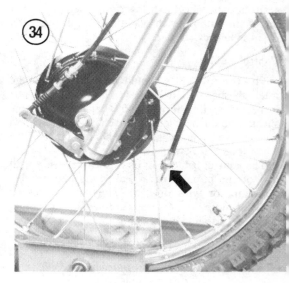

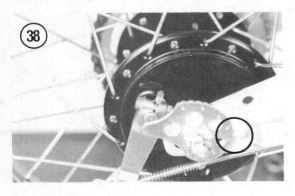

PERIODIC MAINTENANCE

Drive Chain

The drive chain should be checked and adjusted every 300 miles (500 km).

Chain tension check

1. Place a milk crate or wood block(s) under the engine to support the bike securely with the rear wheel off the ground.
2. Shift the transmission into NEUTRAL.
3. Rotate the rear wheel to move the chain to different positions, checking the chain tension at each position. Chains rarely wear or stretch evenly and, as a result, the free play will not remain constant. Locate the tightest point along the chain path to check the free play.
4. The correct amount of chain free play, when pushed up midway between the sprockets on the lower chain run (**Figure 35**) is:
   a. *XT125 and XT200*: 1 7/8-2 1/8 in. (45-55 mm).
   b. *XT250*: 2-2 3/8 in. (50-60 mm).
5. If the chain tension is incorrect, adjust as described in this chapter.

Chain adjustment

1. Place a milk crate or wood block(s) under the engine to support the bike securely with the rear wheel off the ground.
2. Shift the transmission into NEUTRAL.
3. Loosen the rear brake adjuster (**Figure 36**).
4. Loosen the axle nut.
5. Turn both axle snail adjusters (**Figure 37**) in equal amounts to either increase or decrease chain tension. After adjustment is complete, make sure that the same snail adjuster mark aligns with the stopper pin on either side of the swing arm (**Figure 38**).
6. If the chain cannot be adjusted to within specifications, it is excessively worn and stretched and should be replaced. Always replace both sprockets when replacing the drive chain; never install a new chain over worn sprockets.
7. Tighten the axle nut as follows:
   a. *XT125 and XT200*: 61 ft.-lb. (85 N•m).
   b. *XT250*: 77 ft.-lb. (106 N•m).
8. After the drive chain has been adjusted, the rear brake pedal free play must be adjusted as described in this chapter.

Drive Chain Cleaning, Inspection and Lubrication

Yamaha does not specify mileage intervals for cleaning the drive chain but it is a good practice to remove, thoroughly clean and lubricate the chain every 2,000 miles (3,200 km) or more frequently if ridden in dusty or muddy terrain. After riding in sand, remove and clean the chain as soon as possible. Service intervals for lubrication are every 300 miles (500 km).

1. Remove the drive chain as described in Chapter Nine.

2. Immerse the chain in a pan of cleaning solvent and allow it to soak for about half an hour. Move it around and flex it during this period so that dirt between the pins and rollers may work its way out.

3. Scrub the rollers and side plates with a stiff brush and rinse away loosened grit. Rinse it a couple of times to make sure all dirt is washed out. Hang up the chain and allow it to thoroughly dry.

4. After cleaning the chain, examine it carefully for wear or damage. If any signs are visible, replace the chain.

> *CAUTION*
> *Always check both sprockets (**Figure 39**) every time the drive chain is removed. If any wear is visible on the teeth, replace the sprockets. Never install a new chain over worn sprockets or a worn chain over new sprockets.*

5. Check the inner face of the inner plates (**Figure 40**). They should be lightly polished on both sides.

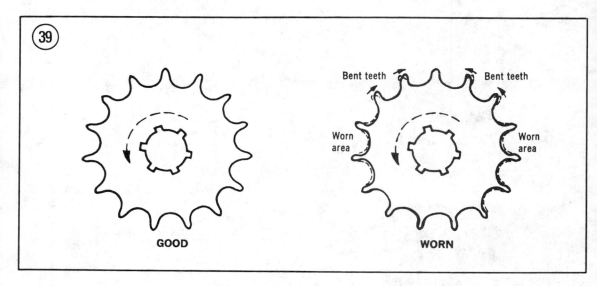

GOOD **WORN**

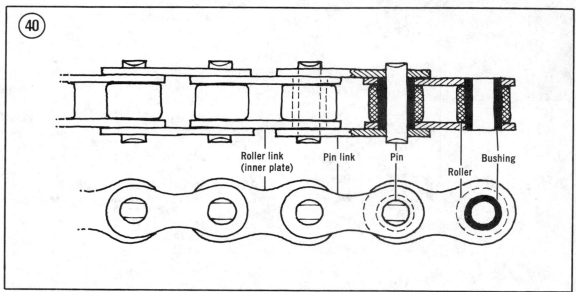

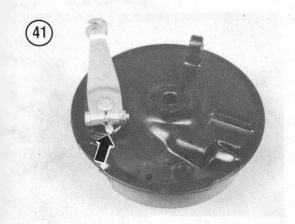

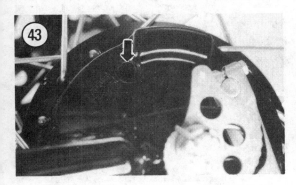

If they show considerable wear on both sides, the sprockets are not aligned. Adjust alignment as described under *Drive Chain Adjustment* in this chapter.

6. Lubricate the chain with a good grade of chain lubricant carefully following the manufacturer's instructions.

7. Reinstall the chain as described in Chapter Nine.

8. Adjust chain free play as described in this chapter.

Brake Lining Inspection

The brake linings should be inspected at the intervals specified in **Table 1**. If the brake shoes must be replaced, refer to Chapter Ten. Always replace brake shoes in sets; never replace a single brake shoe.

XT250

Remove the inspection cover from the front and rear wheel backing plates (**Figure 43**). Observe the thickness of the brake shoes. The thickness of new brake linings is 0.16 in. (4 mm). The brake shoes should be replaced when shoe thickness is 0.08 in. (2 mm) or less.

XT125 and XT200

Apply the brake fully; if the wear indicator arrow on the brake arm aligns with the wear limit line on the brake backing plate the brake shoes must be replaced. See **Figure 41** (front) and **Figure 42** (rear).

> *WARNING*
> *After inspecting the brakes, reinstall the inspection cover(s); failure to do so will allow water to enter the brake area, causing loss of braking power.*

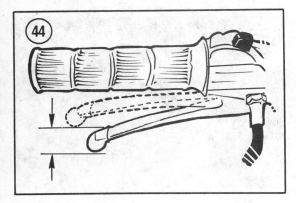

Front Brake Lever Adjustment

The front brake cable must be adjusted so that 3/16-5/16 in. (5-8 mm) of brake lever movement (**Figure 44**) is required to actuate the brake, but it must not be adjusted so closely that the brake shoes contact the drum with the lever relaxed. Minor adjustments should be made at the brake lever and major adjustments made at the brake panel at the wheel.

1. Slide back the rubber brake lever cover.

2. Loosen the adjuster locknut (A, **Figure 45**). Turn the adjuster (B, **Figure 45**) to obtain a free

play measurement of 3/16-5/16 in. (5-8 mm). Tighten the locknut.

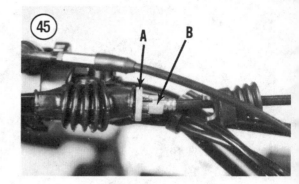

NOTE
Because of normal brake wear, this adjustment will eventually be "used up." When this occurs, proceed to Step 3.

3. Loosen the locknut and screw the brake lever adjuster all the way toward the hand grip. Tighten the locknut.
4. At the brake panel, loosen the locknut (A, **Figure 46**) and turn the adjuster (B, **Figure 46**) until the brake lever can be used once again for the minor adjustment. Tighten the locknut.
5. At the hand lever, loosen the locknut and turn the adjuster (B, **Figure 45**) to achieve the correct amount of free play. Tighten the locknut.
6. Slide the rubber brake lever cover back into place.

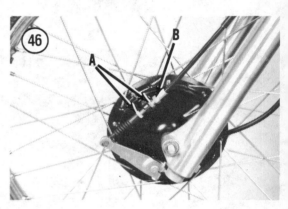

Rear Brake Pedal
Height Adjustment

The rear brake pedal height should be adjusted at the intervals specified in **Table 1** or anytime the brake shoes are replaced. The height positon should be set to your own personal preference.
1. Place the bike on the sidestand.
2. Check to be sure the brake pedal is in the at-rest position.
3. To change height position, loosen the locknut and turn the adjuster. See **Figure 47** (XT125 and XT200) or **Figure 48** (XT250).
4. Tighten the locknut and adjust the brake pedal free play as described in this chapter.

Rear Brake Pedal
Free Play Adjustment

Adjust the brake pedal to the correct height as described in this chapter. Then turn the adjustment nut on the end of the brake rod (**Figure 36**) until the brake pedal has 3/4-1 1/4 in. (20-30 mm) free play. Free play is the distance the pedal travels from the at-rest position to the applied position when the pedal is depressed lightly by hand.

Rotate the rear wheel and check for brake drag. Also operate the pedal several times to make sure it returns to the at-rest position immediately after release.

Adjust the rear brake light switch as described in Chapter Seven.

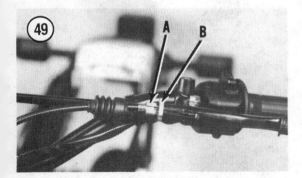

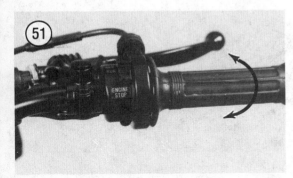

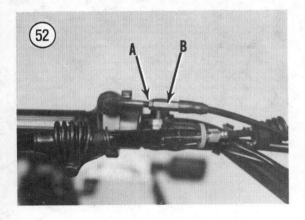

Clutch Cable Adjustment

The clutch cable free play should be adjusted at the intervals specified in **Table 1**.

> *NOTE*
> *When rebuilding or reassembling the clutch assembly, perform the **Clutch Mechanism Adjustment** in Chapter Five before adjusting the clutch cable.*

1. Slide back the rubber clutch lever cover.
2. Loosen the adjuster locknut (A, **Figure 49**). Turn the adjuster (B, **Figure 49**) to obtain a free play measurement of 1/8 in. (2-3 mm). Tighten the locknut.

> *NOTE*
> *If the proper amount of free play cannot be achieved at the hand lever, additional adjustment can be made close to the clutch actuating lever on the right-hand side of the engine.*

3. At the hand lever, loosen the locknut and turn the adjuster all the way in toward the hand lever. Tighten the locknut.
4. On the right-hand side of the engine, loosen the locknut and turn the adjuster barrel until the correct amount of lever free play is obtained. See **Figure 50**. Tighten the locknut.
5. If necessary, repeat Step 2 for fine adjustment.
6. After adjustment is completed, check that the locknuts are tight both at the hand lever and at the right-hand side of the engine.
7. Test ride the bike and make sure the clutch is operating correctly.

Throttle Operation/Adjustment

The throttle grip should have 1/8-1/4 in. (2-5 mm) of rotational play (**Figure 51**). Make sure there is free play in the cable so the carburetor will be able to close completely when the throttle is let off. If adjustment is necessary, perform the following.

1A. *XT125 and XT200*: Slide back the rubber cover at the cable adjuster. Loosen the cable locknut (A, **Figure 52**) and turn the adjuster (B, **Figure 52**) in or out to achieve the proper play. Tighten the locknut (A). If the proper amount of free play cannot be produced by the adjuster at the throttle grip there is an additional adjustment point at the top of the carburetor. Remove the fuel tank as described in Chapter Six. Loosen the locknut and turn the adjuster (**Figure 53**) to achieve the proper amount of free play. Tighten the locknut.

3

1B. *XT250*: Referring to **Figure 54**, loosen the adjuster locknuts on cable No. 1 and turn the adjuster in or out to obtain the correct free play. Tighten the locknut after making the adjustment.

2. Check the throttle cable(s) from grip to carburetors. Make sure they are not kinked or chafed. Replace them if necessary.

3. Make sure that the throttle grip rotates smoothly from fully closed to fully open. Check at center, full left and full right position of steering.

Decompression Cable Adjustment (XT250)

1. Place the bike on the sidestand.

2. Remove the fuel tank as described in Chapter Six.

3. Remove the spark plug. This will make it easier to rotate the engine with a wrench.

4. Remove the alternator cover (**Figure 55**) from the left-hand side of the engine.

5. Rotate the crankshaft with a wrench on the alternator nut (**Figure 56**). Turn the nut *counterclockwise* to align the "T" mark on the flywheel with the crankcase timing mark. This positions the piston at top dead center (TDC) on the compression stroke.

> *NOTE*
> *A piston at TDC will have both of its rocker arms loose, indicating that both the exhaust and intake valves are closed. Remove the valve adjustment covers (**Figure 57**) and check. If both rocker arms are not loose, turn the engine an additional 180°.*

6. Measure the free play at the end of the decompression cam lever as shown in A, **Figure 58**. The correct amount of free play is 1/32-1/8 in. (1-3 mm).

7. To adjust the free play, loosen the locknut (B, **Figure 58**) and turn the adjuster until the correct amount of free play is achieved. Tighten the locknut.

CAUTION
If the free play is not adjusted correctly, it will result in hard starting (excessive free play) or cause erratic engine idle and possibly a burned exhaust valve (insufficient free play).

8. Install the valve adjusting covers, the spark plug, the alternator cover and the fuel tank.

Fuel Shutoff Valve/Filter

Refer to Chapter Six for complete details on removal, cleaning and installation.

Fuel Line Inspection

Inspect the fuel line(s) (**Figure 59**) for cracks or deterioration; replace if necessary. Make sure the hose clamps are in place and holding securely.

Exhaust System

Check for leakage at all fittings. Tighten all bolts and nuts; replace the gasket at the cylinder head if necessary.

Spark Arrester Cleaning

Periodically remove the screw holding the spark arrester (**Figure 60**) and remove it from the end of the exhaust pipe. Clean the pipe of all exhaust residue with a wire brush and solvent.

Air Cleaner
Removal/Cleaning/Installation

The service intervals specified in **Table 1** should be followed with general use. However, the air cleaner should be serviced more often if the bike is ridden in dusty areas.

The air cleaner removes dust and abrasive particles from the air before it enters the carburetor and engine. Without the air cleaner, very fine particles could enter into the engine and cause rapid wear of the piston rings, cylinder and bearings. They also might clog small passages in the carburetor. Never run the bike without the air cleaner element installed.

1. Place the bike on the sidestand.
2. Remove the screws securing the side cover from the left-hand (XT125 and XT200) or right-hand (XT250) side.
3. Remove the screw(s) securing the air filter cover and remove the cover. See **Figure 61** (XT125 and XT200) or **Figure 62** (XT250).

4A. *XT125 and XT200*: Pull back on the rear filter stop and pull the filter element out of the housing. See **Figure 63**.

4B. *XT250 models*: Pull the air filter out of the air box (**Figure 64**).

5. Remove the air filter element from the holder. See **Figure 65** (XT125 and XT200) or **Figure 66** (XT250).

6. Wipe out the interior of the air box with a shop rag and cleaning solvent. Remove any foreign matter that may have passed through a broken filter. Make sure the drain hole is open.

7. Clean the filter gently in cleaning solvent until all dirt is removed. Thoroughly dry in a clean shop cloth until all solvent residue is removed. Let it dry for about one hour.

CAUTION
Inspect the filter; if it is torn or broken in any area it should be replaced. Do not run with a damaged element as it will allow dirt to enter the engine.

8. Pour a small amount of foam air filter oil into the filter and work it into the porous foam material. Do not oversaturate the filter as too much oil will restrict air flow. The filter will be discolored by the oil and should have an even color indicating that the oil is distributed evenly. Let the filter dry for another hour prior to installation. If installed too soon, the chemical carrier in the special foam air filter oil will be drawn into the engine and may cause damage.

9. Install the air filter element onto the holder.

10. On XT125 and XT200 models, coat the mouth of the air filter where it seats against the air box with waterproof grease. On XT250 models, coat all 4 edges of the filter with grease. This

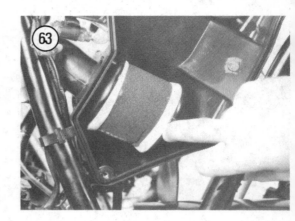

application of grease will help to provide an air-tight seat between the air box and filter.

11. Install the filter assembly into the air box. Make sure that the air filter element is properly seated against the air box. On XT250 models, make sure the fuzzy side of the air filter faces the rear of the bike.

> *CAUTION*
> *An improperly installed air cleaner element will allow dirt and grit to enter the carburetor and engine, causing expensive engine damage.*

12. Install the air filter cover and the side cover.

Wheel Bearings

The wheel bearings should be cleaned and repacked at the intervals specified in **Table 1**. Refer to Chapter Eight and Chapter Nine for complete service procedures.

Steering Head Check

The steering head is fitted with loose ball bearings. It should be checked at the intervals specified in **Table 1**.
1. Prop up the motorcycle so that the front tire clears the ground.

2. Center the front wheel. Push lightly against the left handlebar grip to start the wheel turning to the right, then let go. The wheel should continue turning under its own momentum until the forks hit their stop.
3. Center the wheel and push lightly against the right handlebar grip.
4. If, with a light push in either direction, the front wheel will turn all the way to the stop, the steering adjustment is not too tight.
5. Center the front wheel and kneel in front of it. Grasp the bottoms of the 2 front fork slider legs. Try to pull the forks toward you and then try to push them toward the engine. If no play is felt, the steering adjustment is not too loose.
6. If the steering adjustment is too tight or too loose, readjust it as described in Chapter Eight.

Steering Head Bearings

The steering head bearings should be repacked every 9,500 miles (15,000 km) as described in Chapter Eight.

Wheel Hubs, Rims and Spokes

Check wheel hubs and rims for bends and other signs of damage. Check both wheels for broken or bent spokes. Replace damaged or broken spokes as described in Chapter Eight. Pluck each spoke with your finger like a guitar string or tap each one lightly with a spoke wrench. All spokes should emit the same sound. A spoke that is too tight will have a higher pitch than the others; one that is too loose will have a lower pitch. If only one or two spokes are slightly out of adjustment, adjust them with a spoke wrench made for this purpose. If more are affected, the wheel should be removed and trued. Refer to Chapter Eight.

Front Suspension Check

1. Apply the front brake and pump the fork up and down as vigorously as possible. Check for smooth operation and check for any oil leaks.
2. Make sure the upper and lower fork bridge bolts (**Figure 67**) are tight.
3. Check the tightness of the handlebar holder bolts (**Figure 68**).
4. Make sure that the front axle nut is tight and that the cotter pin is in place.

> *CAUTION*
> *If any of the previously mentioned bolts and nuts are loose, refer to Chapter Eight for correct procedures and torque specifications.*

Rear Suspension Check

1. Place a milk crate or wood block(s) under the engine to support it securely with the rear wheel off the ground.
2. Push hard on the rear wheel sideways to check for side play in the rear swing arm bushings or bearings.
3. Check that the front monoshock bolt is tight and that the rear monoshock bolt is held securely with the cotter pin.
4. Make sure the rear axle nut is tight and the cotter pin is still in place.

> *CAUTION*
> *If any of the previously mentioned nuts or bolts are loose, refer to Chapter Nine for correct procedures and torque specifications.*

Nuts, Bolts and Other Fasteners

Constant vibration can loosen many fasteners on a motorcycle. Check the tightness of all fasteners, especially those on:
  a. Engine mounting hardware.
  b. Engine crankcase covers.
  c. Handlebar and front forks.
  d. Gearshift and kickstarter levers.
  e. Sprocket bolts and nuts.
  f. Brake pedal and lever.
  g. Exhaust system.

TUNE-UP

A complete tune-up should be performed at the intervals specified in **Table 1**. More frequent tune-ups may be required if the bike is ridden primarily in stop-and-go traffic or off-road. The purpose of the tune-up is to restore the performance lost due to normal wear and deterioration of parts.

Table 6 summarizes tune-up specifications.

Before starting a tune-up procedure, make sure to first have all new parts on hand.

Because different systems in an engine interact, the procedures should be done in the following order:
  a. Clean or replace the air cleaner element.
  b. Tighten cylinder head bolts.
  c. Adjust valve clearance.
  d. Adjust camshaft chain tension.
  e. Check engine compression.
  f. Check or replace spark plug.
  g. Check ignition timing.
  h. Adjust carburetor idle speed.

Tools

To perform a tune-up on your Yamaha, you will need the following tools:
  a. Spark plug wrench.
  b. Socket wrench and assorted sockets.
  c. Flat feeler gauge.
  d. Compression gauge.
  e. Spark plug wire feeler gauge and gapper tool.
  f. Ignition timing light.
  g. Portable tachometer.
  h. Torque wrench.

Cylinder Head Fasteners

The engine must be at room temperature for this procedure (95° F/35° C or cooler).
1. Place the bike on the sidestand.
2. Remove the seat and fuel tank as described in Chapter Six.
3. Tighten the cylinder head fasteners in a crisscross pattern to the specifications in **Table 6**.
4. The fuel tank and cam cover should be left off at this time for the following procedures.

Valve Adjustment

Valve clearance measurement must be made with the engine cool, at room temperature.
1. Place the bike on the sidestand.
2. Remove the seat and fuel tank as described in Chapter Six.
3. Remove the spark plug (this makes it easier to turn the engine by hand).
4. Remove both valve adjustment covers (**Figure 69**).
5A. *XT125 and XT200*: Remove the 2 inspection hole covers (**Figure 70**) located on the left-hand crankcase.

5B. *XT250*: Remove the left-hand crankcase cover (**Figure 71**).

6. Rotate the engine by turning the crankshaft. Use either a socket (XT125 and XT200) or wrench (XT250) on the nut located on the left-hand end of the crankshaft. See **Figure 72**. Turn it *counterclockwise* until the piston is at top dead center (TDC) on the compression stroke.

NOTE
A piston at TDC on its compression stroke will have free play in both of its rocker arms, indicating that both the intake and exhaust valves are closed.

7. Make sure the "T" mark on the flywheel is aligned with the stationary pointer on the crankcase.

8. If the engine timing mark is aligned with the "T" mark but both rocker arms are not loose, rotate the engine an additional 180° until both valves have free play.

9. Check the intake and exhaust valve clearance by inserting a flat feeler gauge between the rocker arm pad and the camshaft lobe (**Figure 73**). When the clearance is correct, there will be a slight resistance on the feeler gauge when it is inserted and withdrawn. Refer to **Table 6** for the correct valve clearance specification for your model.

NOTE
Step 9 describes valve adjustment. The valve adjusting wrench used in the following procedures is provided in your bike's tool kit or it may be purchased from a Yamaha dealer.

10. To correct the clearance, use the valve adjusting wrench (**Figure 74**) and back off the locknut. Turn the adjuster in or out so there is a slight resistance felt on the feeler gauge. Hold the adjuster to prevent it from turning further and tighten the locknut securely. Recheck the clearance

3

to make sure the adjuster did not slip when the locknut was tightened. Readjust if necessary.

11. Rotate the engine 360° and repeat Step 8 to make sure the adjustment is correct. If the clearance is still not correct, repeat Step 9 until it is correct.

12. Inspect the rubber O-ring on each valve adjusting cover. Replace if they are starting to deteriorate or harden; replace as a set even if only one is bad. Install both covers and tighten securely.

13. Install the spark plug.

14. On XT250 models, adjust the starter decompressor as described in this chapter.

15. Install all parts previously removed.

Camshaft Chain
Tensioner Adjustment

In time the camshaft chain and guide will wear and develop slack. This will cause engine noise and if neglected too long will cause engine damage. The cam chain tension should be adjusted at the specified intervals (**Table 1**) or whenever it becomes noisy.

1. Place the bike on the sidestand.

2. Remove the fuel tank as described in Chapter Six.

3. Remove both valve covers (**Figure 69**).

4A. *XT125 and XT200*: Remove the 2 inspection hole covers (**Figure 70**) located on the left-hand crankcase.

4B. *XT250*: Remove the left-hand crankcase cover (**Figure 71**).

5. Rotate the engine by turning the crankshaft. Use either a socket (XT125 and XT200) or wrench (XT250) on the nut located on the left-hand end of the crankshaft. See **Figure 72**. Turn it *counterclockwise* until the piston is at top dead center (TDC) on the compression stroke.

> *NOTE*
> *A piston at TDC on its compression stroke will have free play in both of its rocker arms, indicating that both the intake and exhaust valves are closed.*

6. Make sure the "T" mark on the flywheel is aligned with the stationary pointer on the crankcase.

7. Grasp and attempt to move both rocker arms. If both rocker arms are not loose, rotate the engine an additional 180° until both valves have free play. Reinstall the valve adjustment covers.

> *NOTE*
> *On XT250 models, adjust the starter decompressor as described in this chapter after completing Step 7.*

8. Remove the cam chain adjuster cover (**Figure 75**).

9. Loosen the adjuster locknut (A, **Figure 76**) and turn the adjuster (B, **Figure 76**) until the push rod (inside the adjuster) is flush with the end of the adjuster. Do not tighten the locknut or install the cover at this point; continue with Step 10.

10. Start the engine and allow it to idle. Check the movement of the pushrod. If it moves slightly, the adjustment is correct. If the pushrod does not move, the adjuster is too tight. Loosen the adjuster so that the pushrod moves slightly when the engine is running.

11. When the adjuster operates as described in Step 9, turn the engine off and tighten the adjuster locknut.

12. Install all parts previously removed.

Compression Test

At every tune-up check cylinder compression. Record the results and compare them at the next check. A running record will show trends in

deterioration so that corrective action can be taken before complete failure occurs.

The results, when properly interpreted, can indicate general cylinder, piston ring and valve condition.

1. Place the bike on the sidestand.
2. Start the engine and let it warm to normal operating temperature. Shut the engine off.
3. Remove the spark plug. Install the spark plug back into the plug cap to ground the wire (**Figure 77**).
4. Connect the compression tester to the cylinder following manufacturer's instructions (**Figure 78**).
5. Turn the throttle all the way open.
6. Operate the kickstarter several times while watching the gauge. Stop turning the engine over when the pressure reading stops climbing.
7. Remove the tester and record the reading.
8. When interpreting the results, actual readings are not as important as the difference between the readings. Compare readings to specifications in **Table 6**. If a reading is higher than normal, there

may be a buildup of carbon deposits in the combustion chamber or on the piston crown. If a low reading (10% or more) is obtained it can be caused by one or more of the following faulty items:

    a. A leaking cylinder head gasket.
    b. Incorrect valve clearance.
    c. Valve leakage (burned valve face).
    d. Worn or broken piston ring.
    e. Misadjusted starter decompressor lever (XT250 only).

9. If the head gasket is okay, perform a "wet" test to determine which other component is faulty. Pour a teaspoon of engine oil through the spark plug hole onto the top of the piston. Turn the engine over once to clear some of the excess oil, then take another compression test and record the reading. If the compression returns to normal, the valves are good but the rings are defective. If compression does not increase, the valves require servicing (providing the starter decompressor lever is adjusted correctly on XT250 models). A valve could be hanging open but not burned or a piece of carbon could be on a valve seat.
10. Install the spark plug and connect the spark plug lead.

Spark Plug Heat Selection

Spark plugs are available in various heat ranges that are hotter or colder than the spark plugs originally installed at the factory.

Select a plug in a heat range designed for the loads and temperature conditions under which the engine will operate. Use of incorrect heat ranges can cause a seized piston, scored cylinder wall or damaged piston crown.

In general, use a hot plug for low speeds, low loads and low temperatures. Use a cold plug for high speeds, high engine loads and high temperatures. The plug should operate hot enough to burn off unwanted deposits, but not so hot that it is damaged or causes preignition. A spark plug of the correct heat range will show a light tan color on the portion of the insulator within the cylinder after the plug has been in service.

The reach (length) of a plug is also important. A longer than normal plug could interfere with the valves and pistons causing permanent and severe damage; refer to **Figure 79**. The standard heat range spark plugs are listed in **Table 6**.

Spark Plug Cleaning/Replacement

1. Grasp the spark plug lead (**Figure 80**) as near to the plug as possible and pull it off the plug.

2. Blow away any dirt that has accumulated in the spark plug well.

> *CAUTION*
> *The dirt could fall into the cylinder when the plug is removed, causing serious engine damage.*

3. Remove the spark plug with a spark plug wrench.

> *NOTE*
> *If the plug is difficult to remove, apply penetrating oil such as WD-40 or Liquid Wrench around base · of plug and let it soak in about 10-20 minutes.*

4. Inspect spark plug carefully. Look for a broken center porcelain, excessively eroded electrodes and excessive carbon or oil fouling. If any problems are found, replace the plug. If deposits are light, the plug may be cleaned with a wire brush. Regap the plug as described in this chapter.

Spark Plug
Gapping and Installation

A spark plug should be carefully gapped to ensure a reliable, consistent spark. You must use a special spark plug gapping tool with a wire gauge.

1. Remove the new spark plug from the box. *Do not* screw on the small cap that is loose in the box; it is not used.
2. Insert a wire gauge between the spark plug's center and side electrode (**Figure 81**). The correct gap is listed in **Table 6**. If the gap is correct, you will feel a slight drag as you pull the wire through. If there is no drag or the gauge won't pass through, bend the side electrode *with the gapping tool* (**Figure 82**) to set the proper gap (**Table 6**).
3. Put a small drop of oil or anti-seize compound on the threads of the spark plug.
4. Screw the spark plug in by hand until it seats. Very little effort is required. If force is necessary, you have the plug cross-threaded; unscrew it and try again.
5. Tighten the spark plugs to specifications (**Table 6**). If you don't have a torque wrench, an additional 1/4 to 1/2 turn is sufficient after the gasket has made contact with the head. If you are reinstalling the old, regapped plug and are reusing the old gasket, only tighten an additional 1/4 turn.

> *NOTE*
> *Do not overtighten. This will only squash the gasket and destroy its sealing ability.*

6. Install the spark plug wire. Make sure it is on tight.

Reading Spark Plugs

Much information about engine and spark plug performance can be determined by careful examination of the spark plug. This information is only valid after performing the following steps.

1. Ride bike a short distance at full throttle in any gear.
2. Turn off kill switch before closing throttle. Simultaneously pull in clutch and coast and brake to a stop. *Do not* downshift transmission while stopping.
3. Remove spark plug and examine it. Compare to the illustrations in Chapter Two:
   a. If the insulator is white or burned, the plug is too hot and should be replaced with a colder one.
   b. A too-cold plug will have sooty deposits ranging in color from dark brown to black.

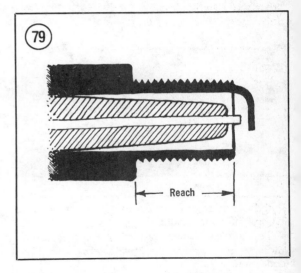

Replace with a hotter plug and check for too-rich carburetion or evidence of oil blow-by at the piston rings.

c. If the plug has a light tan or gray colored deposit and no abnormal gap wear or electrode erosion is evident, the plug and the engine are running properly.

d. If the plug exhibits a black insulator tip, a damp and oily film over the firing end or a carbon layer over the entire nose, it is oil or gas fouled. An oil or gas fouled plug can be cleaned, but it is better to replace it.

Ignition Timing

All models are equipped with a capacitor discharge ignition system (CDI). Timing is set on all models and is not adjustable (the base plate screws have no slots for adjustment). The following procedure can be used to check ignition timing only.

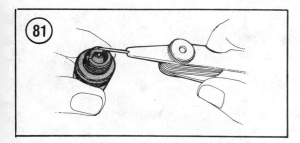

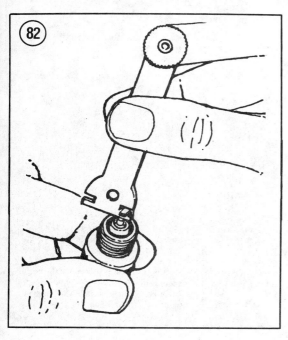

NOTE
Before starting this procedure, check all electrical connections related to the ignition system. Make sure all connections are tight and free of corrosion and that all ground connections are tight.

1. Place the bike on the sidestand.
2. Start the engine and let it reach normal operating temperature. Turn the engine off.
3. Connect a portable tachometer following the manufacturer's instructions.
4. Remove the timing mark inspection cover (XT125 and XT200) or the magneto cover (XT250). See **Figure 70** or **Figure 71**.
5. Connect a timing light following the manufacuturer's instructions.
6. Restart the engine and let it idle at the specified rpm. See **Table 6**.
7. Adjust the idle speed if necessary as described in this chapter.
8. Aim the timing light toward the timing marks and pull the trigger (**Figure 84**). The timing is correct if the marks are aligned as follows:
   a. *XT125 and XT200*: The stationary pointer in the timing window should be within the firing range shown on the flywheel. See **Figure 85**.
   b. *XT250*: The stationary pointer on the crankcase should be between the two firing marks as shown in **Figure 86**.
9. If the ignition timing is incorrect, proceed as follows:
   a. *XT125 and XT200*: Remove the left-hand side cover and check the tightness of the coils in the cover (**Figure 87**).
   b. *XT250*: Remove the magneto (see Chapter Seven) and check the timing plate screws for tightness (**Figure 88**).
   c. If these are okay, refer to Chapter Seven for ignition system troubleshooting. Ignition timing cannot be adjusted.

Carburetor Idle Mixture

The idle mixture (pilot screw) is preset at the factory and it is *not to be reset*.

Carburetor Idle Speed Adjustment

Before making this adjustment, the air cleaner must be clean and the engine must have adequate compression. Otherwise this procedure cannot be done properly.

1. Place the bike on the centerstand.
2. Attach a portable tachometer following the manufacturer's instructions.

(83) **SPARK PLUG CONDITION**

NORMAL

- Identified by light tan or gray deposits on the firing tip.
- Can be cleaned.

GAP BRIDGED

- Identified by deposit buildup closing gap between electrodes.
- Caused by oil or carbon fouling. If deposits are not excessive, the plug can be cleaned.

OIL FOULED

- Identified by wet black deposits on the insulator shell bore and electrodes.
- Caused by excessive oil entering combustion chamber through worn rings and pistons, excessive clearance between valve guides and stems, or worn or loose bearings. Can be cleaned. If engine is not repaired, use a hotter plug.

CARBON FOULED

- Identified by black, dry fluffy carbon deposits on insulator tips, exposed shell surfaces and electrodes.
- Caused by too cold a plug, weak ignition, dirty air cleaner, too rich a fuel mixture, or excessive idling. Can be cleaned.

LEAD FOULED

- Identified by dark gray, black, yellow, or tan deposits or a fused glazed coating on the insulator tip.
- Caused by highly leaded gasoline. Can be cleaned.

WORN

- Identified by severely eroded or worn electrodes.
- Caused by normal wear. Should be replaced.

FUSED SPOT DEPOSIT

- Identified by melted or spotty deposits resembling bubbles or blisters.
- Caused by sudden acceleration. Can be cleaned.

OVERHEATING

- Identified by a white or light gray insulator with small black or gray brown spots and with bluish-burnt appearance of electrodes.
- Caused by engine overheating, wrong type of fuel, loose spark plugs, too hot a plug, or incorrect ignition timing. Replace the plug.

PREIGNITION

- Identified by melted electrodes and possibly blistered insulator. Metallic deposits on insulator indicate engine damage.
- Caused by wrong type of fuel, incorrect ignition timing or advance, too hot a plug, burned valves, or engine overheating. Replace the plug.

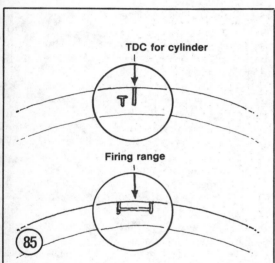

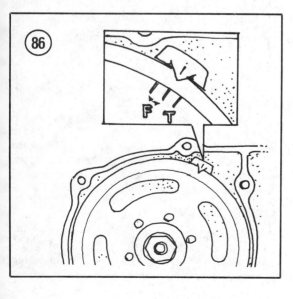

3. Start the engine and let it warm up to normal operating temperature.

4. Set the idle speed by turning the idle speed stop screw in to increase or out to decrease idle speed. See **Figure 89** (XT125 and XT200) or **Figure 90** (XT250). The correct idle speed is listed in **Table 6**.

5. Open and close the throttle a couple of times; check for variation in idle speed. Readjust if necessary.

> *WARNING*
> *With the engine idling, move the handlebar from side to side. If idle speed increases during this movement, the throttle cable(s) needs adjusting or may be incorrectly routed through the frame. Correct this problem immediately. Do not ride the bike in this unsafe condition.*

6. Turn the engine off and disconnect the portable tachometer. Install all parts previously removed.

STORAGE

Several months of inactivity can cause serious problems and a general deterioration of your machine. This is especially true in areas with extremely cold winters. During the winter, you should prepare your bike carefully for "hibernation".

Selecting a Storage Area

Most riders store their bikes in their home garage. If you do not have a garage, there are other facilities for rent or lease in most areas. When selecting an area, consider the following points.

1. The storage area must be dry; there should be no dampness or excesseive humidity. A heated area is not necessary, but it should be insulated to minimize extreme temperature variations.
2. Avoid buildings with large window areas. If unavailable, block off the windows to keep direct sunlight off the bike.
3. Avoid buildings in industrial areas where factories are liable to emit corrosive fumes. Also avoid buildings near large bodies of salt water.
4. Select an area where there is a minimum risk of fire, theft or vandalism. Check with your insurance agent to make sure that your insurance covers the bike where it is stored (the agent may also be able to suggest an area for consideration).

Preparing Bike for Storage

Careful preparation will minimize deterioration and make it easier to restore the bike to service later. Use the following procedures.

1. Wash the bike completely. Make certain you remove any road salt which may have accumulated during the first few weeks of winter. Wax all painted and polished surfaces, including any chromed areas.
2. Run the engine for 20-30 minutes to stabilize oil temperature. Drain oil, regardless of mileage since the last oil change. Replace the oil filter with a new one and fill the engine with the normal quantity of fresh oil.
3. Remove the battery and coat the cable terminals with petroleum jelly (Vaseline). If there

is evidence of acid spillage in the battery box, neutralize with baking soda, wash clean and repaint the damaged area. Store the battery in a warm area and recharge it every 2 weeks during storage.
4. Drain all gasoline from the fuel tank, interconnecting hoses and carburetors. Leave the fuel petcock in the RESERVE position. As an alternative, a fuel preservative may be added to the fuel. This preservative is available from many motorcycle shops and marine equipment suppliers.
5. Lubricate the drive chain and control cables.
6. Tie or tape a heavy plastic bag over the outlet of the mufflers to prevent the entry of moisture.
7. Check tire pressure, inflate to the proper pressure and move the bike to the storage area. Place it on the centerstand.
8. Cover the bike with a tarp, blanket or heavy plastic drop cloth. Place this cover over the bike mainly as a dust cover—do not wrap it tightly (especially any plastic material) as it may trap moisture. Leave room for air to circulate around the bike.

Inspection During Storage

Try to inspect the bike weekly while in storage. Any deterioration can then be corrected quickly. For example, if corrosion of bright metal parts is observed, cover them with a light coat of grease or silicone spray after a thorough polishing. Turn the engine over a couple of times—don't start it, use the kickstarter with the ignition OFF. Pump the front forks to keep the seals lubricated.

Restoring Bike to Service

A bike that has been properly prepared and stored in a suitable area requires only light maintenance to restore it to service. It is advisable however, to perform a spring tune-up.

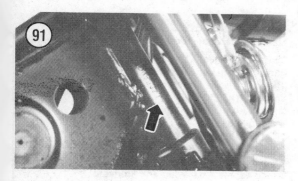

NOTE
If a fuel preservative was used, drain the system and refill with fresh gasoline.

4. Remove the spark plug and squirt a small amount of fuel into the cylinder to help remove the oil coating.
5. Install a fresh spark plug.
6. Perform a tune-up as described in this chapter.
7. Check the operation of the lighting, charging and ignition systems. Oxidation on the switch contacts during storage may make one or more of these systems inoperable.
8. Clean and test ride the motorcycle.

WARNING
If any type of preservative (Armor-All or equivalent) has been applied to the tire treads, be sure the tires are well "scrubbed-in" prior to any fast riding or cornering on a hard surface. If not, they will slip right out from under you.

GENERAL SPECIFICATIONS

General information and specifications are listed in **Table 7**.

SERIAL NUMBERS

You must know the model serial numbers and VIN number for registration purposes and sometimes when ordering replacement parts.

The frame serial number is stamped on the right-hand side of the steering head (**Figure 91**). The vehicle identification number (VIN) is on the left-hand side of the steering head (**Figure 92**). The engine serial number is located on the right-hand crankcase (**Figure 93**).

PARTS REPLACEMENT

Yamaha makes frequent changes during a model year, some minor and some relatively major. When you order parts from a dealer or other parts distributor, always order by engine or chassis number. Write down and carry them with you. Compare new parts to old parts before purchasing them. If they are not alike, have the parts manager explain the difference to you. This is especially true with electrical components as few dealers or parts houses will allow you to return them for an exchange or refund.

1. Before removing the bike from the storage area, reinflate the tires to the correct pressures. Air loss during storage may have nearly flattened the tires and moving the bike can cause damage to the tire and wheel assembly.
2. When the bike is brought to the work area, turn the fuel petcock to the PRI position.
3. Check the fuel system for leaks. Open the carburetor drain screw and allow several cups of fuel to pass through the system. Install the drain screws. Turn the petcock to the ON position.

WARNING
Place a metal container under the drain tubes to catch the expelled fuel—this presents a real fire danger if allowed to drain onto the floor. Dispose of fuel properly.

Table 1 MAINTENANCE SCHEDULE*

Every 300 miles (500 km) or as needed	Lubricate and adjust drive chain
First 600 miles (1,000 km) and first 2,500 miles (4,000 km); then every 2,000 miles (3,000 km) or 6 months	Check and adjust cam chain tension Check and adjust valve clearance Check and adjust decompression cable free play (XT250 only) Change engine oil and replace filter Clean oil strainer Clean and re-oil air filter Adjust brake free play Adjust clutch free play Check cables for fraying and lubricate
First 2,500 miles (4,000 km); then every 2,000 miles (3,000 km) or 6 months	Check exhaust system for leakage; repair as necessary Check and adjust engine idle speed
Adjust throttle cable free play if necessary	Lubricate the brake pedal shaft Lubricate clutch and brake lever pivot shafts Lubricate kick crank boss and sidestand pivot shaft Check steering for looseness Check wheel bearings for proper operation; replace if necessary Check battery specific gravity; fill as necessary
First 2,500 miles (4,000 km); then every 4,000 miles (6,000 km) or 1 year	Check crankcase ventilation hose for cracks or damage; replace hose if necessary Check emission control system (1983 California models) Check fuel line for damage; replace if necessary
Every 9,500 miles (15,000 km) or 2 years	Replace spark plug Change fork oil Lubricate rear swing arm pivot shaft Replace steering bearings

* This Yamaha factory maintenance schedule should be considered as a guide to general maintenance and lubrication intervals. Harder than normal use and exposure to mud, water, sand, high humidity, etc. will naturally dictate more frequent attention to most maintenance items.

Table 2 TIRE INFLATION PRESSURE

Tire size	Air pressure
Front tire	
2.75 x 21—4 PR	
Cold	18 psi (1.3 kg/cm²)
Maximum load limit*	18 psi (1.3 kg/cm²)
Off-road	14 psi (1.0 kg/cm²)
3.00 x 21—4PR	
Cold	18 psi (1.3 kg/cm²)
Maximum load limit**	22 psi (1.5 kg/cm²)
High-speed riding	22 psi (1.5 kg/cm²)
Rear tire	
100/80 x 17—52P	
Cold	22 psi (1.5 kg/cm²)
Maximum load limit*	26 psi (1.8 kg/cm²)
Off-road	14 psi (1.0 kg/cm²)

(continued)

Table 2 TIRE INFLATION PRESSURE (continued)

Tire size	Air pressure
4.60 x 17—4PR	
Cold	22 psi (1.5 kg/cm²)
Maximum load limit**	26 psi (1.8 kg/cm²)
High-speed riding	26 psi (1.8 kg/cm²)

* Maximum load limit: 201-351 lb. (91-159 kg).
** Maximum load limit: 198-353 lb. (90-160 kg).

Table 3 BATTERY STATE OF CHARGE

Specific gravity	State of charge
1.110-1.130	Discharged
1.140-1.160	Almost discharged
1.170-1.190	One-quarter charged
1.200-1.220	One-half charged
1.230-1.250	Three-quarters charged
1.260-1.280	Fully charged

Table 4 RECOMMENDED LUBRICANTS

Engine oil	
Temperatures 40° and up	SAE 20W-40 SE/SF
Temperatures below 40°	SAE 10W-30 SE/SF
Battery refilling	Distilled water
Fork oil	SAE 10 or equivalent
Cables and pivot points	Yamaha chain and cable lube or SAE 10W-30 motor oil
Air filter	Special air filter oil

Table 5 APPROXIMATE REFILL CAPACITIES

Engine oil	
XT250	
Oil change*	1.4 qt. (1,300 cc)
Engine overhaul	1.7 qt. (1,600 cc)
XT125, XT200	
Oil change*	1.1 qt. (1,000 cc)
Engine overhaul	1.4 qt. (1,300 cc)
Front forks**	
XT125	6.50 oz. (192 cc)
XT200	8.42 oz. (250 cc)
XT250	9.10 oz. (270 cc)

* With filter change.
** Capacity for each fork leg.

Table 6 TUNE-UP SPECIFICATIONS

Valve clearance	
Intake	
XT125, XT200	0.0028 in. (0.07 mm)
XT250	0.0020-0.0039 in. (0.05-0.10 mm)
Exhaust	
XT125, XT200	0.0051 in. (0.13 mm)
XT250	0.0047-0.0067 in. (0.12-0.17 mm)
Compression pressure	
XT125, XT200	128-149 psi (9-10.5 kg/cm²)
XT250	142-185 psi (10-13 kg/cm²)
Spark plug	
Type	
XT125, XT200	NGK D8EA
	ND X24ES-U
XT250	NGK BP-7ES
	ND W22EP
Gap	
XT125, XT200	0.024-0.028 in. (0.6-0.8 mm)
XT250	0.027-0.032 in. (0.7-0.9 mm)
Torque specification	14 ft.-lb. (20 N•m)
Ignition timing	Fixed
Idle speed	
XT125	1,300 ±50 rpm
XT200	1,250 ±50 rpm
XT250	1,200 rpm
Cylinder head torque	
XT125 and XT250	16 ft.-lb. (22 N•m)
XT250	
M10	27 ft.-lb. (37 N•m)
M8	14 ft.-lb. (20 N•m)
M6	7 ft.-lb. (10 N•m)

Table 7 GENERAL SPECIFICATIONS

Engine type	4-stroke, air-cooled, SOHC
Bore and stroke	
XT125	2.24 x 1.92 in. (57.0 x 48.4 mm)
XT200	2.64 x 2.15 in. (67.0 x 55.7 mm)
XT250	2.95 x 2.22 in. (75.0 x 56.5mm)
Displacement	
XT125	124 cc
XT200	196 cc
XT250	249cc
Compression ratio	
XT125	10:1
XT200	9.5:1
XT250	9.2:1
Lubrication	Wet sump
Carburetion	
Type	
XT125 and XT200	TK
XT250	Mikuni
Model	
XT125	15E00
XT200	15A00
XT250	VM28SS
Ignition	Capacitor discharge ignition (CDI)
Clutch	Wet, multiple-disc

(continued)

Table 7 GENERAL SPECIFICATIONS (continued)

Transmission type	
XT125	6-speed constant mesh
XT200 and XT250	5-speed constant mesh
Transmission ratios (XT125)	
1st	2.923
2nd	1.888
3rd	1.428
4th	1.125
5th	0.925
6th	0.793
Transmission ratios (XT200)	
1st	2.833
2nd	1.789
3rd	1.318
4th	1.040
5th	0.821
Transmission ratios (XT250)	
1st	2.642
2nd	1.684
3rd	1.260
4th	1.000
5th	0.821
Final reduction ratio	
XT125	3.857
XT200	3.133
XT250	3.133
Starting system	Kickstarter only
Battery	
XT125 and XT200	6V 4AH
XT250	6V 6AH

3

NOTE: If you own a 1984 model, first check the Supplement at the back of the book for any new service information.

CHAPTER FOUR

ENGINE

All models covered in this book are equipped with an air-cooled, 4-stroke single cylinder engine with a single overhead camshaft. The crankshaft is supported by 2 main ball bearings. The camshaft is chain-driven from the timing sprocket on the left-hand side of the crankshaft and operates rocker arms that are individually adjustable.

The engine used in the various models is the same basic unit with different bore and stroke dimensions to achieve varying displacements.

This chapter contains information for removal, inspection, service and reassembly of the engine. **Table 1** (XT125 and XT200) and **Table 2** (XT250) provide complete specifications for the engines. **Table 3** and **Table 4** list torques for specific engine fasteners. For those fasteners which are not listed in **Table 3** or **Table 4**, **Table 5** lists general torque specifications for nuts and bolts for all models. To use the table, first determine the size of the nut or bolt. **Figure 1** and **Figure 2** show how this is done.

Tables 1-5 are located at the end of this chapter.

Although the clutch and transmission are located within the engine they are covered in Chapter Five to simplify this material. The alternator is covered in Chapter Seven.

Before beginning work, re-read Chapter One. You will do a better job with this information fresh in your mind.

ENGINE PRINCIPLES

Figure 3 explains how the engine works. This will be helpful when troubleshooting or repairing the engine.

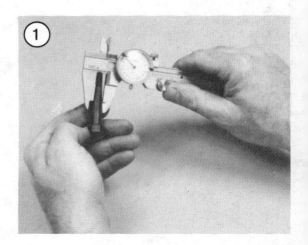

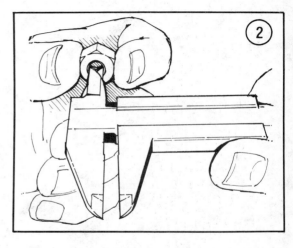

③

4-STROKE OPERATING PRINCIPLES

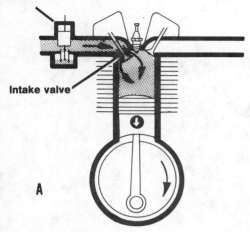

Carburetor

Intake valve

A

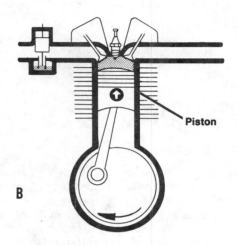

Piston

B

As the piston travels downward, the exhaust valve is closed and the intake valve opens, allowing the new air-fuel mixture from the carburetor to be drawn into the cylinder. When the piston reaches the bottom of its travel (BDC), the intake valve closes and remains closed for the next 1 1/2 revolutions of the crankshaft.

While the crankshaft continues to rotate, the piston moves upward, compressing the air-fuel mixture.

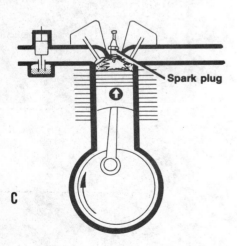

Spark plug

C

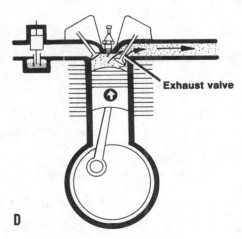

Exhaust valve

D

As the piston almost reaches the top of its travel, the spark plug fires, igniting the compressed air-fuel mixture. The piston continues to top dead center (TDC) and is pushed downward by the expanding gases.

When the piston almost reaches BDC, the exhaust valve opens and remains open until the piston is near TDC. The upward travel of the piston forces the exhaust gases out of the cylinder. After the piston has reached TDC, the exhaust valve closes and the cycle starts all over again.

ENGINE COOLING

Cooling is provided by air passing over the cooling fins on the cylinder head and cylinder. It is very important to keep these fins free from buildup of dirt, oil, grease and other foreign matter. Brush out the fins with a whisk broom or small stiff paint brush.

> *CAUTION*
> *Remember, these fins are thin in order to dissipate heat and may be damaged if struck too hard. The loss of cooling fins will cause overheating and internal engine damage.*

SERVICING ENGINE IN FRAME

The engine must be removed from the frame to remove the cylinder head, cylinder and piston. The crankcase studs are too long to allow the removal of the cylinder head with the engine in the frame.

The following components can be serviced while the engine is mounted in the frame (the bike's frame is a great holding fixture for breaking loose stubborn bolts and nuts):

    a. Carburetor (Chapter Six).
    b. Alternator (Chapter Seven).
    c. Clutch assembly (Chapter Five).
    d. External shift mechanism (Chapter Five).
    e. Oil pump.
    f. Primary drive and balancer gears.
    g. Kickstarter.

ENGINE

Removal/Installation

1. Drain the engine oil as described in Chapter Three.
2. Remove the side covers and seat.
3. Remove the fuel tank as described in Chapter Six.
4. Remove the exhaust system as described in Chapter Six.
5. Remove the carburetor as described in Chapter Six.
6. Remove the bolts securing the skid plate (**Figure 4**) and remove the skid plate.
7. Disconnect the spark plug lead and tie it up out of the way.
8. On XT250 models, disconnect the starter decompression cable at the cylinder head and remove the cable and brackets. See **Figure 5**.

9. On all 1980-1982 and 1983 non-California models, disconnect the engine breather hose (**Figure 6**) from the crankcase.

> *NOTE*
> *On 1983 California models, refer to Chapter Six for identification of emission control hoses and components.*

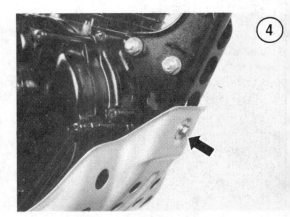

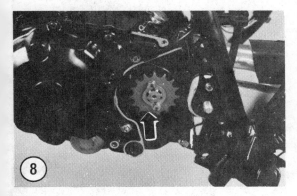

10. Remove the alternator as described in Chapter Seven.

11. Remove the drive chain master link (**Figure 7**) and remove the bolts securing the drive sprocket (**Figure 8**). Remove the sprocket holder and the drive sprocket.

12. Remove the clutch assembly as described in Chapter Five.

13. Remove the balancer shaft and gear as described in this chapter.

14. Remove the left foot-rest.

15. Take a final look all over the engine to make sure everything has been disconnected.

16. Remove the upper engine hanger bolts and nuts and remove the hanger plates. See **Figure 9**.

17. Place a suitable size hydraulic jack, with a piece of wood to protect the crankcase, under the engine. Apply a *small* amount of jack pressure up on the engine.

18. Remove the bolts and nuts securing the front engine hanger bolts and remove the engine hanger. See **Figure 10**.

19. Remove the bottom engine mount bolt (A, **Figure 11**) on XT125 and XT200 models.

> *WARNING*
> *The rear engine mount and swing arm use the same bolt. Thus, when performing Step 20, make sure that the bolt is removed only as far as required to allow engine removal. Complete removal will cause separation of the swing arm from the frame and the bike may then fall to the floor.*

20. With an assistant steadying the engine, remove the rear engine mounting bolt (B, **Figure 11**). Pull the engine slightly forward and remove it from the right-hand side. Take it to a workbench or engine stand for further disassembly.

21. Install bolts through the frame and swing arm as shown in **Figure 12** so that the bike can be safely moved out of the way.

22. While the engine is removed, check all frame-to-engine mount areas for cracks or other damage. See **Figure 13**.

23. Install by reversing these removal steps, noting the following.

24. Place the engine on wood blocks to help alignment (**Figure 14**).

25. Tighten the rear engine through bolt (B, **Figure 11**) to the following torque specifications:
   a. XT125 and XT200: 58 ft.-lb. (80 N•m).
   b. XT250: 47 ft.-lb. (65 N•m).

26. Tighten the front hanger bolts (**Figure 10**) to the following torque specifications:
   a. XT125 and XT200: 23 ft.-lb. (32 N•m).
   b. XT250: 23 ft.-lb. (32 N•m).

27. Tighten the upper hanger bolts (**Figure 9**) to the following torque specifications:
   a. XT125 and XT200: 23 ft.-lb. (32 N•m).
   b. XT250: 14.5 ft.-lb. (20 N•m).

28. Tighten the lower engine mounting bolt (A, **Figure 11**) on XT125 and XT200 models to 23 ft.-lb. (32 N•m).

29. Fill the engine with the recommended type and quantity of oil; refer to Chapter Three.

30. Adjust the clutch, drive chain and rear brake pedal as described in Chapter Three. On XT250 models, adjust the starter decompression cable as described in Chapter Three.

31. Start the engine and check for leaks.

CYLINDER HEAD

The cylinder head carries the rocker arm assemblies, valves and camshaft. The cover also carries the starter decompressor lever assembly on XT250 models. This procedure describes all service procedures for cylinder head removal, inspection and installation. While the camshaft, rocker assemblies and valves are also carried in the cylinder head, their service and inspection procedures are under separate headings in this chapter.

Removal

> *CAUTION*
> *To prevent any warpage and damage, remove the cylinder head cover and cam only when the engine is at room temperature.*

1. Place a milk crate or wood block(s) under the engine to support the bike securely.

2. Remove the side covers and seat.

3. Remove the fuel tank as described in Chapter Six.

4. Remove the carburetor as described in Chapter Six.

5. Remove the bolts securing the side cover to the left-hand side of the engine (**Figure 15**) and remove it.

(15)

(16)

(17)

(18)

6. Remove the cam chain tensioner cap (**Figure 16**).

7. Loosen the cam chain tensioner locknut (**Figure 17**) and remove the chain tensioner assembly (**Figure 18**).

8. Remove the alternator cover as described in Chapter Seven.

9. Using a wrench to hold the left-hand crankshaft nut, loosen but do not remove the cam sprocket bolt (**Figure 19**).

10. Remove the spark plug (this will make it easier to rotate the engine).

11. Remove the alternator as described in Chapter Seven.

12. Remove the engine as described in this chapter.

13. Place the engine on a suitable workbench or engine stand (**Figure 20**).

4

> *NOTE*
> *If the engine is placed on a workbench, set the engine on 2 wood blocks or fabricate a holding fixture of 2×4 inch boards.*

(19)

(20)

14. On XT250 models, loosen the chain guide stopper locking nut and bolt (**Figure 21**).

15. Unscrew the cam sprocket bolt (loosened previously) and remove it.

16. Slide the cam sprocket (**Figure 22**) off the camshaft and drop it down slightly. Detach it from the cam chain and remove it. Drop the cam chain down and remove it from the crankshaft sprocket.

17. Loosen and remove the cylinder head bolts in the order shown in **Figure 23** (XT125 and XT200) or **Figure 24** (XT250).

18. Loosen the head by tapping around the perimeter with a rubber or plastic mallet.

> *CAUTION*
> *Remember, the cooling fins are fragile and may be damaged if tapped or pried on too hard. Never use a metal hammer.*

19. Remove the cylinder head (**Figure 25**) by pulling it straight up and off the cylinder.

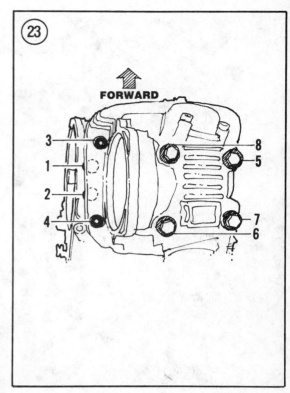

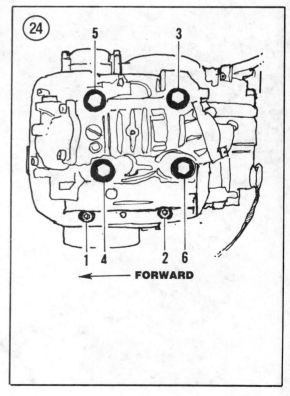

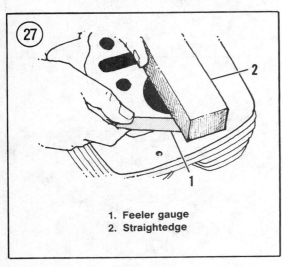

1. Feeler gauge
2. Straightedge

20. Remove the cylinder head gasket and discard it.

NOTE
Don't lose the 2 (XT250) or 3 (XT125 and XT200) locating dowels in the top of the cylinder. **Figure 26** *shows the locating dowels for the XT125 and XT200 models. Discard the small O-ring.*

Inspection

1. Remove all traces of gasket material from the cylinder head mating surfaces.
2. *Without* removing the valves, remove all carbon deposits from the combustion chambers and valve ports with a wire brush. A blunt screwdriver or chisel may be used if care is taken not to damage the head, valves and spark plug threads.
3. After the carbon is removed from the combustion chamber and the valve intake and exhaust ports, clean the entire head in cleaning solvent. Blow dry with compressed air.
4. Clean away all carbon from the piston crown. Do not remove the carbon ridge at the top of the cylinder bore.
5. Check for cracks in the combustion chamber and exhaust port. A cracked head must be replaced.
6. After the head has been thoroughly cleaned, place a straightedge across the cylinder head/cylinder gasket surface (**Figure 27**) at several points. Measure the warp by inserting a flat feeler gauge between the straightedge and the cylinder head at each location. There should be no warpage; if a small amount is present, the head should be taken to a Yamaha dealer to determine if it is possible to resurface it slightly.
7. Check the camshaft and rocker arm components as described in this chapter.
8. Check the valves and valve guides as described in this chapter.

Installation

1. Clean the mating surfaces of the head and cylinder block of any gasket material.
2. Install the locating dowels in the cylinder as follows:
   a. XT125 and XT200: Install 2 locating dowels on the left-hand side. On the right-hand rear hole, install a locating dowel and a new O-ring. See **Figure 26**.
   b. XT250: Install 2 locating dowels on the right-hand side. On the right-rear hole, install a new O-ring over the locating dowel.

3. Install the front cam chain guide (A, **Figure 28**) through the cylinder cavity and into the bracket in the lower crankcase (B, **Figure 28**).

4. Tie a piece of wire to the cam chain.

5. Install a new cylinder head gasket (**Figure 29**).

6. Loosen all valve adjusters fully (**Figure 30**). This relieves strain on the rocker arms and cylinder head during installation.

7. Align the cylinder head over the cylinder. Then guide the cam chain (using the wire) up through the cylinder head. Lower the cylinder head onto the cylinder. Secure it with the long stud bolts and the shorter bolts (**Figure 31**). Tighten all cylinder head bolts in the sequence shown in **Figure 23** (XT125 and XT200) or **Figure 24** (XT250) to the specifications listed in **Table 3** or **Table 4**.

8. Temporarily install the alternator rotor and rotate the crankshaft to align the timing mark on the crankshaft sprocket with the crankcase cover mark (**Figure 32**).

9. Turn the camshaft in the cylinder head until the cam drive sprocket locating pin (A, **Figure 33**) is

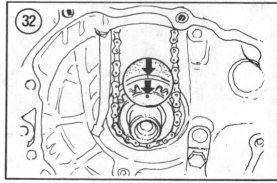

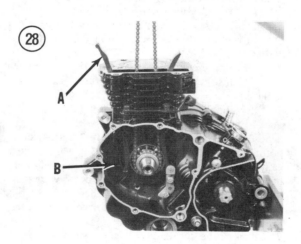

pointing up at the alignment mark in the cylinder head (B, **Figure 33**).

10. Pull up on the cam chain and remove the wire from it.

Continue to pull up on the cam chain and make sure the chain is meshed properly with the drive sprocket on the crankshaft.

11. With the timing slot in the cam chain sprocket pointing up at the 12 o'clock position, slide the sprocket into the cam chain and install the

sprocket onto the end of the camshaft. The alignment mark on the sprocket must be aligned with the fixed pointer on the cylinder head housing as shown in **Figure 34**.

CAUTION
*Check the cam chain alignment at the top and bottom. All timing marks must be aligned as shown in **Figure 32** and **Figure 34**. If alignment is not correct, reposition the cam chain on the sprocket so alignment is correct. Very expensive damage could result from improper cam and chain alignment. Recheck your work several times to be sure alignment is correct.*

12. When alignment is correct, install the cam sprocket bolt (**Figure 35**) and tighten to specifications. See **Table 3** or **Table 4**.

13. Make one final check to make sure alignment is correct. The alignment mark on the lower sprocket must be aligned with the fixed mark on the crankcase (**Figure 32**) and the alignment mark on the top sprocket must be aligned with the fixed pointer on the cylinder head housing (**Figure 34**).

14. Insert the cam chain tensioner into the cylinder (**Figure 18**). Do not tighten it at this time.

15. After the engine has been installed in the frame, adjust the valves and cam chain tension as described in Chapter Three.

CAMSHAFT AND ROCKER ARMS

Disassembly

When performing this procedure, label and package each part in individual plastic bags to avoid interchanging them.

1. Remove the cylinder head as described in this chapter.

2. Remove the intake and exhaust valve covers.

3. Flatten the bearing retainer lockwasher and remove the bolts securing the bearing retainer in the cylinder head.

4. Lift the bearing retainer (**Figure 36**) out of the cylinder head.

5. Thread a 6 mm screw into the end of one rocker arm shaft and remove the shaft and rocker arm (**Figure 37**). If the shaft is difficult to remove, use a special knock puller as shown in **Figure 38**. Repeat for the opposite rocker arm shaft.

NOTE
*The knock puller used in Step 5 (**Figure 39**) can be fabricated by obtaining a long bolt with 6 mm threads and drilling a guide hole in a heavy piece of metal stock.*

6. Thread a 10 mm bolt into the end of the camshaft (**Figure 40**) and remove it (**Figure 41**) and the bushing (XT125 and XT200) or bearing (XT250) carefully through the cylinder head.

> *CAUTION*
> *Use care when removing the camshaft to prevent damaging the journals on the camshaft or in the cylinder head.*

Camshaft Inspection

1A. *XT125 and XT200*: Remove the camshaft bushing (**Figure 42**) and check the cam bearing journals for wear and scoring (**Figure 43**). Check the camshaft bushing (**Figure 44**) inner and outer surfaces for pitting or any other signs of wear or damage. If any abnormal conditions are detected, replace the worn part.

1B. *XT250*: A bearing is pressed onto the left-hand side of the camshaft. Check the right-hand cam bearing journal as described in Step 1A. Then check the camshaft bearing races for pits, chatter marks or other signs of abnormal wear or damage. If the bearing is okay, lubricate it with engine oil to prevent rust formation. If the bearing is damaged, have it replaced by a Yamaha dealer.

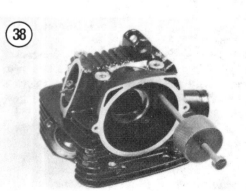

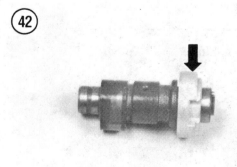

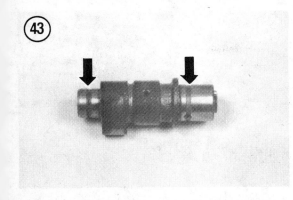

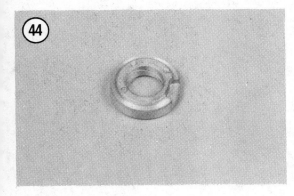

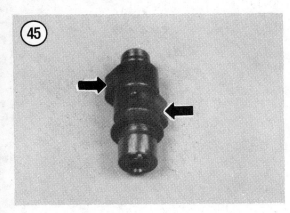

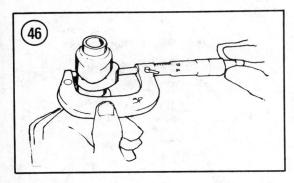

2. Even though the cam journals appear to be satisfactory, the bearing journals should be measured with a micrometer. Compare to dimensions given in **Table 1** or **Table 2**. If worn to the service limit the cam must be replaced.

3. Check the cam lobes for wear (**Figure 45**). The lobes should show no signs of scoring and the edges should be square. Slight damage may be removed with a silicone carbide oilstone. Use No. 100-120 grit stone initially, then polish with a No. 280-320 grit stone.

4. Even if the cam lobe surface appears to be satisfactory, with no visible signs of wear, the cam lobes must be measured with a micrometer as shown in **Figure 46**. Compare to dimensions given in **Table 1** or **Table 2**.

NOTE
Measuring the cam lobes with a micrometer is important in maintaining engine performance. If the cam lobe wear exceeds factory wear limits, valve lift and timing will be affected.

5. On XT250 models, the camshaft rides on a needle bearing installed in the right-hand side of the cylinder head. Inspect this bearing for any signs of wear or damage. If necessary, have the bearing replaced by a Yamaha dealer. On XT125 and XT200 models, no removable is used. Instead, check the bearing surface in the cylinder head itself. If this surface is damaged, the cylinder head must be replaced.

6. Check the left-hand side cam bushing or bearing surface in the cylinder head. The surface should not be scored or excessively worn. Replace the cylinder head if wear is evident.

7. Inspect the cam sprocket for wear; replace if necessary.

NOTE
If the sprocket is worn, inspect the camshaft chain as described in this chapter.

**Rocker Arm and
Shaft Inspection**

1. On XT250 model rocker arms, remove the O-rings from the rocker arm shafts and discard them.

2. Wash all parts in cleaning solvent and thoroughly dry.

3. Inspect the rocker arm pad (**Figure 47**) where it rides on the cam lobe and where the adjuster rides on the valve stem. If the pad is scratched or unevenly worn, inspect the cam lobe for scoring,

chipping or flat spots. Replace the rocker arm if defective.

4. Measure the inside diameter of the rocker arm bore (A, **Figure 48**) with an inside micrometer and check against dimensions in **Table 1** or **Table 2**. Replace if worn to the service limit or greater.

5. Inspect the rocker arm shaft for signs of wear or scoring. Measure the outside diameter (B, **Figure 48**) with a micrometer and check against dimensions in **Table 1** or **Table 2**. Replace if worn to the service limit or less.

Assembly

1. Coat the camshaft and bore and the rocker arm shafts and rocker arm bore with assembly oil.

2. On XT250 models, install a new O-ring on each rocker arm shaft.

3. Install the rocker arm shaft with the threaded hole facing *out*. Partially insert the rocker arm shaft into the cover (**Figure 49**) and position the rocker arm into the cylinder head cover.

> *CAUTION*
> *If the rocker arm shaft is installed in the wrong direction, it will be difficult or impossible to remove later.*

4. Make sure the locking relief in the rocker arm shaft (if so equipped) is aligned with the hole in the cylinder head to allow the cylinder head stud to pass by it during installation.

5. Repeat Step 2 and Step 3 for the opposite rocker arm and shaft.

6. Install the bushing (XT125 and XT200) or bearing (XT250) onto the left-hand side of the camshaft. See **Figure 42**.

7. Insert the camshaft into the cylinder head (**Figure 41**). Install the bearing retainer (**Figure 36**), lockwashers and bolts. Tighten the bolts securely. Bend the lockwasher tabs over the bolts to lock them.

CAMSHAFT CHAIN

Removal/Installation

To remove the cam chain, remove the cylinder head as described in this chapter. The crankcase halves do not have to be separated.

Chain tensioner removal is described under *Cylinder Head Removal* in this chapter.

Chain guide removal is described under *Crankcase Disassembly* in this chapter.

Inspection

Referring to **Figure 50**, inspect the surface of the chain guide (A) and chain tensioner (B). If either is

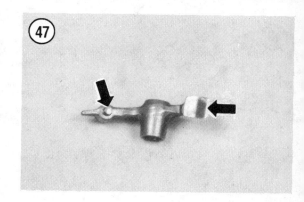

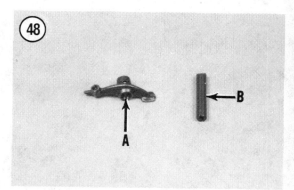

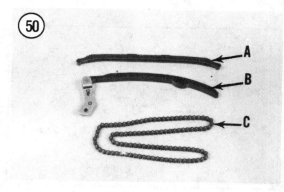

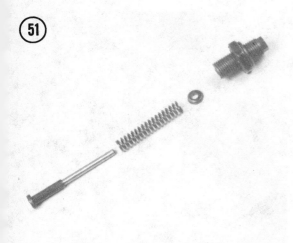

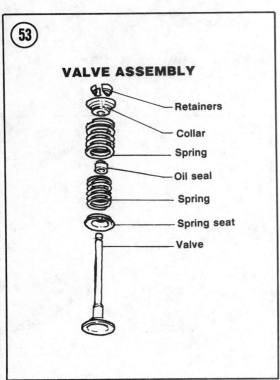

VALVE ASSEMBLY

— Retainers
— Collar
— Spring
— Oil seal
— Spring
— Spring seat
— Valve

worn or disintegrating it must be replaced. This may indicate a worn cam chain or improper cam chain adjustment.

Inspect the cam drive chain (C, **Figure 50**) for wear and damage. If the chain needs replacing, also replace the drive sprocket on the crankshaft and the cam sprocket. Intermixing new and worn parts will cause premature failure of the new part.

Disassemble the cam chain tensioner as shown in **Figure 51**. Replace any parts that appear worn or damaged. Check the O-ring in the tensioner cap (**Figure 52**) and replace it if worn.

VALVES AND VALVE COMPONENTS

Refer to **Figure 53** for this procedure.

> *CAUTION*
> *All component parts of each valve assembly must be kept together; do not mix with like components from the opposite valve or excessive wear may result.*

1. Remove the cylinder head as described in this chapter.
2. Remove the rocker arms and camshaft as described in this chapter.
3. Install a valve spring compressor squarely over valve retainer with other end of tool placed against valve head (**Figure 54**).
4. Tighten valve spring compressor until split valve keeper separates. Lift out split keeper with needlenose pliers.
5. Gradually loosen valve spring compressor and remove from head. Lift off valve retainer.

> *CAUTION*
> *Remove any burrs from the valve stem grooves before removing the valve (**Figure 55**). Otherwise the valve guides will be damaged.*

6. Remove inner and outer springs and valve (**Figure 56**).

7. Remove the seal (**Figure 57**).

8. Repeat Steps 3-7 and remove opposite valve.

Inspection

1. Clean valves with a wire brush and solvent.

2. Inspect the contact surface of each valve for burning (**Figure 58**). Minor roughness and pitting can be removed by lapping the valve as described in this chapter. Excessive unevenness of the contact surface is an indication that the valve is not serviceable. The contact surface of the valve may be ground on a valve grinding machine, but it is best to replace a burned or damaged valve with a new one.

3. Inspect the valve stems for wear and roughness and measure the vertical runout of the valve stem as shown in **Figure 59**. The runout should not exceed 0.0012 in. (0.03 mm).

4. Measure valve stems for wear using a micrometer (**Figure 60**). Compare with specifications in **Figure 61**.

5. Remove all carbon and varnish from the valve guides with a stiff spiral wire brush.

> *NOTE*
> *Step 6 requires special measuring equipment to measure the diameter of the valve guides. If you do not have the required measuring devices, proceed to Step 8.*

6. Measure each valve guide at top, center and bottom with a small hole gauge. Compare measurements with specifications in **Table 1** or **Table 2**.

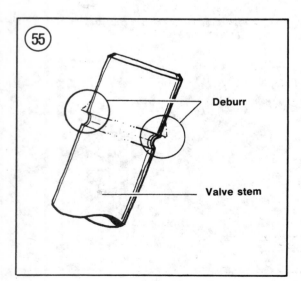

Deburr

Valve stem

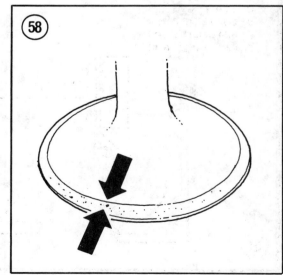

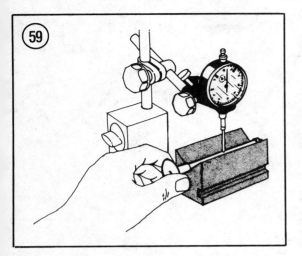

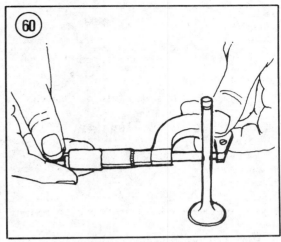

4

INTAKE AND EXHAUST VALVE SPECIFICATIONS—INTAKE

XT125
A. 1.142 in. (29 mm)
B. 0.236 in. (6.010 mm)
C. 45 degrees
D. 0.089 in. (2.26 mm)
E. 0.039 in. (1.0 mm)
F. 0.039 in. (1.0 mm)

XT200
A. 1.339 in. (34 mm)
B. 0.236 in. (6.010 mm)
C. 45 degrees
D. 0.089 in. (2.26 mm)
E. 0.039 in. (1.0 mm)
F. 0.039 in. (1.0 mm)

XT250
A. 1.496 in. (38 mm)
B. 0.276 in. (7.010 mm)
C. 45 degrees
D. 0.089 in. (2.26 mm)
E. 0.043 in. (1.1 mm)
F. 0.047 in. (1.2 mm)

EXHAUST

XT125
A. 0.945 in. (24 mm)
B. 0.236 in. (6.025 mm)
C. 45 degrees
D. 0.089 in. (2.26 mm)
E. 0.039 in. (1.0 mm)
F. 0.039 in. (1.0 mm)

XT200
A. 1.122 in. (28.5 mm)
B. 0.236 in. (6.025 mm)
C. 45 degrees
D. 0.089 in. (2.26 mm)
E. 0.039 in. (1.0 mm)
F. 0.039 in. (1.0 mm)

XT250
A. 1.260 in. (32 mm)
B. 0.276 in. (7.010 mm)
C. 45 degrees
D. 0.089 in. (2.26 mm)
E. 0.043 in. (1.1 mm)
F. 0.039 in. (1.1 mm)

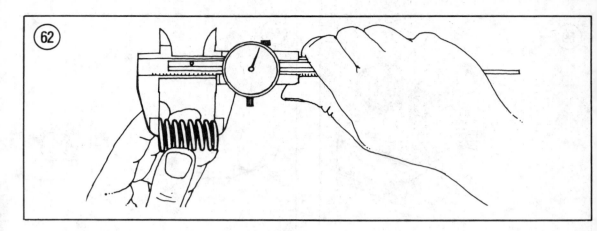

7. Subtract the measurement in Step 4 from the measurement in Step 6. The difference is the valve guide-to-valve stem clearance. See specifications in **Table 1** or **Table 2** for correct clearance. Replace any guide or valve that is not within tolerance.

8. Insert each valve in its guide. Hold the valve just slightly off its seat and rock it sideways. If it rocks more than slightly, the valve or guide is probably worn and should be replaced. As a final check, take the head to a dealer and have the valves and guides measured.

9. Measure the valve spring heights with a vernier caliper (**Figure 62**). All should be of length specified in **Table 1** or **Table 2** with no bends or other distortion. Replace defective springs in pairs (inner and outer). See **Figure 63**.

10. Measure the tilt of all valve springs as shown in **Figure 64**. Compare with specifications shown in **Table 1** or **Table 2**.

11. Check the valve spring retainer and valve keepers. If they are in good condition, they may be reused.

12. Inspect valve seats. If worn or burned, they must be reconditioned. This should be performed by your dealer or local machine shop, although the procedure is described in this chapter. Seats and valves in near-perfect condition can be reconditioned by lapping with fine carborundum paste. Lapping, however, is always inferior to precision grinding.

Installation

1. Coat the valve stems with molybdenum disulfide paste and insert into cylinder head.

2. Install bottom spring retainers and new seals (**Figure 57**).

> NOTE
> *Oil seals should be replaced whenever a valve is removed or replaced.*

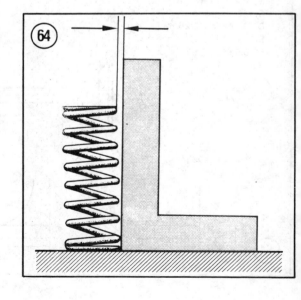

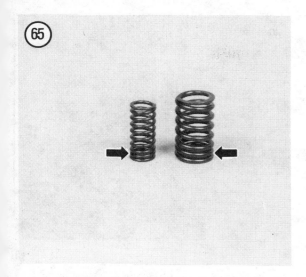

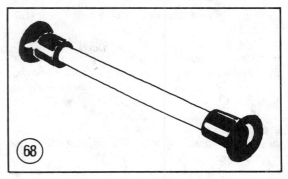

3. Install valve springs with the narrow pitch end (end with coils closest together) facing the head (**Figure 65**) and install upper valve spring retainers.
4. Push down on upper valve spring retainers with the valve spring compressor and install valve keepers. After releasing tension from compressor, examine valve keepers and make sure they are seated correctly. See **Figure 66**.

Valve Guide Replacement

When guides are worn so that there is excessive stem-to-guide clearance or valve tipping, they must be replaced as a set. This job should only be done by a Yamaha dealer as special tools are required.

Valve Seat Reconditioning

This job is best left to your dealer or local machine shop. They have the special equipment and knowledge for this exacting job. You can still save considerable money by removing the cylinder head and taking just the head to the shop.
1. With a 30 degree valve seat cutter, remove just enough metal to make bottom of seat concentric (**Figure 67**).
2. With a 60 degree valve seat cutter, remove just enough metal from top of seat to make it concentric.
3. With a 45 degree valve seat cutter, cut a seat that measures 0.0390-0.0433 in. (1.0-1.1 mm). See **Figure 67**.

Valve Lapping

Valve lapping is a simple operation which can restore the valve seal without machining if the amount of wear or distortion is not too great.
1. Smear a light coating of fine grade valve lapping compound on seating surface of valve.
2. Insert the valve into the head.
3. Wet the suction cup of the lapping stick (**Figure 68**) and stick it onto the head of the valve. Lap the valve to the seat by spinning tool between hands

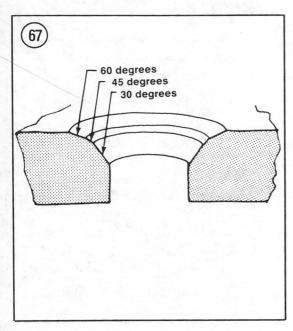

60 degrees
45 degrees
30 degrees

while lifting and moving valve around seat 1/4
turn at a time.

4. Wipe off valve and seat frequently to check
progress of lapping. Lap only enough to achieve a
precise seating ring around valve head. Measure
width of seat. If seat width is not within tolerance
in **Figure 61**, valve seat in cylinder head must be
resurfaced.

5. Closely examine valve seat in cylinder head. It
should be smooth and even with a smooth,
polished seating ring.

6. Thoroughly clean the valves and cylinder in
solvent to remove all grinding compound. Any
compound left on the valves or the cylinder head
will end up in the engine and will cause damage.

7. After the lapping has been completed and the
valve assemblies have been reinstalled into the
head, check the seal of each valve by pouring
solvent into the intake and exhaust ports. There
should be no leakage past the seat. If so,
combustion chamber will appear wet. If fluid leaks
past any of the seats, disassemble that valve
assembly and repeat the lapping procedure until
there is no leakage.

CYLINDER

Removal

1. Remove the cylinder head as described in this
chapter.

2. Remove the cylinder holding bolts (**Figure 69**).

3. Loosen the cylinder by tapping around the
perimeter with a rubber or plastic mallet.

4. Pull the cylinder straight up and off the
crankcase studs.

5. Remove the cylinder base gasket and discard it.
Remove the dowel pins from the crankcase studs.

6. Install a piston holding fixture under the piston
(**Figure 70**) to protect the piston skirt from damage.
This fixture may be purchased or may be a
homemade unit of wood. See **Figure 71**.

7. Stuff clean shop rags into the crankcase to
prevent objects from falling undetected into the
crankcase.

Inspection

1. Measure the cylinder bores with a cylinder
gauge (**Figure 72**) or inside micrometer at the
points shown in **Figure 73**.

2. Measure in 2 axes—in line with the piston pin
and at 90° to the pin. If the taper or out-of-round is
greater than specifications (**Table 1** or **Table 2**), the

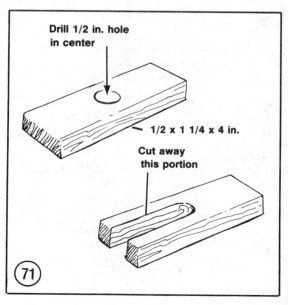

Drill 1/2 in. hole
in center

1/2 x 1 1/4 x 4 in.

Cut away
this portion

72

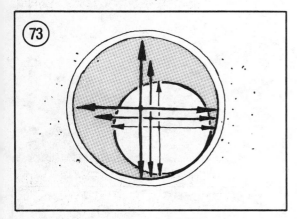

73

74

75

cylinder must be rebored to the next oversize and new pistons and rings installed.

> *NOTE*
> *The new piston should be obtained first before the cylinder is bored so that the piston can be measured; slight manufacturing tolerances must be taken into account to determine the actual size and the working clearance. Piston-to-cylinder clearance is specified in **Table 1** and **Table 2**.*

3. Check the cylinder wall (**Figure 74**) for scratches; if scratched, the cylinder should be rebored.

Installation

1. If the base gasket is stuck to the bottom of the cylinder it should be removed and the cylinder surface cleaned thoroughly.

2. Check that the top cylinder surface (**Figure 75**) is clean of all old gasket material.

3. Install the locating dowels and O-rings as follows:

   a. XT125 and XT200: Install 2 dowel pins on the left hand crankcase stud holes and the O-ring on right-rear stud hole. See **Figure 76**.

   b. XT250: Install 2 dowel pins on the right hand side crankcase stud holes. Install O-ring on the right-rear dowel pin.

4. Install a new cylinder base gasket. Make sure all holes align.

5. Install a piston holding fixture under the piston (**Figure 70**).

76

6. Carefully install the cylinder over the piston (**Figure 77**). Slowly work the piston past each piston ring.

7. Continue to slide the cylinder down until it bottoms on the piston holding fixture.

8. Remove the piston holding fixture and push the cylinder down until it bottoms on the crankcase.

9. Install the cylinder holding bolts and tighten them to specifications in **Table 3** or **Table 4**.

10. Install the cylinder head as described in this chapter.

PISTON AND PISTON PIN

The piston is made of an aluminum alloy. It should be handled carefully during all service operations. The piston pin is made of steel and is machined to a precision fit in the piston. The piston pin is held in place by a clip at each end.

Piston Removal

1. Remove the cylinder head and cylinder as described in this chapter.

2. Stuff the crankcase with a clean shop rag to prevent objects from falling into the crankcase. See **Figure 78**.

> *WARNING*
> *The edges of all piston rings are very sharp. Be careful when handling them to avoid cut fingers.*

3. Remove the top ring first by spreading the ends with your thumbs just enough to slide it up over the piston (**Figure 79**). Repeat for the remaining rings.

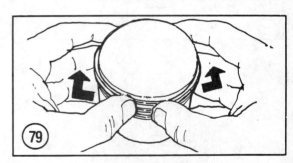

> *NOTE*
> *If the rings are difficult to remove, they can be removed with a ring expander tool.*

4. Before removing the piston, hold the rod tightly and rock piston as shown in **Figure 80**. Any rocking motion (do not confuse with the normal sliding motion) indicates wear on the piston pin, rod bushing, pin bore or more likely, a combination of all three.

5. Remove the circlips from the piston pin bore (**Figure 81**).

6. Heat the piston and pin with a small butane torch. The pin will probably push right out. If it doesn't, heat the piston to about 140° F (60° C), i.e., until it is too warm to touch, but not excessively hot. If the pin is still difficult to push out, use a homemade tool as shown in **Figure 82**.

7. Lift the piston off the connecting rod.

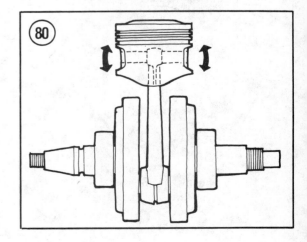

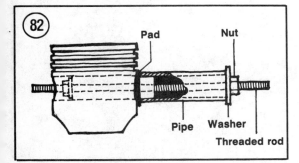

Piston Inspection

1. Carefully clean the carbon from the piston crown with a chemical remover or with a soft scraper (**Figure 83**). Do not remove or damage the carbon ridge around the circumference of the piston above the top ring (**Figure 84**). If the piston, rings and cylinder are found to be dimensionally correct and can be reused, removal of the carbon ring from the top of piston or the carbon ridge from the cylinder will promote excessive oil consumption.

> *WARNING*
> *The rail portions of the oil scraper can be very sharp. Be careful when handling them to avoid cut fingers.*

> *CAUTION*
> *Do not wire brush piston skirts.*

2. Examine each ring groove for burrs, dented edges and wide wear. Pay particular attention to the top compression ring groove, as it usually wears more than the others.
3. Clean the oil transfer holes in the piston (**Figure 85**) of all carbon deposits.
4. Measure piston-to-cylinder clearance as described in this chapter.
5. If damage or wear indicate piston replacement, select a new piston as described under *Piston Clearance Measurement* in this chapter.

Piston Clearance Measurement

1. Make sure the piston and cylinder walls are clean and dry.
2. Measure the inside diameter of the cylinder bore at a point 13 mm (1/2 in.) from the upper edge with a bore gauge (**Figure 72**).
3. Measure the outside diameter of the piston (**Figure 86**) at a specified point from the lower edge

of the piston 90°degrees to piston pin axis (**Figure 87**). The correct measurement points are:

a. XT125: 9/32 in. (7.0 mm).
b. XT200: 5/16 in. (7.5 mm).
c. XT250: 3/16 in. (5.5 mm).

4. Piston clearance is the difference between the maximum piston diameter and the minimum cylinder diameter. Subtract the dimension of the piston from the cylinder dimension. If the clearance exceeds specifications (**Table 1** or **Table 2**), the cylinder should be rebored to the next oversize and a new piston installed.

5. Obtain the new piston before having the cylinder bored. Measure the new piston and add the specified clearance to determine the proper cylinder bore dimension.

Piston Installation

1. Apply molybdenum disulfide grease to the inside surface of the connecting rod.

2. Oil the piston pin with assembly oil and install it in the piston until its end extends slightly beyond the inside of the boss (**Figure 88**).

3. Place the piston over the connecting rod. Make sure the arrow on the piston crown (**Figure 89**) is facing toward the front of the engine.

4. Line up the piston pin with the hole in the connecting rod. Push the piston pin through the connecting rod and into the other side of the piston until it is even with the piston pin clip grooves.

> *CAUTION*
> *If the piston pin does not slide easily, heat the piston until it is too warm to touch but not excessively hot (140° F or 60° C). Continue to drive the piston in while holding the piston so that the rod does not have to take any shock. Otherwise, it may be bent. Drive the pin in until it is centered in the rod. If pin is still difficult to install, use the homemade tool (**Figure 82**) but eliminate the piece of pipe.*

> *NOTE*
> *In the next step, install the clips with the gap away from the cutout in the piston (**Figure 90**).*

5. Install new piston pin clips in both ends of the pin boss. Make sure they are seated in the grooves in the piston.

6. Check the installation by rocking the piston back and forth around the pin axis and from side to side along the axis. It should rotate freely back and forth but not from side to side.

7. Install the piston rings as described in this chapter.

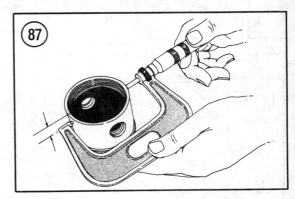

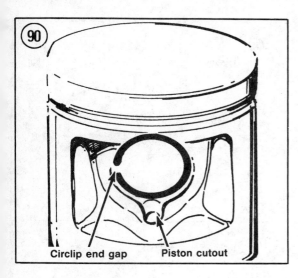

Circlip end gap   **Piston cutout**

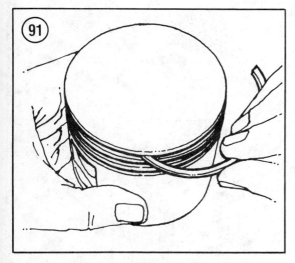

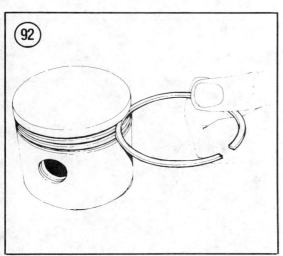

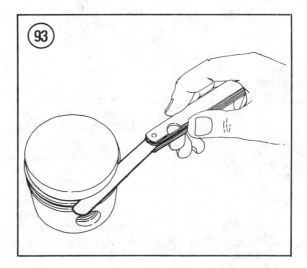

8. Install the cylinder and cylinder head as described in this chapter.

PISTON RINGS

Replacement

> *WARNING*
> *The edges of all piston rings are very sharp. Be careful when handling them to avoid cut fingers.*

1. Remove the old rings with a ring expander tool or by spreading the ring ends with your thumbs and lifting the rings up evenly (**Figure 79**).

2. Using a broken piston ring, remove all carbon from the piston ring grooves (**Figure 91**). Inspect grooves carefully for burrs, nicks or broken or cracked lands. Recondition or replace piston if necessary.

3. Roll each ring around its piston groove as shown in **Figure 92** to check for binding. Minor binding may be cleaned up with a fine-cut file.

4. Measure the side clearance of each ring in its groove with a flat feeler gauge (**Figure 93**) and compare to specifications in **Table 1** or **Table 2**. If the clearance is greater than specified, the rings must be replaced. If the clearance is still excessive with the new rings, the piston must also be replaced.

5. Check end gap of each ring. To check ring, insert the ring into the bottom of the cylinder bore and square it with the cylinder wall by tapping with the piston. The ring should be in about 3/4 in. (20 mm). Insert a feeler gauge as shown in **Figure 94**. Compare gap with **Table 1** or **Table 2**. If the gap is greater than specified, the rings should be replaced. When installing new rings, measure their end gap in the same manner as for old ones. If the gap is

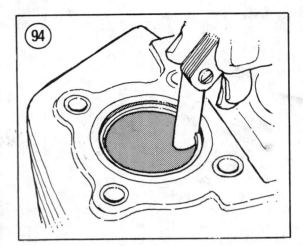

less than specified, carefully file the ends with a fine-cut file until the gap is correct.

6. Install the piston rings in the order shown in **Figure 95**.

> *NOTE*
> *Install all rings with their markings facing up.*

7. Install oil ring in oil ring groove with a ring expander tool or by spreading the ends with your thumbs.

8. Install 2 compression rings carefully with a ring expander tool or by spreading the ends with your thumbs.

9. Distribute ring gaps around piston as shown in **Figure 95**. The important thing is that the ring gaps are not aligned with each other when installed.

10. If new rings were installed, measure the side clearance of each ring in its groove with a flat feeler gauge (**Figure 93**). Compare to specifications given in **Table 1** or **Table 2**.

11. Follow the *Break-in Procedure* in this chapter if a new piston or piston rings have been installed or the cylinder was rebored or honed.

OIL PUMP

The oil pump is located on the right-hand side of the engine behind the clutch assembly. The oil pump can be removed with the engine in the frame.

Removal/Installation

1. Remove the clutch assembly as described in Chapter Five.

2A. *XT125 and XT200*: Turn pump gear and align slots in gear with 3 oil pump attachment screws. Remove 3 screws and remove oil pump assembly. See **Figure 96**.

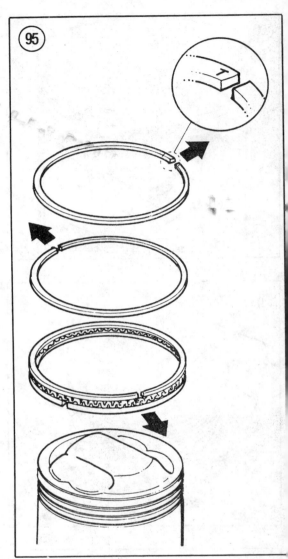

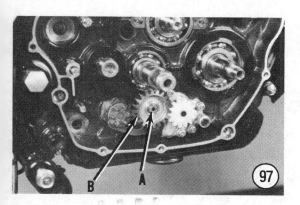

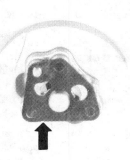

4

2B. *XT250*: Remove the oil pump as follows:
  a. Remove the circlip securing the oil pump idler gear (A, **Figure 97**). Then remove washer (**Figure 98**), idler gear (B, **Figure 97**) and washer (**Figure 99**).
  b. Remove oil pump screws (**Figure 100**) and remove pump.
3. Inspect all parts as described in this chapter.
4. Install by reversing the removal steps, noting the following.
  a. *XT125 and XT200*: Check that the oil pump gasket is installed correctly on the backside of the pump and that it is not torn. Install a new gasket if necessary. See **Figure 101**.
  b. *XT250*: Before installing pump, check O-ring (**Figure 102**). Replace it if necessary.

Disassembly/Inspection/Assembly

1. Inspect the outer housing for cracks.
2. *XT250*: Remove the screw (**Figure 103**) and separate the oil pump assembly.

NOTE
Steps 3-6 describe disassembly of the oil pump on XT125 and XT200 models.

3. Remove the gasket from the backside of the housing (**Figure 101**).

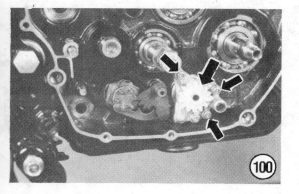

4. Remove the screw (**Figure 104**) securing the oil pump housings. Then lift the rear housing off (**Figure 105**).

5. Remove the inner and outer rotors (**Figure 106**).

6. Remove the pin (**Figure 107**) and separate the pump gear from the front housing (**Figure 108**).

7. Clean all parts (**Figure 109**) in solvent and thoroughly dry with compressed air.

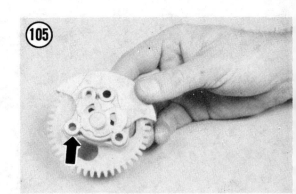

NOTE
The oil pump on all models is not rebuildable. If any part is found to be worn or damaged, the oil pump must be replaced with a new unit; replacement parts are not available from Yamaha.

8. Check the inner housing rotor surface for any signs of wear or galling (**Figure 110**).

9. Check the oil pump gear and shaft (**Figure 111**) for gear breakage, wear or shaft galling.

10. Install the inner rotor and check the clearance between the inner and outer rotor (**Figure 112**) with a flat feeler gauge. The clearance should be within the specifications listed in **Table 1** or **Table 2**. If the clearance is greater, replace the oil pump.

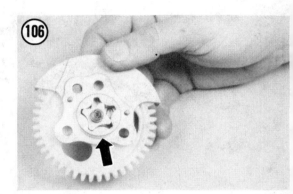

NOTE
Proceed with Step 11 only when the above inspection and measurement steps indicate that the parts are in good condition.

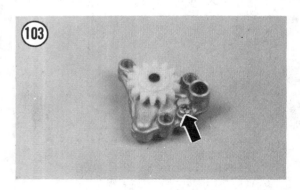

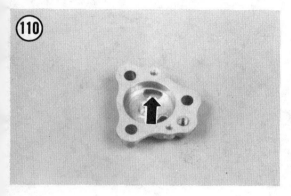

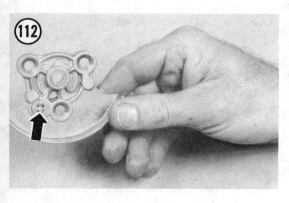

11. Assembly is the reverse of Step 2 (XT250) or Steps 3-6 (XT125 and XT200), noting the following:

  a. Coat all parts with fresh engine oil prior to assembly.

  b. On XT125 and XT200 models, insert the oil pump housing fastening screw into the outer housing (**Figure 112**) before installing the oil pump gear.

PRIMARY DRIVE AND BALANCER GEARS

The primary drive and balancer gears may be removed with the engine in the frame.

Removal/Installation (XT125 and XT200)

NOTE
*The gears are identified in **Figure 113**:*
A, primary drive gear; B, balancer driven gear; C, balancer drive gear.

1. Remove the clutch assembly as described in Chapter Five.
2. Remove the oil pump as described in this chapter.
3. Flatten the primary drive gear lockwasher. Place a folded rag between the balancer drive gear and balancer driven gear at the point indicated in **Figure 114** and loosen and remove the locknut.
4. Remove the following parts in order:
  a. Primary drive gear (**Figure 115**).
  b. Washer (**Figure 116**).
5. Flatten the balancer driven gear lockwasher (A, **Figure 117**). Place a folded rag between the balancer gears at the point indicated in B, **Figure 117** and loosen the locknut.

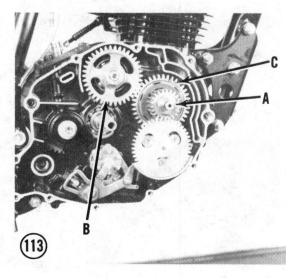

6. Remove the following parts in order:
   a. Balancer drive gear (**Figure 118**).
   b. Woodruff key (A, **Figure 119**).
   c. Washer (B, **Figure 119**).
   d. Locknut and washer (**Figure 120**).
   e. Balancer driven gear (**Figure 121**).
   f. Woodruff key (**Figure 122**).
7. Inspect the drive and balancer gears as described in this chapter.
8. Installation is the reverse of these steps, noting the following.
9. When installing the balancer drive and driven gears, align the timing marks on both gears as shown in **Figure 123**.
10. Tighten the balancer driven gear and primary drive locknuts to the specifications in **Table 3**.
11. After tightening the locknuts, bend the lockwasher tabs over the locknuts.

Removal/Installation (XT250)

> *NOTE*
> *The gears are identified in **Figure 124**: A, primary drive gear; B, balancer driven gear; C, balancer drive gear.*

1. Remove the clutch assembly as described in Chapter Five.
2. Flatten the primary drive gear lockwasher. Place a folded rag between the balancer drive gear and balancer driven gear at the point indicated in **Figure 125** and loosen the locknut.
3. Flatten the balancer driven gear lockwasher (A, **Figure 126**). Place a folded rag between the

(115)

(116)

(117)

(114)

(118)

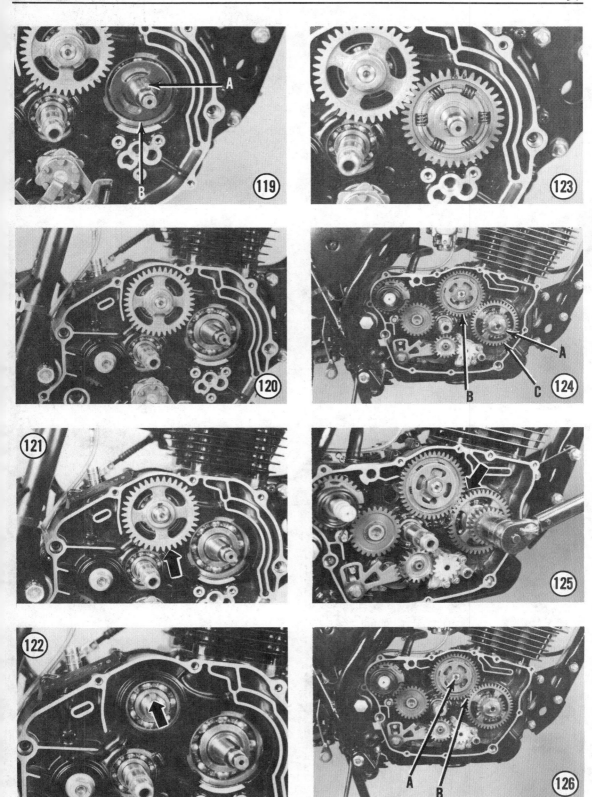

balancer gears at the point indicated in B, **Figure 126** and loosen the locknut.

4. Remove the following parts in order:
   a. Locknut and lockwasher (**Figure 127**).
   b. Washer (**Figure 128**).
   c. Balancer driven gear (**Figure 129**).
   d. Woodruff key (A, **Figure 130**).
   e. Washer (B, **Figure 130**).
   f. Washer (**Figure 131**).

5. Remove the following parts in order:
   a. Primary drive nut.
   b. Washer (**Figure 132**).
   c. Primary drive gear (**Figure 133**).
   d. Woodruff key (A, **Figure 134**).
   e. Balancer drive gear (B, **Figure 134**).

6. Inspect the drive and balancer gears as described in this chapter.

7. Installation is the reverse of these steps, noting the following.

8. When installing the balancer drive and driven gears, align the timing marks on both gears as shown in **Figure 135**.

9. Tighten the balancer driven gear and primary drive locknuts to the specifications in **Table 4**.

10. After tightening the locknuts, bend the lockwasher tabs over the locknuts.

Inspection (All Models)

After the drive and balancer gears have been cleaned, visually inspect the components (**Figure**

(133)

(134)

(135)

(136)

136) for excessive wear. Any burrs, pitting or roughness on the teeth of a gear will cause wear on the mating gear.

NOTE
Defective gears should be replaced. It's a good idea to replace the mating gear on the other shaft (even though it may not show as much wear or damage) to prevent excessive wear to the new gear.

CRANKCASE AND CRANKSHAFT

Disassembly of the crankcase (splitting the cases) and removal of the crankshaft require that the engine be removed from the frame.

The crankcase is made in 2 halves of precision diecast aluminum alloy and has very thin walls. To avoid damage, do not hammer or pry on any of the interior or exterior projected walls. These areas are easily damaged. The cases on all Yamaha XT models are manufactured as a matched set. Thus if one case is damaged, both cases must be replaced. The cases are assembled with sealant; dowel pins align the halves when they are bolted together.

The crankshaft assembly is made up of 2 flywheels pressed together on a hollow crankpin. The connecting rod big-end bearing on the crankpin is a needle bearing assembly. The crankshaft assembly is supported by 2 ball bearings in the crankcase. Service to the crankshaft for the home mechanic is limited to removal and installation. However, well-equipped Yamaha dealers or machine shops can disassemble and rebuild the crankshaft when necessary.

Crankcase Disassembly

1. Remove the engine as described in this chapter.
2. Remove the cam chain adjuster (**Figure 137**).
3. Remove the cam chain.

(137)

4. Remove the exterior engine assemblies as described in this chapter and other related chapters:

    a. Cylinder head.

    b. Cylinder.

    c. Piston.

    d. Alternator.

    e. Clutch.

    f. Oil pump.

    g. Primary drive and balancer gears.

    h. External shift mechanism.

5. Remove the chain guide stopper bolts and remove the chain guide. See **Figure 138** (XT125 and XT200) or **Figure 139** (XT250).

6. Remove the crankcase bolts as follows:

    a. On XT125 and XT200 models, remove the crankcase bolts on both sides of the crankcase.

    b. On XT250 models, remove the bolts from the left-hand side.

    c. To prevent crankcase warpage, loosen the bolts in a crisscross pattern.

NOTE
Set the engine on wood blocks or fabricate a holding fixture of 2 x 4 inch wood as shown in Figure 140.

CAUTION
Perform the next step directly over and close to the workbench as the crankcase halves may separate easily. Do not hammer on the crankcase halves or they will be damaged.

7. Perform the following to separate the crankcase assemblies:

    a. Place the engine assembly on wood blocks with the right-hand side facing up.

    b. Yamaha has provided pry slots in the left- and right-hand crankcase assemblies to help with disassembly. Carefully pry the right-hand crankcase up until the crankshaft and crankcase separate. See **Figure 141**.

8. If the crankcase and crankshaft will not separate using this method, check to make sure that all screws are removed. If you still have a problem, take the crankcase assembly to a dealer and have them separate it.

CAUTION
Never pry between the case halves. Doing so may result in oil leaks, requiring replacement of the case halves.

9. Don't lose the 2 locating dowels if they came out of the case. They do not have to be removed from the case if they are secure.

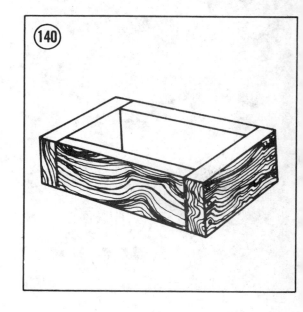

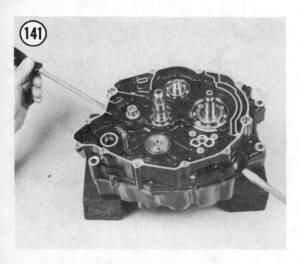

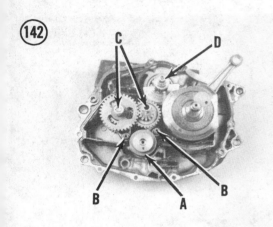

10. Referring to **Figure 142**, lift up and carefully remove the following parts:
   a. Shift drum (A).
   b. Shift forks (B).
   c. Transmission shafts (C).
   d. Balancer shaft (D).

11. Carefully remove the crankshaft assembly from the crankcase half (**Figure 143**). If the crankshaft is difficult to remove, a crankcase separation tool (**Figure 144**) will have to be used as shown in **Figure 145**.

12. Inspect the crankcase halves, crankshaft and balancer shaft as described in this chapter.

Crankcase Assembly

1. Apply assembly oil to the inner race of all bearings in both crankcase halves.

NOTE
Set the left-hand crankcase assembly on wood blocks or the wood holding fixture shown in the disassembly procedure.

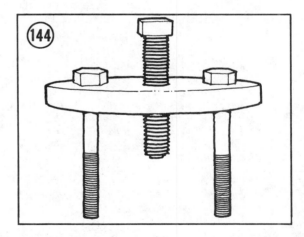

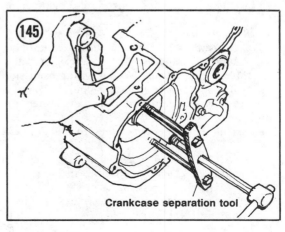

Crankcase separation tool

2. Install the crankshaft (**Figure 143**) by tapping the end of the crankshaft with a plastic mallet.
3. Install the balancer shaft (D, **Figure 142**).
4. Install the transmission assemblies, shift shafts and shift drum into the crankcase. Lightly oil all shaft ends. Refer to Chapter Five for the correct procedure.

NOTE
Make sure the mating surfaces are clean and free of all old sealant.

5. Install the 2 locating dowels (**Figure 146**) if they were removed.
6. Apply a light coat of non-hardening liquid gasket (**Figure 147**) such as Yamabond No. 4, 4-Three Bond or equivalent to the mating surfaces of both crankcase halves.
7. Set the upper crankcase half over the one on the blocks. Push it down squarely into place until it reaches the crankshaft bearing; there is usually about 1/2 inch left to go.
8. Lightly tap the case halves together with a plastic or rubber mallet until they seat. After the cases are assembled, tap on the end of each shaft to make sure it is free and rotates smoothly.

CAUTION
Crankcase halves should fit together without force. If the crankcase halves do not fit together completely, do not attempt to pull them together with the crankcase screws. Separate the crankcase halves and investigate the interference. If the transmission shafts were disassembled, recheck to make sure that a gear is not installed backwards. Crankcase halves are very expensive. Do not risk damage by trying to force the cases together.

9. Install all the crankcase screws and tighten only finger-tight at first.
10. Securely tighten the screws in 2 stages in a crisscross pattern until they are firmly hand-tight.
11. After the crankcase halves are completely assembled, rotate the crankshaft and transmission shafts to make sure there is no binding. If any is present, disassemble the crankcase and correct the problem.
12. Install the rear chain guide. See **Figure 138** (XT125 and XT200) or **Figure 139** (XT250).
13. Install all exterior engine assembles as described in this chapter and other chapters:
   a. External shift mechanism.
   b. Primary drive and balancer gears.
   c. Oil pump.
   d. Clutch.
   e. Alternator.
   f. Piston.
   g. Cylinder.
   h. Cylinder head.
14. Install the cam chain tensioner assembly. See **Figure 148**.

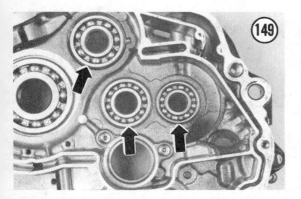

Crankcase and Crankshaft Inspection

1. Clean both crankcase halves inside and out with cleaning solvent. Thoroughly dry with compressed air and wipe off with a clean shop cloth. Be sure to remove all traces of old gasket material from all mating surfaces.

2. Check the transmission and balancer shaft bearings (**Figure 149** and **Figure 150**) and the shift drum bearing (**Figure 151**) for roughness, galling and play by rotating them slowly by hand. If any roughness or play can be felt in the bearing it must be replaced.

3. Carefully inspect the cases for cracks and fractures, especially in the lower areas; they are vulnerable to rock damage. Also check the areas around the stiffening ribs, bearing bosses and threaded holes. If any are found, replace the crankcases.

4. Check that bolt threads in cases are clean and free of any thread damage. See **Figure 152** and **Figure 153**. Clean thread holes by blowing out with compressed air. If threads are damaged, use a tap of the correct size to repair them.

5. Check the crankshaft main bearings (**Figure 154** and **Figure 155**) for roughness, pitting, galling and

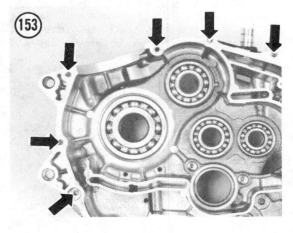

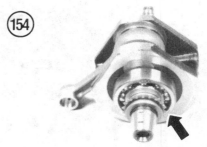

play by rotating them slowly by hand. If any roughness or play can be felt in the bearing it must be replaced. Replace the crankcase bearing (**Figure 155**) as described in this chapter. The bearing on the crankshaft (**Figure 154**) should be replaced by a dealer as special tools are required.

6. Inspect the cam chain sprocket (A, **Figure 156**) for wear or missing teeth. If damaged, the sprocket should be replaced by a dealer as special tools are required.

NOTE
*If the cam chain sprocket requires replacement, the camshaft sprocket and cam chain (**Figure 157**) should also be replaced to prevent premature wear to the new part.*

7. Check the camshaft keyways (B and C, **Figure 156**) for signs of damage. If damaged, refer further service to a Yamaha dealer.

8. Check the connecting rod small end (**Figure 158**) for any signs of galling or discoloration. If damaged, replace the connecting rod and piston pin.

9. Check the condition of the connecting rod big end bearing by grasping the rod in one hand and lifting up on it. With the heel of your other hand, rap sharply on the top of the rod. A sharp metallic sound, such as a click, is an indication that the bearing or crankpin or both are worn. The crankshaft assembly should be disassembled and new parts installed.

10. Check the connecting rod-to-crankshaft side clearance with a flat feeler gauge (**Figure 159**). Compare to dimensions given in **Table 1** or **Table 2**. If the clearance is greater than specified the crankshaft assembly should be disassembled and new parts installed.

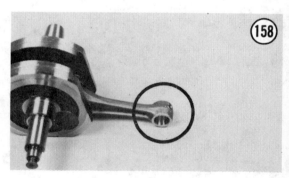

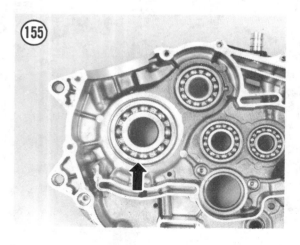

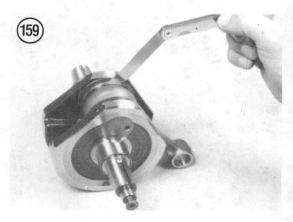

11. Check the balancer shaft bearing surfaces (**Figure 160**) for any signs of wear or discoloration and the keyway (**Figure 161**) for any signs of damage. If damage is found, replace the balancer shaft.

12. Replace the oil seals as described in this chapter. They should always be replaced when the crankcase is disassembled.

Bearing and Oil Seal Replacement

When replacing oil seals and bearings, always place the crankcase halves on wood blocks to protect the sealing surfaces from damage.

1. Pry out the oil seals (**Figure 162**) with a small screwdriver, taking care not to damage the

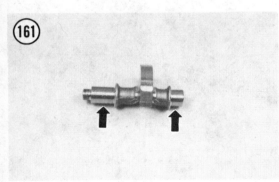

crankcase bore. If the seals are old and difficult to remove, heat the cases as described in Step 2 and use an awl to punch a small hole in the steel backing of the seal. Install a small sheet metal screw part way into the seal and pull the seal out with a pair of pliers.

> *CAUTION*
> *Do not install the screw too far or it may contact and damage the bearing behind it.*

2. The bearings are installed with a slight interference fit. The crankcase must be heated in an oven to a temperature of about 212° F (100° C). An easy way to check the proper temperature is to drop tiny drops of water on the case; if they sizzle and evaporate immediately, the temperature is correct. Heat only one case at a time.

> *CAUTION*
> *Do not heat the cases with a torch (propane or acetylene); never bring a flame into contact with the bearing or case. The direct heat will destroy the case hardening of the bearing and will likely cause warpage of the case.*

3. Remove the case from the oven and hold onto the 2 crankcase studs with a kitchen pot holder, heavy gloves or heavy shop cloths—*it is hot.*

4. Hold the crankcase with the bearing side down and tap it squarely on a piece of soft wood. Continue to tap until the bearing(s) fall out. Repeat for the other half.

> *CAUTION*
> *Be sure to tap the crankcase squarely on the piece of wood. Avoid damaging the sealing surface of the crankcase.*

5. If the bearings are difficult to remove, they can be gently tapped out with a socket or piece of pipe the same size as the bearing outer race.

> *CAUTION*
> *If the bearings or seals are difficult to remove or install, don't take a chance on expensive damage. Have the work performed by a dealer or competent machine shop.*

6. While heating up the crankcase halves, place the new bearings in a freezer. Chilling them will slightly reduce their overall diameter while the hot crankcase is slightly larger due to heat expansion. This will make bearing installation much easier.

7. While the crankcase is still hot, press each new bearing(s) into place in the crankcase by hand until

it seats completely. Do not hammer it in. If the bearing will not seat, remove it and cool it again. Reheat the crankcase and install the bearing again.

8. Oil seals can be installed with a proper size socket or piece of pipe. Make sure that the bearings and oil seals are not cocked in the crankcase hole and that they are seated properly.

9. After installing bearings and seals, apply a light amount of lightweight lithium base grease to the seal lips. Coat the bearings with engine oil to prevent rust.

KICKSTARTER

The kickstarter can be removed with the engine in the frame.

Removal/Installation
(XT125 and XT200)

1. Remove the clutch as described in Chapter Five.
2. Remove the following in order:
   a. Idler gear circlip (**Figure 163**).
   b. Washer (A, **Figure 164**).
   c. Idler gear (B, **Figure 164**).

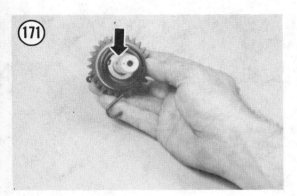

d. Washer (**Figure 165**).

e. Circlip (**Figure 166**).

3. Disconnect the kickstarter return spring from the crankcase post (A, **Figure 167**). Then remove the kickstarter assembly (B, **Figure 167**).

4. Installation is the reverse of these steps. Refill the engine oil as described in Chapter Three.

Disassembly/Assembly
(XT125 and XT200)

1. Clean the assembled shaft in solvent and dry with compressed air.

2. Remove the following parts in order:

a. Washer (**Figure 168**).

b. Plate washer (**Figure 169**).

c. Circlip (**Figure 170**).

d. Spacer (**Figure 171**).

e. Return spring (**Figure 172**).

f. Washer (**Figure 173**).

g. Kick gear and clip (**Figure 174**).

3. Inspect the kickstarter assembly as described in this chapter.

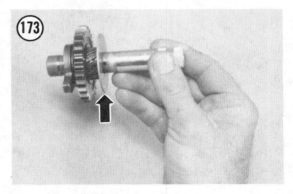

4

4. Apply assembly oil to all sliding surfaces of all parts prior to assembly.

5. Make sure the clip is installed on the kick gear as shown in **Figure 175**.

6. Install the kick gear and clip (**Figure 174**).

7. Install the large washer (**Figure 173**).

8. Slide the return spring onto the shaft. Then insert the end of the spring into the hole in the shaft as shown in **Figure 172**.

9. Install the spacer so that the slot (**Figure 176**) fits around the end of the spring. **Figure 171** shows the spacer correctly installed.

10. Install the circlip (**Figure 170**).

11. Install the plate washer (**Figure 169**) so that the tangs on the washer fit into the slots in the side of the spacer.

12. Install the plain washer (**Figure 168**).

NOTE
*Prior to installing the assembled shaft into the crankcase, check with **Figure** 177 for correct placement of all components.*

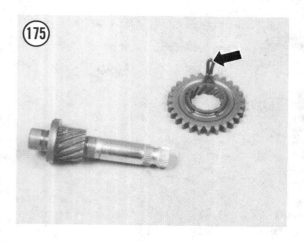

Removal/Installation (XT250)

1. Remove the clutch as described in Chapter Five.
2. Disconnect the kickstarter return spring from the crankcase post (A, **Figure 178**). Then remove the kickstarter assembly (B, **Figure 178**).
3. Remove the following in order:

   a. Idler gear circlip (**Figure 179**).
   b. Washer.
   c. Idler gear (**Figure 180**).
   d. Washer (**Figure 181**).
   e. Circlip (**Figure 182**).

4. Installation is the reverse of these steps. Refill the engine with oil as described in Chapter Three.

Disassembly/Assembly (XT250)

1. Clean the assembled shaft in solvent and dry with compressed air.
2. Remove the following parts in order:

   a. Washer (**Figure 183**).
   b. Circlip (**Figure 184**).
   c. Washer.
   d. Spring (**Figure 185**).
   e. Ratchet (**Figure 186**).

f. Circlip (**Figure 187**).

g. Gear (**Figure 188**).

h. Spring (**Figure 189**).

3. Inspect the kickstarter assembly as described in this chapter.

4. Apply assembly oil to all sliding surfaces of all parts prior to assembly.

5. Install the spring on the shaft in the direction shown in **Figure 189** and insert the spring hook in the slot.

6. Install the gear with the ratchet teeth facing in the direction shown in **Figure 188**. Secure the gear with the circlip (**Figure 187**).

7. Install the ratchet so that it meshes with the gear (**Figure 186**).

8. Install the spring (**Figure 185**), washer, circlip (**Figure 184**) and washer (**Figure 183**).

NOTE
*Prior to installing the assembled shaft into the crankcase, check with **Figure** 190 for correct placement of all components.*

Inspection (All Models)

1. Check for chipped, broken or missing teeth on the gears (A, **Figure 191**). Replace parts as necessary.

2. Check the kick shaft for signs of wear, fatigue or damage (B, **Figure 191**). Replace the shaft if necessary.

3. Check all parts for uneven wear; replace any that are questionable.

BREAK-IN

Following cylinder servicing (boring, honing, new rings, etc.) and major lower end work, the engine should be broken in just as if it were new. The performance and service life of the engine depends greatly on a careful and sensible break-in.

For the first 500 miles, no more than one-third throttle should be used and speed should be varied as much as possible within the one-third throttle limit. Prolonged, steady running at one speed, no matter how moderate, is to be avoided, as is hard acceleration.

Following the 500-mile service, increasingly more throttle can be used but full throttle should not be used until the motorcycle has covered at least 1,000 miles and then it should be limited to short bursts until 1,500 miles have been logged.

The mono-grade oils recommended for break-in and normal use provide a better bedding pattern for rings and cylinders than do multi-grade oils. As a result, piston ring and cylinder bore life are greatly increased. During this period, oil consumption will be higher than normal. It is therefore important to frequently check and correct the oil level. At no time, during break-in or later, should the oil level be allowed to drop below the bottom line on the inspection window; if the oil level is low, the oil will become overheated resulting in insufficient lubrication and increased wear.

500-mile Service

It is essential that oil and filter be changed after the first 500 miles. In addition, it is a good idea to change the oil and filter at the completion of break-in (about 1,500 miles) to ensure that all of the particles produced during break-in are removed from the lubrication system. The small added expense may be considered a smart investment that will pay off in increased engine life.

Table 1 ENGINE SPECIFICATIONS (XT125 AND XT200)

Item	Specification in. (mm)	Wear limit in. (mm)
General		
Type	4-stroke, air-cooled, SOHC	
Number of cylinders	1	
Bore and stroke		
XT125	2.24 x 1.92	
	(57.0 x 48.4)	
XT200	2.64 x 2.15	
	(67.0 x 55.7)	
Displacement		
XT125	124 cc	
XT200	196 cc	
Compression ratio		
XT125	10:1	
XT200	9.5:1	
Lubrication	Wet sump	
Cylinder		
Bore		
XT125	2.244-2.248	
	(57.000-57.010)	
XT200	2.640-2.644	
	(67.000-67.010)	
Taper	—	0.003
	—	(0.008)
Cylinder head		
Warp limit	—	0.0012
	—	(0.03)
Piston		
Size		
XT125	2.2430-2.2424	—
	(57.025-57.040)	—
XT200	2.6390-2.6384	—
	(67.025-67.040)	—
	(continued)	

Table 1 ENGINE SPECIFICATIONS (XT125 AND XT200) (continued)

Item	Specification in. (mm)	Wear limit in. (mm)
Piston (continued)		
Clearance		
XT125	0.0010-0.0018	—
	(0.025-0.045)	—
XT200	0.0013-0.0018	—
	(0.032-0.045)	—
Piston rings		
Number of rings		
Compression	2	—
Oil control	1	—
End gap		
Top/second	0.0059-0.0138	0.0236
	(0.15-0.35)	(0.6)
Oil	0.0118-0.0354	—
	(0.3-0.9)	—
Side clearance		
Top	0.0012-0.0028	0.0059
	(0.03-0.07)	(0.15)
Second	0.0008-0.0024	0.0059
	(0.02-0.06)	(0.15)
Camshaft		
Clearance	0.0083-0.0024	—
	(0.021-0.061)	—
Runout	—	0.001
	—	(0.03)
Lobe height		
Intake	1.438-1.442	—
	(36.54-36.64)	—
Exhaust	1.440-1.444	—
	(36.58-36.68)	—
Diameter		
Intake		
XT125 models	1.186-1.190	—
	(30.13-30.23)	—
XT200 models	1.17-1.21	—
	(30.18-30.28)	—
Exhaust		
XT125 models	1.189-1.193	—
	(30.21-30.31)	—
XT200 models	1.191-1.195	—
	(30.25-30.35)	—
Rocker arm/shaft		
Clearance	0.0004-0.0015	—
	(0.009-0.037)	—
Shaft diameter	0.4712-0.4716	—
	(11.981-11.991)	—
Valve		
Stem runout	—	0.0012
	—	(0.03)
	(0.9-1.1)	—
Valve dimensions	See text	—
Valve spring free length		
Inner	1.40	—
	(35.5)	—
	(continued)	

Table 1 ENGINE SPECIFICATIONS (XT125 AND XT200) (continued)

Item	Specification in. (mm)	Wear limit in. (mm)
Valve spring free length (cont.)		
Outer	1.46	—
	(37.2)	—
Crankshaft		
Runout	—	0.0012
	—	(0.03)
Oil pump		
Side clearance	0.0012-0.0035	—
	(0.03-0.09)	—
Tip clearance	0.006	—
	(0.15)	—

4

Table 2 ENGINE SPECIFICATIONS (XT250)

Item	Specification in. (mm)	Wear limit in. (mm)
General		
Type	4-stroke, air-cooled, SOHC	
Number of cylinders	1	
Bore and stroke	2.95 x 2.22	
	(75 x 56.5)	
Displacement	249 cc	
Compression ratio	9.2:1	
Lubrication	Wet sump	
Cylinder		
Bore	2.9530-2.9538	2.992
	(75.00-75.02)	(75.1)
Taper	—	0.003
	—	(0.008)
Cylinder head		
Warp limit	—	0.0012
	—	(0.03)
Piston		
Clearance	0.0014-0.0022	0.0039
	(0.035-0.055)	(0.1)
Piston rings		
Number of rings		
Compression	2	—
Oil control	1	—
End gap		
Top/second	0.0079-0.0157	—
	(0.2-0.4)	—
Oil	0.012-0.035	—
	(0.3-0.9)	—
Side clearance		
Top	0.0016-0.0031	—
	(0.04-0.08)	—
Second	0.0012-0.0028	—
	(0.03-0.07)	—
Camshaft		
Runout	—	0.001
	—	(0.03)

(continued)

Table 2 ENGINE SPECIFICATIONS (XT250) (continued)

Item	Specification in. (mm)	Wear limit in. (mm)
Camshaft (continued)		
Lobe height		
Intake	1.581-1.585	—
	(40.15-40.25)	—
Exhaust	1.583-1.587	—
	(40.20-40.30)	—
Diameter		
Intake	1.263-1.267	1.26
	(32.09-32.19)	(31.99)
Exhaust	1.264-1.268	1.221
	(32.11-32.21)	(31.01)
Rocker arm/shaft		
Clearance	0.0004-0.0017	—
	(0.009-0.043)	—
Shaft diameter	0.471-0.4726	—
	(11.975-11.990)	—
Rocker arm inside diameter		
	0.472-0.473	—
	(12.000-12.018)	—
Valve		
Stem runout	—	0.0012
	—	(0.03)
Valve spring free length		
Inner	1.57	—
	(40.0)	—
Outer	1.70	—
	(43.2)	—
Crankshaft		
Runout	—	0.0012
	—	(0.03)
Oil pump		
Rotor to rotor clearance		
	0.0012-0.0035	—
	(0.03-0.09)	—

Table 3 TIGHTENING TORQUES (XT125 AND XT200)

Item	ft.-lb.	N•m
Cylinder head	16	22
Cylinder		
M6	7	10
M8	14	20
Cylinder head cover		
Bolt	7	10
Screw	5	7
Camshaft bearing plate	6	8
Oil check screw	5	7
Balancer weight bolt	36	50
Camshaft sprocket	43	60
Drain plug	31	43
Chain guide	6	8
Oil pump	5	7
Oil filter cover	7	10
Crankcase	5	7

Table 4 TIGHTENING TORQUES (XT250)

Item	ft.-lb.	N•m
Cylinder head and cylinder		
M10	27	37
M8	14	20
M6	7	10
Cylinder head cover		
Bolt	7	10
Screw	5	7
Camshaft bearing plate	6	8
Oil check bolt	5	7
Balancer nut	43	60
Balancer bearing cover	5	7
Camshaft sprocket	40	55
Chain tensioner		
Bolt	6	8
Nut	9	12
Plug	22	30
Oil pump	5	7
Drain plug	23	32
Oil filter cover		
Bolt	7	10
Screw	5	7
Oil bleed bolt	4	5
Crankshaft boss	14	20
Decompression cam stopper	6	8
Decompression lever	6	8
Valve cover	7	10

Table 5 GENERAL TORQUE SPECIFICATIONS*

Item	ft.-lb.	N•m
Bolt		
6 mm	4.5	6
8 mm	11	15
10 mm	22	30
12 mm	40	55
14 mm	61	85
16 mm	94	130
Nut		
10 mm	4.5	6
12 mm	11	15
14 mm	22	30
17 mm	40	55
19 mm	61	85
22 mm	94	130

* Use these torque figures for all fasteners not individually listed.

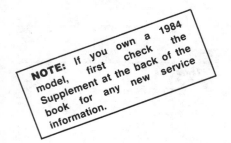

NOTE: If you own a 1984 model, first check the Supplement at the back of the book for any new service information.

CHAPTER FIVE

CLUTCH AND TRANSMISSION

This chapter contains removal, inspection, overhaul and installation of the clutch, transmission and shift mechanism (external and internal). **Table 1** (clutch specifications) and **Table 2** (tightening torques) are at the end of the chapter.

CLUTCH

The clutch used on all XT models is a wet multiplate type which operates immersed in the oil supply it shares with the transmission. The clutch boss is splined to the transmission main shaft. The clutch housing can rotate freely on the main shaft but is geared to the primary drive gear attached to the crankshaft.

During disassembly pay particular attention to the location and positioning of spacers and washers to make assembly easier.

The clutch can be removed with the engine in the frame.

Refer to **Figure 1** for the clutch assembly used on the various models.

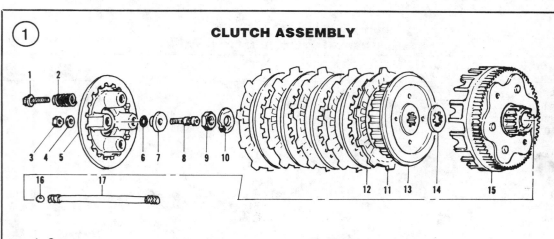

① CLUTCH ASSEMBLY

1. Screw
2. Spring
3. Nut
4. Washer
5. Pressure plate
6. O-ring
7. Plate
8. Adjust screw
9. Nut
10. Washer
11. Friction disc
12. Clutch plate
13. Clutch boss
14. Spacer
15. Clutch housing/primary driven gear
16. Ball
17. Pushrod

CLUTCH TROUBLESHOOTING

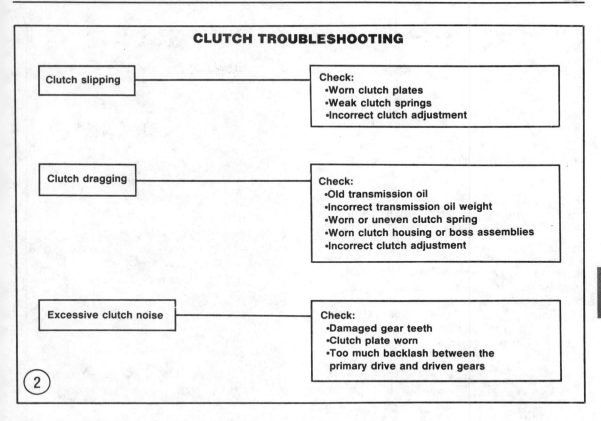

Clutch slipping	**Check:** •Worn clutch plates •Weak clutch springs •Incorrect clutch adjustment
Clutch dragging	**Check:** •Old transmission oil •Incorrect transmission oil weight •Worn or uneven clutch spring •Worn clutch housing or boss assemblies •Incorrect clutch adjustment
Excessive clutch noise	**Check:** •Damaged gear teeth •Clutch plate worn •Too much backlash between the primary drive and driven gears

②

③

④

Troubleshooting

The XT clutch is relatively bulletproof. However, when clutch problems occur, they can be difficult to diagnose. The troubleshooting chart in **Figure 2** lists typical clutch problems and their probable causes.

Removal

1. Support the bike on the kickstand.
2. Drain the transmission oil as described in Chapter Three.
3. Remove the footpeg from the right-hand side (**Figure 3**). Then remove the brake lever assembly as described in Chapter Ten.
4. Remove the bolt securing the kickstarter lever (**Figure 4**) and remove the lever.

> *NOTE*
> *Steps 5 and 6 apply to XT250 models only.*

5. Loosen the decompressor cable locknuts (**Figure 5**) and turn the cable adjuster to provide as much slack as possible.

6. Remove the bolts securing the decompressor cable bracket to the right-hand crankcase cover (**Figure 6**).

7. Remove the oil filter cover (**Figure 7**) and pull the filter out of its housing (**Figure 8**). Do not lose the special O-ring (**Figure 9**).

8. Remove the remaining bolts securing the right-hand crankcase cover and remove the cover.

9. Loosen the clutch bolts (**Figure 10**) securing the pressure plate in a crisscross pattern. Remove the bolts and clutch springs.

10. Remove the pressure plate (**Figure 11**). Be sure to store the plate so that the pushrod assembly (**Figure 12**) is not damaged.

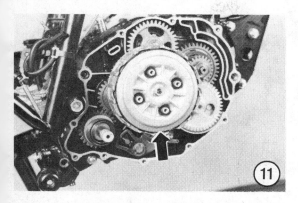

11. Remove the friction (**Figure 13**) and clutch (**Figure 14**) plates.

12. Using a magnet inserted into the main shaft, remove the clutch ball (**Figure 15**) and pushrod (**Figure 16**).

13. Pry back the lockwasher tab from the clutch nut. Then attach a special tool like the "Grabbit" (**Figure 17**) to the clutch housing and remove the clutch nut and lockwasher.

CAUTION
Do not insert a screwdriver or pry bar between the clutch housing and the clutch boss. The fingers on the clutch housing are fragile and can be broken very easily.

NOTE
The "Grabbit" is available from Precision Mfg. and Sales Co., P.O. Box 149, Clearwater, FL 33517.

14. Slide the clutch boss (**Figure 18**) off the main shaft.

15. Remove the thrust washer (**Figure 19**) and slide the clutch housing (**Figure 20**) off of the main shaft.

Inspection

1. Clean all clutch parts in a petroleum-based solvent such as kerosene and thoroughly dry with compressed air.

2. Measure the free length of each clutch spring with a caliper. Replace any springs that are too short (**Table 1**). For best performance, replace all springs as a set.

3. Check the clutch metal plates (A, **Figure 21**) for warpage as shown in **Figure 22**. If any plate is warped more than specified (**Table 1**), replace the entire set of plates. Do not replace only a few plates.

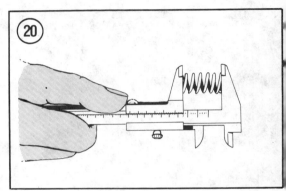

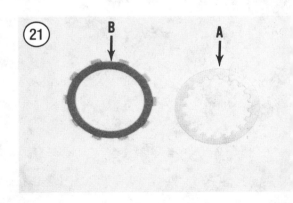

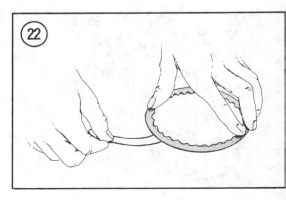

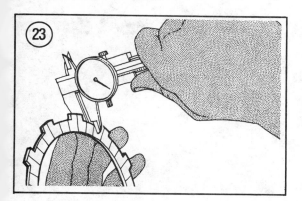

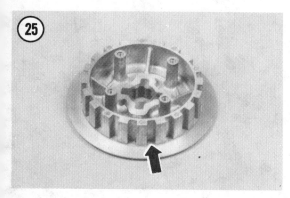

4. Measure the thickness of each friction disc (B, **Figure 21**) at several places around the disc as shown in **Figure 23**. See **Table 1** for specifications. Replace all friction discs if any one is found too thin. Do not replace only a few discs.

5. Check the tangs on the outside of the friction discs (B, **Figure 21**). If any plate is worn or damaged, the discs must be replaced as a set.

6. Inspect the clutch housing (**Figure 24**) and the clutch boss assembly (**Figure 25**) for cracks or galling in the grooves where the clutch plates slide. They must be smooth for good clutch operation. Remove any small burrs with a fine-cut file; if damage is severe, replace the component.

7. Check the teeth on the clutch housing gears (**Figure 26**). If the teeth are damaged, replace the clutch housing assembly.

8. Check the pushrod assembly (**Figure 27**) in the pressure plate for any signs of wear or damage. If the pushrod is bent or damaged on the contact end, it should be replaced. Examine the pushrod O-ring and replace it if worn or damaged.

9. Inspect both ends of the long pushrod. If either end has a worn depression, the pushrod should be replaced.

Assembly/Installation

1. Lubricate all bearing surfaces with clutch/transmission oil.

2. Slide the clutch housing (**Figure 20**) onto the main shaft, making sure to engage the gears on the rear of the housing.

3. Install the thrust washer (**Figure 19**).

4. Install the clutch boss (**Figure 18**). Then install the lockwasher and locknut (**Figure 28**).

5. Using the same tool to hold the clutch housing as during disassembly (**Figure 29**), tighten the

5

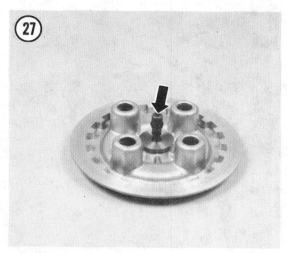

clutch nut to specifications (**Table 2**). Bend over the lockwasher tabs to lock the clutch nut.

6. Install the pushrod (**Figure 30**) and steel ball (**Figure 31**) into the main shaft.

7. Install a friction disc first (**Figure 32**) and then a clutch plate. Continue to install a friction disc and then a clutch plate until all plates are installed.

> *CAUTION*
> *If either or both friction and/or clutch plates have been replaced with new ones or if they were cleaned, apply new clutch/transmission oil to all plate surfaces. This will prevent the plates from burning up when used for the first time.*

8. Install the pressure plate (A, **Figure 33**).

> *NOTE*
> *On XT250 models only, align the arrow on the pressure plate with the index mark on the clutch boss. See **Figure 34**.*

9. Install the clutch springs (B, **Figure 33**) and bolts. Tighten the bolts in a crisscross pattern in 2-3 stages.

10. Perform the *Clutch Mechanism Adjustment* described in this chapter.

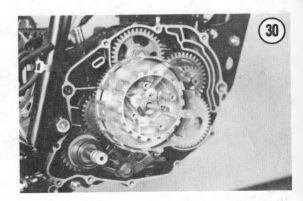

11. Install the right-hand side crankcase housing (**Figure 35**). Install and tighten all screws (except decompression plate screws on XT250 models) in a crisscross pattern. Install the oil filter and cover as described in Chapter Three.

CAUTION
Do not install any of the crankcase cover screws until the crankcase cover is snug against the crankcase surface. Do not try to force the cover into place with the screws.

NOTE
Steps 12 and 13 pertain to XT250 models only.

12. Install the washer and spring (**Figure 36**) onto the decompressor lever on the right-hand crankcase cover. Then install the bracket and connect the decompressor cable as shown in **Figure 37**.

13. Adjust the decompressor cable as described in Chapter Three.

14. Install the kickstarter lever and bolt. Tighten the bolt securely.

15. Install the rear brake pedal assembly as described in Chapter Ten. Install the right-hand side footpeg.

16. Refill the engine with the recommended type and quantity of oil; refer to Chapter Three.

17. Adjust the clutch cable as described in Chapter Three.

Clutch Mechanism Adjustment

This procedure should be performed whenever the clutch assembly is disassembled.

1. Remove the right-hand side crankcase cover as described under *Clutch Removal/Installation* in this chapter.

2. Loosen the clutch cable adjusters at the engine (A, **Figure 38**) and at the handlebar (**Figure 39**).

Turn both adjusters to obtain as much clutch cable slack as possible.

3. Loosen the clutch mechanism adjuster locknut (A, **Figure 40**).

4. Push the clutch push lever (**Figure 41**) toward the front of the engine until it stops and hold it in this position. Turn the clutch mechanism adjuster (B, **Figure 40**) in or out to align the clutch push lever mark with the crankcase match mark (**Figure 41**). Tighten the locknut (A, **Figure 40**) and recheck the adjustment.

5. Install the right-hand side crankcase cover as described in this chapter.

6. Adjust the clutch cable as described under *Clutch Adjustment* in Chapter Three.

CLUTCH CABLE

Replacement

In time the clutch cable will stretch to the point that it will have to be replaced.

1. Remove the side covers and seat.

2. Remove the fuel tank as described in Chapter Six.

3. At the clutch lever, pull back the rubber protective boot covering the cable adjuster.

4. At the clutch lever, loosen the locknut and turn the adjuster barrel (**Figure 39**) all the way toward the cable sheath. Slip the cable end out of the hand lever.

5. At the left-hand side of the engine, loosen the locknut and turn the cable adjuster (A, **Figure 38**) all the way in. Slip the cable end out of the push lever (B, **Figure 38**).

> *NOTE*
> *The piece of string attached in the next step will be used to pull the new clutch cable back through the frame so it will be routed in the same position as the old one.*

6. Tie a piece of heavy string or cord (approximately 6 feet/2 m long) to the clutch mechanism end of the cable. Wrap this end with masking or duct tape. Do not use an excessive amount of tape. Tie the other end of the string to the footpeg.

7. At the handlebar end of the cable, carefully pull the cable (and attached spring) out through the frame and from behind the steering head area. Be sure the attached string follows the same path of the cable through the frame and behind the steering head area.

8. Remove the tape and untie the string from the old cable.

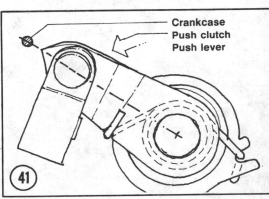

Crankcase
Push clutch
Push lever

9. Lubricate the new cable as described in Chapter Three.

10. Tie the string to the clutch mechanism end of the new clutch cable and wrap it with tape.

11. Carefully pull the string back through the frame, routing the new cable through the same path as the old cable.

12. Remove the tape and untie the string from the cable and the footpeg. Attach the new cable to the clutch lever and the clutch mechanism.

13. Install all components which were removed.

14. Check the clutch mechanism adjustment as described in this chapter. Adjust the mechanism if necessary.

15. Adjust the clutch cable as described in Chapter Three.

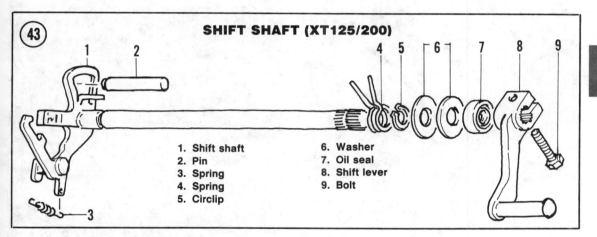

SHIFT SHAFT (XT125/200)

1. Shift shaft
2. Pin
3. Spring
4. Spring
5. Circlip
6. Washer
7. Oil seal
8. Shift lever
9. Bolt

5

EXTERNAL SHIFT MECHANISM

The external shift mechanism is located on the same side of the crankcase as the clutch assembly and can be removed with the engine in the frame. To remove the shift drum and shift forks (internal shift mechanism), it is necessary to remove the engine and split the crankcases. See *Transmission and Internal Shift Mechanism* in this chapter.

The gearshift lever is subject to a lot of abuse. If the bike has been in a hard spill, the gearshift lever may have been hit and the shift shaft bent. It is very hard to straighten the shaft without subjecting the crankcase to abnormal stress where the shaft enters the case. If the shaft is bent enough to prevent it from being withdrawn from the crankcase, it is necessary to cut the shaft off with a hacksaw very close to the crankcase. Then file the end of the shaft to remove all burrs before withdrawing the shaft. It is much cheaper in the long run to replace the shaft than risk damaging a very expensive crankcase.

Removal/Installation

1. Drain the engine oil as described in Chapter Three.
2. Support the bike on the kickstand or by placing a milk crate or wood block(s) under the engine for support.
3. Remove the clutch assembly as described in this chapter.
4. Remove the gearshift lever from the left-hand side (**Figure 42**).
5. Complete removal and installation of the external shift mechanism by performing the appropriate procedure for your specific model.

XT125 and XT200

Refer to **Figure 43**.
1. Remove the oil pump as described in Chapter Four.
2. Remove the kickstarter as described in Chapter Four.
3. Referring to **Figure 44**, simultaneously pull back on the shift lever arm and the stopper lever.

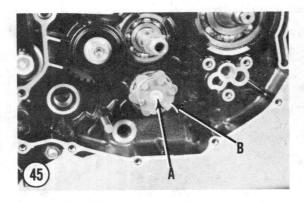

Then pull the shift lever assembly out of the crankcase through the right-hand side.

4. Using a No. T-30 Torx socket, remove the Torx screw (A, **Figure 45**) securing the shift cam segment (B, **Figure 45**) and remove the segment.

5. Examine the shift shaft seal in the left-hand side crankcase (**Figure 46**). If damaged, pry it out carefully using a suitable size screwdriver. Install a new seal by tapping it in with a socket the same diameter as the seal. Make sure the seal seats flush in the crankcase before installing the shift lever.

6. Inspect the external shift mechanism assembly as described in this chapter.

7. Install the segment by aligning the pin in the back of the segment with the hole in the shift cam. See **Figure 47**. Apply a small amount of Loctite to the Torx screw threads and tighten it to 8.7 ft.-lb. (12 Nm) with the No. T-30 Torx socket.

8. Install the shift lever mechanism into the crankcase from the right-hand side.

9. Referring to **Figure 44**, simultaneously pull back on the shift lever arm and the stopper lever and push the mechanism into position. Then release the shift lever arm so that it engages the shift pins in the segment; release the stopper lever so that the round cam engages with the star-shaped locator on the segment. See **Figure 48**.

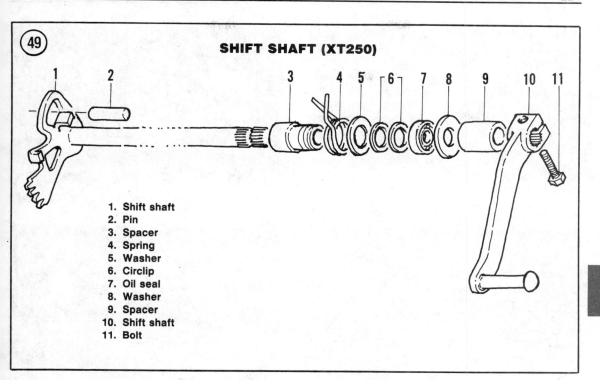

SHIFT SHAFT (XT250)

1. Shift shaft
2. Pin
3. Spacer
4. Spring
5. Washer
6. Circlip
7. Oil seal
8. Washer
9. Spacer
10. Shift shaft
11. Bolt

10. Install the kickstarter and oil pump assemblies as described in Chapter Four.

11. Install the clutch as described in this chapter.

12. Perform the *Clutch Mechanism Adjustment* in this chapter.

13. Refill the engine with the correct type and quantity of oil. Refer to Chapter Three.

14. Adjust the clutch cable as described in Chapter Three.

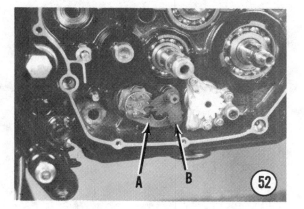

XT250

Refer to **Figure 49**.

1. Remove the oil pump idler gear (A, **Figure 50**) and pull the shift shaft (B, **Figure 50**) out of the crankcase through the right-hand side.

> *NOTE*
> *When removing the oil pump idler gear, note that there are washers on both sides of the gear (Figure 51).*

2. Referring to **Figure 52**, pull the shift arm down (A) and slide the No. 2 shift lever (B) out of the crankcase. Remove the washer (**Figure 53**).

3. Remove the screw (A, **Figure 54**) securing the shift cam segment (B, **Figure 54**) and remove the segment.

4. Examine the shift shaft seal in the left-hand side crankcase (**Figure 46**). If damaged, pry it out carefully using a suitable size screwdriver. Install a new seal by tapping it in with a socket the same diameter as the seal. Make sure the seal seats flush in the crankcase before installing the shift lever.

5. Inspect the external shift mechanism assembly as described in this chapter.

6. Install the segment by aligning the pin in the back of the segment with the hole in the shift cam. See **Figure 47**. Apply a small amount of Loctite to the screw threads and tighten it to 8.7 ft.-lb. (12 Nm).

7. Referring to **Figure 52**, pull the shift arm down (A) and slide the No. 2 shift lever (B) onto the pivot shaft. Release the shift arm so that it engages with the segment shift pins.

8. Install the shift shaft mechanism into the crankcase part-way.

9. Pull up on the No. 2 shift lever and slide in the shift shaft until they engage as shown in **Figure 55**. The alignment dot on the No. 2 shift lever must be indexed correctly (**Figure 55**) to ensure proper shifting.

10. Install the oil pump idler gear (B, **Figure 50**) by installing the washer, idler gear and washer. Secure the gear with the circlip.

11. Install the clutch as described in this chapter.

12. Perform the *Clutch Mechanism Adjustment* in this chapter.

13. Refill the engine with the correct type and quantity of oil. Refer to Chapter Three.

14. Adjust the clutch cable as described in Chapter Three.

Inspection (All Models)

1. Examine the shift lever (A, **Figure 56**). Make sure the shaft is not bent.

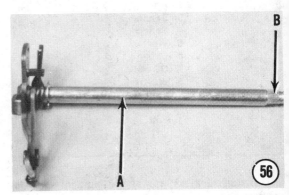

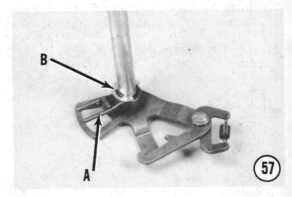

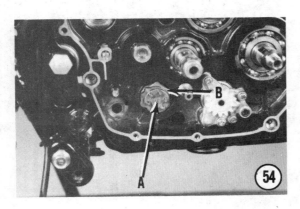

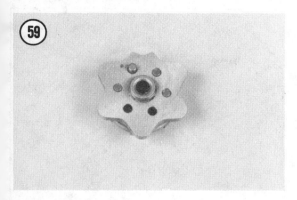

2. Examine the splines on the end of the shift lever (B, **Figure 56**). If the splines are damaged, the shift lever should be replaced. Eventually the splines will deteriorate to a point where the shift pedal will slip during shifting.

3. Check the return spring on the shift lever. See A, **Figure 57**. Replace it if worn or damaged. On XT125 and XT200 models, the spring is secured with a circlip (B, **Figure 57**). Make sure the circlip is positioned correctly before installation.

4. Inspect all accessory shift levers and stopper levers. See **Figure 58**. Look for signs of wear at all contact points. Replace any worn or damaged parts.

5. Examine the shift cam segment (**Figure 59**). If worn or damaged it must be replaced.

DRIVE SPROCKET

1. Push the bike forward until the master link is visible on the driven sprocket.

2. Support the bike on the kickstand.

3. Remove the bolt securing the gearshift pedal (**Figure 42**) and remove the pedal.

4. Remove the screws securing the drive sprocket cover and remove the cover. See **Figure 60** (XT125 and XT200) or **Figure 61** (XT250).

5. Have an assistant hold the rear brake on while you loosen the bolts securing the drive sprocket and drive sprocket holding plate.

6. Remove the drive chain master link clip (**Figure 62**) and remove the drive chain.

7. Remove the bolts (**Figure 63**) securing the drive sprocket and drive sprocket holding plate. Rotate the holding plate in either direction to disengage it from the splines on the shaft; slide off the holding plate and drive sprocket.

8. Install by reversing these removal steps, noting the following.

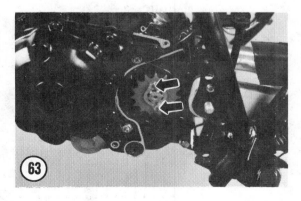

9. Install a new drive chain master link so that the closed end of the clip is facing the direction of chain travel (**Figure 64**).

10. Adjust the drive chain as described in Chapter Three.

Inspection

Inspect the teeth on the drive sprocket. If the teeth are visibly worn (**Figure 65**), replace the sprocket with a new one.

If the sprocket requires replacement, replace the rear sprocket and drive chain also. Combining worn and new parts will rapidly wear out the new parts.

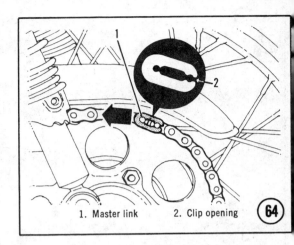

1. Master link   2. Clip opening   64

TRANSMISSION AND INTERNAL SHIFT MECHANISM

The crankcase must be disassembled to gain access to the transmission components. The transmission is shown in **Figure 66** (XT125), **Figure 67** (XT200) and **Figure 68** (XT250).

Troubleshooting

The XT transmission is relatively bulletproof. However, when shifting problems occur they can be difficult to diagnose. The troubleshooting chart in **Figure 69** lists typical transmission problems and probable causes.

Removal

This procedure is shown on an XT200 transmission assembly; where differences occur with XT125 and XT250 models, they are noted.

1. Remove the engine and disassemble the crankcase as described in Chapter Four.

2. Lift up and remove the transmission components in the following order:
    a. Shift fork shafts (A, **Figure 70**).
    b. Shift drum (B, **Figure 70**).
    c. Shift forks (**Figure 71**).
    d. Transmission shafts (**Figure 72**).

3. Disassemble and inspect the shift forks and transmission assemblies as described in this chapter.

4. Installation is the reverse of these steps, noting the following:
    a. If the transmission assemblies were disassembled, make sure all circlips are seated completely in their respective grooves.
    b. Prior to installation, coat all bearing and sliding surfaces of the shift forks shafts, shift drum and transmission shafts with assembly oil.

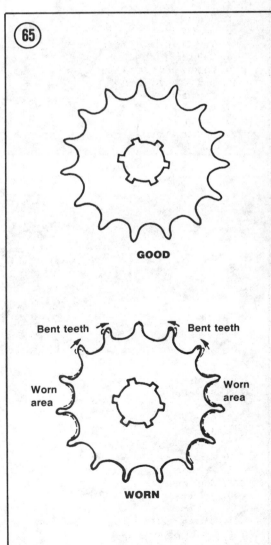

65

GOOD

Bent teeth   Bent teeth
Worn area   Worn area

WORN

(66) XT125 TRANSMISSION

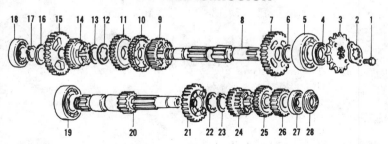

1. Bolt
2. Holder
3. Sprocket
4. Seal
5. Bearing
6. Spacer
7. Countershaft 2nd gear
8. Countershaft
9. Countershaft 5th gear
10. Countershaft 3rd gear
11. Countershaft 4th gear
12. Spacer
13. Circlip
14. Countershaft 6th gear
15. Countershaft 1st gear
16. Spacer
17. Circlip
18. Bearing
19. Bearing
20. Main shaft
21. Main shaft 6th gear
22. Spacer
23. Circlip
24. Main shaft 3rd/4th gear combination
25. Main shaft 5th gear
26. Main shaft 2nd gear
27. Bearing
28. Spacer

(67) XT200 TRANSMISSION

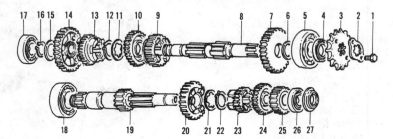

1. Bolt
2. Holder
3. Sprocket
4. Seal
5. Bearing
6. Spacer
7. Countershaft 2nd gear
8. Countershaft
9. Countershaft 4th gear
10. Countershaft 3rd gear
11. Spacer
12. Circlip
13. Countershaft 5th gear
14. Countershaft 1st gear
15. Spacer
16. Circlip
17. Bearing
18. Bearing
19. Main shaft
20. Main shaft 5th gear
21. Spacer
22. Circlip
23. Main shaft 3rd gear
24. Main shaft 4th gear
25. Main shaft 2nd gear
26. Bearing
27. Seal

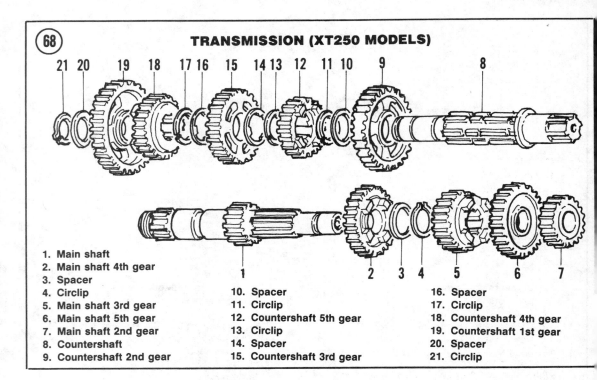

⑥⑧   **TRANSMISSION (XT250 MODELS)**

21 20   19   18   17 16   15   14 13   12   11 10   9   8

1. Main shaft
2. Main shaft 4th gear
3. Spacer
4. Circlip
5. Main shaft 3rd gear
6. Main shaft 5th gear
7. Main shaft 2nd gear
8. Countershaft
9. Countershaft 2nd gear

10. Spacer
11. Circlip
12. Countershaft 5th gear
13. Circlip
14. Spacer
15. Countershaft 3rd gear

16. Spacer
17. Circlip
18. Countershaft 4th gear
19. Countershaft 1st gear
20. Spacer
21. Circlip

c. Make sure all cam pin followers are in mesh with the shift drum grooves.

d. Spin the transmission shafts and shift through the gears using the shift drum. Make sure you can shift into all gears. This is the time to find that something may be installed incorrectly—not after the crankcase is completely assembled.

NOTE
This procedure is best done with the aid of a helper as the assemblies are loose and will not spin very easily. Have the helper spin the transmission shaft while you turn the shift drum through all the gears.

5. Assemble the crankcase as described in Chapter Four.

Preliminary Inspection

Whenever the engine cases are disassembled, the transmission assembly should be cleaned and inspected to locate possible troubles that may not have shown up yet, but would eventually cause shifting problems.

Place the assembled shafts into a large can or plastic bucket and thoroughly clean with solvent and a stiff brush. Dry with compressed air or let sit on rags to drip dry.

TRANSMISSION TROUBLESHOOTING

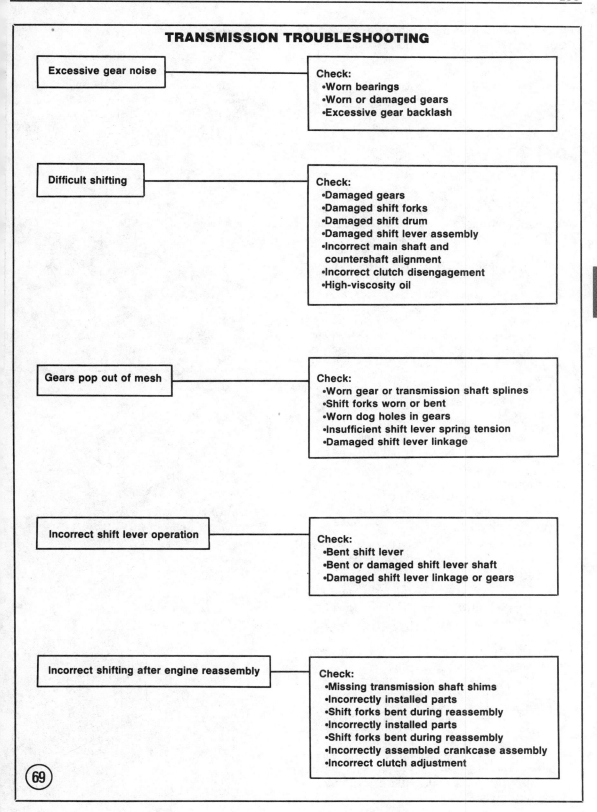

Excessive gear noise

Check:
- Worn bearings
- Worn or damaged gears
- Excessive gear backlash

Difficult shifting

Check:
- Damaged gears
- Damaged shift forks
- Damaged shift drum
- Damaged shift lever assembly
- Incorrect main shaft and countershaft alignment
- Incorrect clutch disengagement
- High-viscosity oil

Gears pop out of mesh

Check:
- Worn gear or transmission shaft splines
- Shift forks worn or bent
- Worn dog holes in gears
- Insufficient shift lever spring tension
- Damaged shift lever linkage

Incorrect shift lever operation

Check:
- Bent shift lever
- Bent or damaged shift lever shaft
- Damaged shift lever linkage or gears

Incorrect shifting after engine reassembly

Check:
- Missing transmission shaft shims
- Incorrectly installed parts
- Shift forks bent during reassembly
- Incorrectly installed parts
- Shift forks bent during reassembly
- Incorrectly assembled crankcase assembly
- Incorrect clutch adjustment

5

1. After they have been cleaned, visually inspect the transmission components for excessive wear. Any burrs, pitting or roughness on the teeth of a gear will cause wear on the mating gear (**Figure 73**). Minor roughness can be cleaned up with an oilstone but there is little point in attempting to remove deep scars.

> *NOTE*
> *Defective gears should be replaced. It's a good idea to replace the mating gear on the other shaft even though it may not show as much wear or damage.*

2. Carefully check the engagement dogs (**Figure 74**). If any are chipped, worn, rounded or missing, the affected gear must be replaced.
3. Rotate the transmission bearings in the crankcases by hand. Refer to **Figure 75** and **Figure 76**. Check for roughness, noise and radial play. Any bearing that is suspect should be replaced. Refer to *Bearing and Oil Seal Replacement* in Chapter Four.
4. If the transmission shafts are satisfactory and are not going to be disassembled, apply engine oil to all components and set aside until reassembly.

**Main Shaft Disassembly/
Assembly (XT125)**

Refer to **Figure 66** for this procedure.

> *NOTE*
> *A helpful "tool" that should be used for transmission disassembly is a large egg carton. As you remove a part from the shaft, identify it and then set it in one of the depressions in the exact same position from which it was removed (**Figure 77**). This is an easy way to remember the correct relationship of all parts.*

1. Place the assembled shaft into a large can or plastic bucket and thoroughly clean with solvent and a stiff brush. Dry with compressed air or let it sit on rags to drip dry.

> *NOTE*
> *A hydraulic press is required to remove some gears from the main shaft. Before disassembly, measure the clearance between each pressed gear (**Figure 78**) with a feeler gauge and record the measurement for reassembly.*

2. Press off 2nd and 5th gears.
3. Slide off 3rd/4th combination gear.
4. Remove the circlip and splined washer.
5. Slide off 6th gear.

6. Inspect the main shaft assembly as described later in this chapter.
7. Make sure that all splined gears slide smoothly on the main shaft splines.
8. Slide on 6th gear and install the splined washer and circlip.
9. Slide on 3rd/4th combination gear.
10. Press on 5th and 2nd gears. Be sure to install gears to specifications measured before disassembly.
11. Make sure all circlips are seated correctly in the main shaft grooves.

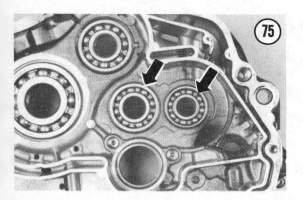

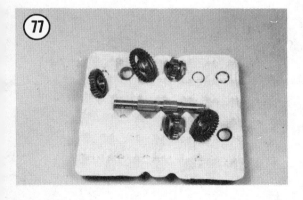

**Countershaft Disassembly/
Assembly (XT125)**

Refer to **Figure 66**.

> *NOTE*
> *A helpful "tool" that should be used for transmission disassembly is a large egg carton. As you remove a part from the shaft, identify it and then set it in one of the depressions in the exact same position from which it was removed (**Figure 77**). This is an easy way to remember the correct relationship of all parts.*

1. Place the assembled shaft into a large can or plastic bucket and thoroughly clean with solvent and a stiff brush. Dry with compressed air or let it sit on rags to drip dry.
2. Remove the washer and slide off 2nd gear.
3. Remove the circlip and washer and slide off 1st gear and 6th gear.
4. Remove the circlip and splined washer.
5. Slide off 4th gear.
6. Slide off 3rd gear.
7. Remove 5th gear.
8. Inspect the countershaft assembly as described later in this chapter.
9. Make sure that all gears slide smoothly on the countershaft splines.
10. Slide on 5th gear.
11. Slide on 3rd gear.
12. Slide on 4th gear.
13. Install the splined washer and install the circlip.
14. Slide on 6th gear.
15. Slide on 1st gear and install the washer and circlip.
16. Slide on 2nd gear and install the washer.
17. After assembly is complete refer to **Figure 66** for the correct placement of all gears. Make sure all circlips are seated correctly in the countershaft grooves.

**Main Shaft Disassembly/
Assembly (XT200)**

Refer to **Figure 67** for this procedure.

> *NOTE*
> *A helpful "tool" that should be used for transmission disassembly is a large egg carton. As you remove a part from the shaft, identify it and then set it in one of the depressions in the exact same position from which it was removed (**Figure 77**). This is an easy way to remember the correct relationship of all parts.*

5

1. Place the assembled shaft into a large can or plastic bucket and thoroughly clean with solvent and a stiff brush. Dry with compressed air or let it sit on rags to drip dry.

> *NOTE*
> *A hydraulic press is required to remove some gears from the main shaft. Before disassembly, measure the clearance between each pressed gear (**Figure 78**) with a feeler gauge and record the measurement for reassembly.*

2. Press off 2nd and 4th gears.
3. Slide off third gear.
4. Remove the circlip and splined washer.
5. Slide off 5th gear.
6. Inspect the main shaft assembly as described later in this chapter.
7. Make sure that all splined gears slide smoothly on the main shaft splines.
8. Slide on 5th gear and install the splined washer and circlip.
9. Slide on third gear.
10. Press on 4th and 2nd gears. Be sure to install gears to specifications measured before disassembly.
11. Make sure all circlips are seated correctly in the main shaft grooves.

**Countershaft Disassembly/
Assembly (XT200)**

Refer to **Figure 67**.

> *NOTE*
> *A helpful "tool" that should be used for transmission disassembly is a large egg carton. As you remove a part from the shaft, identify it and then set it in one of the depressions in the exact same position from which it was removed (**Figure 77**). This is an easy way to remember the correct relationship of all parts.*

1. Place the assembled shaft into a large can or plastic bucket and thoroughly clean with solvent and a stiff brush. Dry with compressed air or let it sit on rags to drip dry.
2. Remove the washer (**Figure 79**) and slide off 2nd gear (**Figure 80**).
3. Slide off 4th gear (**Figure 81**).
4. Remove the circlip and washer (**Figure 82**).

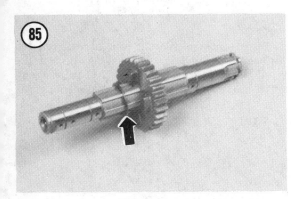

5. Slide off 1st gear (**Figure 83**).

6. Slide off 5th gear (**Figure 84**).

7. Remove the circlip and the splined washer (**Figure 85**).

8. Slide off 3rd gear (**Figure 87**).

9. Inspect the countershaft assembly as described later in this chapter.

10. Make sure that all gears slide smoothly on the countershaft splines.

11. Slide on 3rd gear (**Figure 86**) and install the splined washer (**Figure 85**) and circlip.

12. Slide on 5th gear (**Figure 84**).

13. Slide on 1st gear (**Figure 83**) and install the washer and circlip (**Figure 82**).

14. Slide on 4th gear (**Figure 81**) and 2nd gear (**Figure 80**). Install the washer (**Figure 79**).

15. After assembly is complete, refer to **Figure 87** for the correct placement of all gears. Make sure all circlips are seated correctly in the countershaft grooves.

**Main Shaft Disassembly/
Assembly (XT250)**

Refer to **Figure 68** for this procedure.

> *NOTE*
> *A helpful "tool" that should be used for transmission disassembly is a large egg carton. As you remove a part from the shaft, identify it and then set it in one of the depressions in the exact same position from which it was removed (Figure 77). This is an easy way to remember the correct relationship of all parts.*

1. Place the assembled shaft into a large can or plastic bucket and thoroughly clean with solvent

and a stiff brush. Dry with compressed air or let it sit on rags to drip dry.

> *NOTE*
> *A hydraulic press is required to remove some gears from the main shaft. Before disassembly, measure the clearance between each pressed gear (**Figure 78**) with a feeler gauge and record the measurement for reassembly.*

2. Press off 2nd gear.
3. Slide off 5th and 3rd gears.
4. Remove the circlip and splined washer.
5. Slide off 4th gear.
6. Inspect the main shaft assembly as described in this chapter.
7. Make sure that all splined gears slide smoothly on the main shaft splines.
8. Slide on 4th gear and install the thrust washer and circlip.
9. Slide on 3rd and 5th gears.
10. Press on 2nd gear. Be sure to install gears to specification measured before disassembly.
11. Make sure all circlips are seated correctly in the main shaft grooves.

Countershaft Disassembly/Assembly (XT250)

Refer to **Figure 68** for this procedure.

> *NOTE*
> *A helpful "tool" that should be used for transmission disassembly is a large egg carton. As you remove a part from the shaft, identify it and then set it in one of the depressions in the exact same position from which it was removed (**Figure 77**). This is an easy way to remember the correct relationship of all parts.*

1. Remove the circlip and washer and slide off 1st and 4th gears.
2. Remove the circlip and the splined washer and slide off 3rd gear.
3. Remove the splined washer and circlip and slide off 5th gear.
4. Remove the circlip and washer and slide off 2nd gear.
5. Inspect the countershaft assembly as described later in this chapter.
6. Make sure that all splined gears slide smoothly on the main shaft splines.
7. Slide on 2nd gear so that it rests against the countershaft stop.

8. Slide on the washer and install the circlip. Then install 5th gear.
9. Install the circlip. Then install the splined washer and 3rd gear.
10. Install the splined washer, circlip, 4th gear and 1st gear.
11. Install the washer and circlip.
12. Make sure all circlips are seated correctly in the countershaft grooves.

Inspection

1. Clean all parts in cleaning solvent and thoroughly dry.
2. Inspect the gears visually for cracks, chips and broken or burned teeth. Check lugs on ends of gears (**Figure 88**) to make sure they are not rounded off. If lugs are rounded off, check the shift forks as described in this chapter. One or more of the shift forks may be bent.
3. Check the slots in gears (**Figure 89**) for distortion or flaking that may indicate a bent shift fork.

> *NOTE*
> *Defective gears should be replaced. It is a good idea to replace the mating gear even though it may not show as much wear or damage. Remember that accelerated wear to new parts is normally caused by contact from worn parts.*

4. Inspect all free wheeling gear bearing surfaces for wear, discoloration and galling. Inspect the mating shaft bearing surface also. If there is any metal flaking or visual damage, replace both parts.

5. Inspect the main shaft and countershaft splines for wear or discoloration (**Figure 90**). Check the mating gear internal splines also. If no visual damage is apparent, install each sliding gear on its respective shaft and work the gear back and forth to make sure the gear operates smoothly.

6. Check all circlips and washers. Replace any circlips that may have been damaged during operation or removal as well as any washers that show wear.

7. If some of the transmission components were damaged, inspect the shift drum and shift forks as described in this chapter.

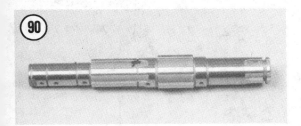

Internal Shift Mechanism Inspection

Refer to **Figure 91** (XT125 and XT200) or **Figure 92** (XT250) for this procedure.

NOTE
Prior to removal or disassembly of any of the components, lay the assembly down on a piece of paper or cardboard and carefully trace around it. Write down the identifying numbers and letter next to each item. This will take a little extra time now but it may save some time and frustration later.

1. Inspect each shift fork (**Figure 93**) for signs of wear or cracking. Examine the shift forks at the points where they contact the slider gear. This surface should be smooth with no signs of wear or damage. Make sure the forks slide smoothly on the shaft (**Figure 94**). Make sure the shaft is not bent.

5

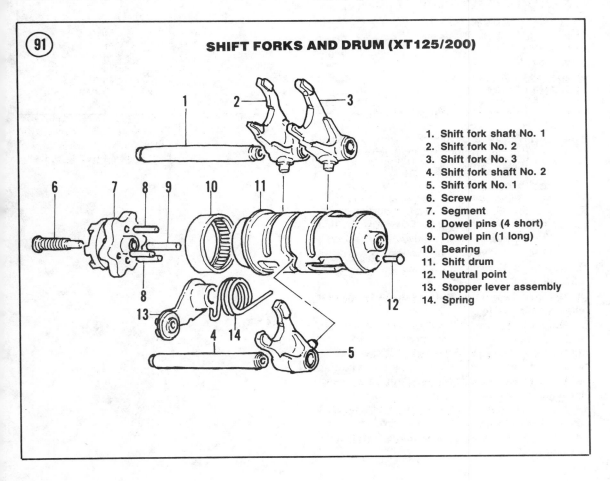

SHIFT FORKS AND DRUM (XT125/200)

1. Shift fork shaft No. 1
2. Shift fork No. 2
3. Shift fork No. 3
4. Shift fork shaft No. 2
5. Shift fork No. 1
6. Screw
7. Segment
8. Dowel pins (4 short)
9. Dowel pin (1 long)
10. Bearing
11. Shift drum
12. Neutral point
13. Stopper lever assembly
14. Spring

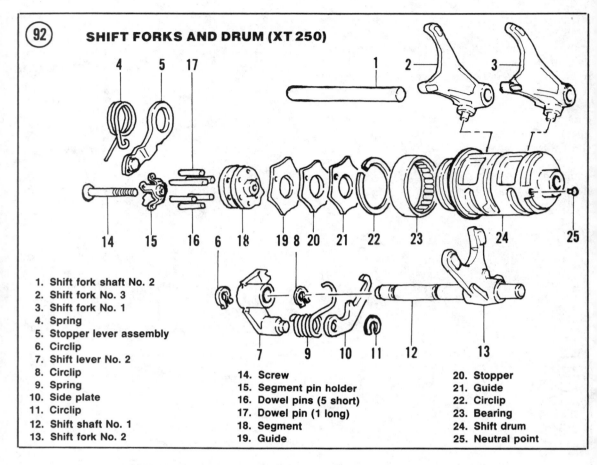

SHIFT FORKS AND DRUM (XT 250)

1. Shift fork shaft No. 2
2. Shift fork No. 3
3. Shift fork No. 1
4. Spring
5. Stopper lever assembly
6. Circlip
7. Shift lever No. 2
8. Circlip
9. Spring
10. Side plate
11. Circlip
12. Shift shaft No. 1
13. Shift fork No. 2
14. Screw
15. Segment pin holder
16. Dowel pins (5 short)
17. Dowel pin (1 long)
18. Segment
19. Guide
20. Stopper
21. Guide
22. Circlip
23. Bearing
24. Shift drum
25. Neutral point

This can be checked by removing the shift forks from the shaft and rolling the shaft on a piece of glass. Any clicking noise detected indicates that the shaft is bent.

2. Check for any arc-shaped wear or burned marks on the shift forks (**Figure 95**). This indicates that the shift fork has come in contact with the gear. The fork fingers have become excessively worn and the fork must be replaced.

3. Check grooves in the shift drum (**Figure 96**) for wear or roughness.

4. Check the shift drum segment (A, **Figure 97**) and alignment pin (B, **Figure 97**). Make sure all parts install easily and that none of the mating surfaces are worn or damaged. Replace the shift drum and segment as a set if any one part is bad.

5. Check the shift drum bearing surface (**Figure 98**) for any signs of wear or damage. Replace the shift drum if necessary.

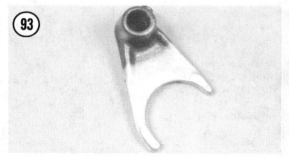

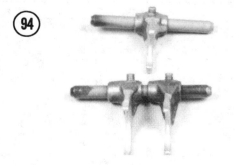

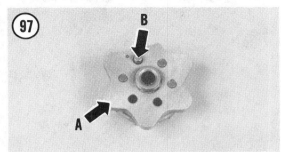

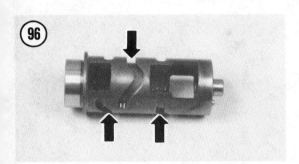

5

Table 1 CLUTCH SPECIFICATIONS

Item	Standard	Wear limit
Friction disc		
Thickness		
XT125 and XT200	0.12 in. (3 mm)	0.11 in. (1.6 mm)
XT250	0.11 in. (2.8 mm)	0.10 in. (2.5 mm)
Clutch plate		
Warp limit		
XT125 and XT200		0.008 in. (0.2 mm)
XT250		0.002 in. (0.05 mm)
Clutch springs		
Free length		
XT125 and XT200	1.37 in. (34.9 mm)	1.34 in. (33.9 mm)
XT250	1.36 in. (34.6 mm)	1.32 in. (33.6 mm)

Table 2 TIGHTENING TORQUES

Item	ft.-lb.	N•m
Primary drive gear		
XT125 and XT200	36	50
XT250	50	70
Clutch boss		
XT125 and XT200	36	50
XT250	50	70
Clutch spring	4.3	6
Neutral switch	14	20
Drive sprocket	7	10

NOTE: If you own a 1984 model, first check the Supplement at the back of the book for any new service information.

CHAPTER SIX

FUEL, EXHAUST AND EMISSION CONTROL SYSTEMS

The fuel system consists of the fuel tank, shutoff valve, a single carburetor and air cleaner. The exhaust system consists of an exhaust pipe assembly and spark arrester.

Emission control equipment is installed on all 1983 California models to conform with California emission requirements. System operation and maintenance are described in this chapter.

This chapter includes service procedures for all parts of the fuel, emission control and exhaust systems. **Table 1** is at the end of the chapter.

AIR CLEANER

The air cleaner must be cleaned frequently. Refer to Chapter Three for specific procedures and service intervals.

CARBURETOR OPERATION

For proper operation, a gasoline engine must be supplied with fuel and air mixed in proper proportions by weight. A mixture in which there is an excess of fuel is said to be rich. A lean mixture is one which contains insufficient fuel. A properly adjusted carburetor supplies the proper mixture to the engine under all operating conditions.

Mikuni carburetors consist of several major systems. A float and float valve mechanism maintain a constant fuel level in the float bowl. The pilot system supplies fuel at low speeds. The main fuel system supplies fuel at medium and high speeds. A starter (choke) system supplies the very rich mixture needed to start a cold engine.

CARBURETOR SERVICE

Major carburetor service (removal and cleaning) should be performed whenever the engine is decarbonized or when poor engine performance, hesitation and little or no response to mixture adjustment is observed.

Refer to **Table 1** at the end of this chapter for carburetor specifications.

Removal/Installation

1. Place a milk crate or wood block(s) under the engine to support it securely.
2. Remove both side covers and seat.
3. Turn the fuel shutoff valve (**Figure 1**) to the OFF position and disconnect the fuel line at the carburetor.
4. Remove the fuel tank as described in this chapter.

5. Place a metal container under the drain tube and open the drain screw (**Figure 2**) on the carburetor. Drain all fuel from the float bowl.

6. On XT250 models, loosen and remove the 2 throttle cables at the carburetor. See **Figure 3**.

7A. On XT125 and XT200 models, loosen the carburetor hose clamps (A, **Figure 4**) and turn the carburetor to the left-hand side of the bike. Then remove the carburetor top cap (B, **Figure 4**) and pull the throttle valve assembly up and out of the carburetor.

NOTE
If the top cap and throttle valve assembly are not going to be removed from the throttle cable for cleaning, wrap them in a clean shop cloth or place them in a plastic bag to help keep them clean.

7B. On XT250 models, remove the front intake manifold with an Allen wrench (**Figure 5**). Do not loosen the front carburetor hose clamp. Then loosen the rear carburetor hose clamp.

8. Label and disconnect all hoses from the carburetor.

9. Carefully work the carburetor free from the rubber boots and remove it. Remove the XT250 carburetor with the intake manifold attached.

10. Take the carburetor to a workbench for disassembly and cleaning.

11. Install by reversing these removal steps. When installing the throttle valve on XT125 and XT200 models, align the slot in the throttle valve with the pin in the carburetor bore. See **Figure 6**. Adjust the throttle cable as described in Chapter Three.

Disassembly/Cleaning/Inspection/Assembly (XT125 and XT200)

Refer to **Figure 7** during this procedure.

1. Remove the fuel line and all drain and overflow hoses.

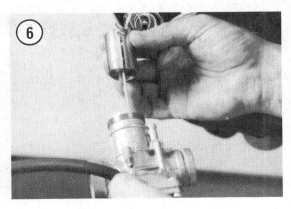

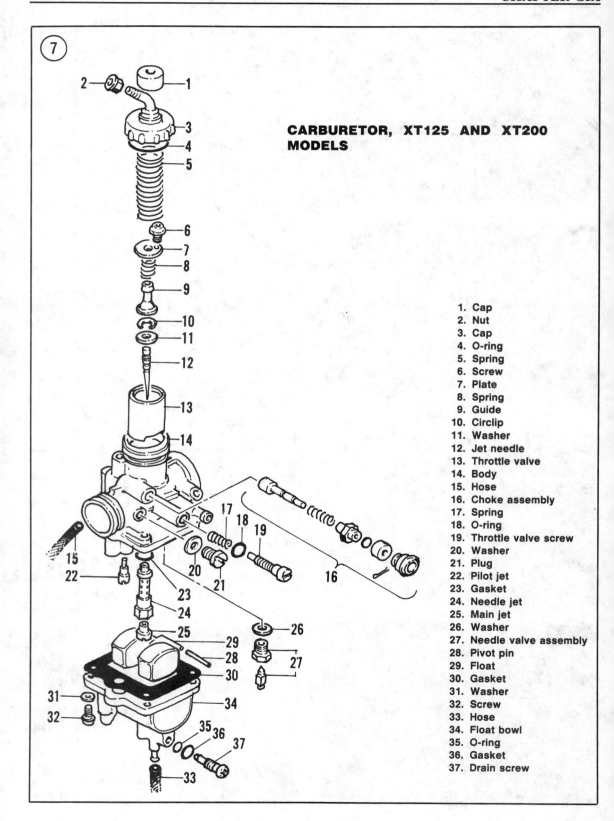

CARBURETOR, XT125 AND XT200 MODELS

1. Cap
2. Nut
3. Cap
4. O-ring
5. Spring
6. Screw
7. Plate
8. Spring
9. Guide
10. Circlip
11. Washer
12. Jet needle
13. Throttle valve
14. Body
15. Hose
16. Choke assembly
17. Spring
18. O-ring
19. Throttle valve screw
20. Washer
21. Plug
22. Pilot jet
23. Gasket
24. Needle jet
25. Main jet
26. Washer
27. Needle valve assembly
28. Pivot pin
29. Float
30. Gasket
31. Washer
32. Screw
33. Hose
34. Float bowl
35. O-ring
36. Gasket
37. Drain screw

2. Unscrew the choke shaft and remove it (**Figure 8**).

3. Remove the screws securing the float bowl (**Figure 9**) and remove it and its gasket.

4. Remove the float pin (**Figure 10**) and float (**Figure 11**).

NOTE
The float valve needle is attached to the float arm. See Figure 12.

5. Remove the needle valve seat (**Figure 13**).
6. Remove the pilot jet (**Figure 14**).
7. Remove the main jet (**Figure 15**).
8. Remove the needle jet (**Figure 16**).
9. Remove the throttle adjust screw (**Figure 17**).
10. Depress the throttle valve spring and remove the throttle cable from the throttle valve.
11. Remove the needle clip retainer and remove the jet needle.
12. Clean all parts, except rubber or plastic parts, in a good grade of carburetor cleaner. This solution is available at most automotive or motorcycle supply stores in a small, resealable tank with a dip basket. If it is sealed when not in use, the solution will last for several cleanings. Follow the manufacturer's instructions for correct soak time (usually about 1/2 hour).

6

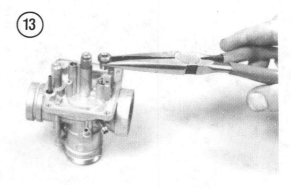

13. Remove all parts from the cleaner and blow dry with compressed air. Blow out the jets with compressed air. *Do not* use a piece of wire to clean them as minor gouges in the jet can alter flow rate and upset the fuel-air mixture.

14. Be sure to clean out the overflow tube from both sides (**Figure 18**).

15. Check the O-rings on the needle jet (**Figure 19**) and the float bowl drain screw (**Figure 20**). Replace the O-rings if worn or damaged.

16. Inspect the tip of the float valve for wear or damage; replace if necessary.

17. Inspect the throttle valve for signs of wear or deep scratches that could cause the throttle to hang open when the engine is operating. Replace the throttle valve (and check the throttle valve bore in the carburetor body) if necessary.

18. The needle valve must close against the needle seat completely to make sure that no gas passes through the seat when it shouldn't. If there are any wear marks or scratches on either mating surface, fuel flow cannot be stopped, resulting in a rich fuel-air mixture. Inspect the needle valve and seat

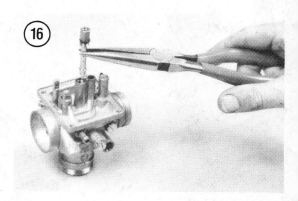

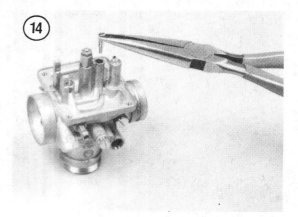

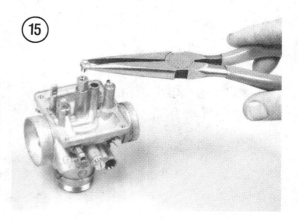

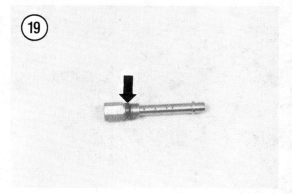

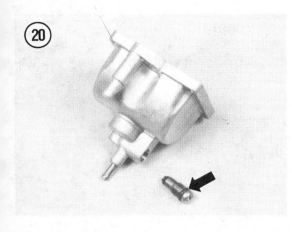

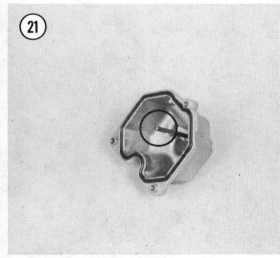

(**Figure 21**). Replace the needle valve and seat as a complete unit if either one is damaged.

NOTE
Damage to the needle valve and seat are normally due to dirt or other debris in the fuel. Check and clean the fuel tank fuel filter more often if this is a problem. Refer to Chapter Three for details.

19. Check the floats for any signs of damage. If the floats are suspected of leaking, shake the floats by hand and listen for fuel sloshing around inside. Another way to check for leakage is by immersing the floats completely in a container of solvent (do not use gasoline) and checking for air bubbles. Replace the floats if necessary.

20. Check the choke shaft (**Figure 22**) and replace it if worn or damaged.
21. Assembly is the reverse of these steps, noting the following.
22. Install a new float bowl gasket (**Figure 23**) if the old one is torn. Make sure the gasket does not cover or block any holes or components.

23. Attach the needle valve onto the float arm (**Figure 24**) before installation.
24. Check the float height and adjust if necessary as described in this chapter.
25. After the carburetor has been assembled, adjust the idle speed as described in this chapter.

Disassembly/Cleaning/
Inspection/Assembly (XT250)

Refer to **Figure 25** for this procedure.

6

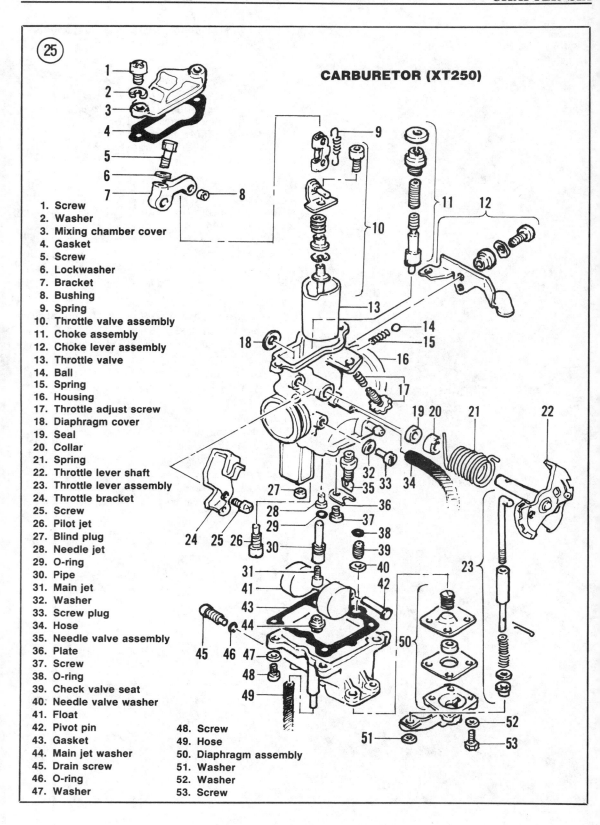

㉕

CARBURETOR (XT250)

1. Screw
2. Washer
3. Mixing chamber cover
4. Gasket
5. Screw
6. Lockwasher
7. Bracket
8. Bushing
9. Spring
10. Throttle valve assembly
11. Choke assembly
12. Choke lever assembly
13. Throttle valve
14. Ball
15. Spring
16. Housing
17. Throttle adjust screw
18. Diaphragm cover
19. Seal
20. Collar
21. Spring
22. Throttle lever shaft
23. Throttle lever assembly
24. Throttle bracket
25. Screw
26. Pilot jet
27. Blind plug
28. Needle jet
29. O-ring
30. Pipe
31. Main jet
32. Washer
33. Screw plug
34. Hose
35. Needle valve assembly
36. Plate
37. Screw
38. O-ring
39. Check valve seat
40. Needle valve washer
41. Float
42. Pivot pin
43. Gasket
44. Main jet washer
45. Drain screw
46. O-ring
47. Washer
48. Screw
49. Hose
50. Diaphragm assembly
51. Washer
52. Washer
53. Screw

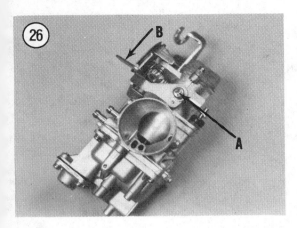

1. Remove the fuel line and all drain and overflow hoses.

2. Remove the screw (A, **Figure 26**) securing the choke lever (B, **Figure 26**) and remove the lever.

3. Remove the accelerator pump cover (**Figure 27**).

4. Remove the spring seat (A, **Figure 28**), ring (B, **Figure 28**) and diaphragm (**Figure 29**).

5. Remove the spring (**Figure 30**).

6. Remove the mixing chamber cover (**Figure 31**).

7. Remove the bolt securing the throttle shaft (**Figure 32**) and pull the throttle shaft out of the carburetor housing. See **Figure 33**.

8. Pull the throttle valve lever (**Figure 34**) up and pull the throttle valve lever assembly out of the carburetor. See **Figure 35**.

9. Remove the screws securing the float bowl (**Figure 36**) and remove it from the carburetor housing.

10. Remove the following from the float bowl:
    a. Main jet washer (**Figure 37**).
    b. O-ring (**Figure 38**).
    c. Check valve seat (**Figure 39**).

11. Remove the float pin and float (**Figure 40**).

12. Remove the float valve (**Figure 41**).

6

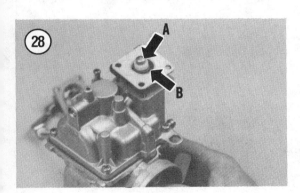

13. Remove the screw (**Figure 42**) securing the float valve seat and remove the float valve seat (**Figure 43**).

14. Remove the pilot jet (**Figure 44**).

15. Remove the main jet (**Figure 45**).

16. Remove the nozzle (**Figure 46**) and the needle jet (**Figure 47**).

17. Clean all parts, except rubber or plastic parts, in a good grade of carburetor cleaner. This solution is available at most automotive or motorcycle supply stores in a small, resealable tank with a dip basket. If it is sealed when not in use, the solution will last for several cleanings. Follow the manufacturer's instructions for correct soak time (usually about 1/2 hour).

18. Remove all parts from the cleaner and blow dry with compressed air. Blow out the jets with compressed air. *Do not* use a piece of wire to clean them as minor gouges in the jet can alter flow rate and upset the fuel-air mixture.

19. Be sure to clean out the overflow tube from both sides (**Figure 48**).

20. Check all O-rings (**Figure 49**). Replace the O-ring(s) if worn or damaged.

21. Inspect the tip of the float valve for wear or damage; replace if necessary.

6

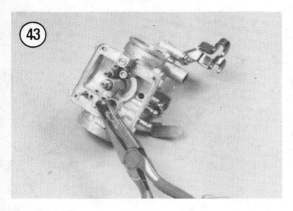

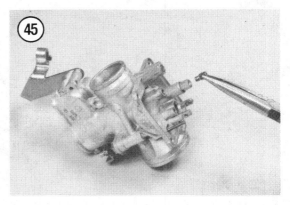

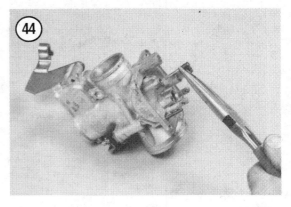

22. Inspect the throttle valve (**Figure 50**) for signs of wear or deep scratches that could cause the throttle to hang open when the engine is operating. Replace the throttle valve (and check the throttle valve bore in the carburetor body) if necessary.

23. The needle valve must close against the needle seat completely to make sure that no gas passes through the seat when it is not required to do so. If there are any wear marks or scratches on either mating surface, fuel flow cannot be stopped, resulting in a rich fuel-air mixture. Inspect the needle valve and seat (**Figure 21**). Replace the needle valve and seat as a complete unit if either one is damaged.

NOTE
Damage to the needle valve and seat are normally due to dirt or other debris in the fuel. Check and clean the fuel tank fuel filter more often if this is a problem. Refer to Chapter Three for details.

24. Check the floats for any signs of damage. If the floats are suspected of leaking, shake the floats by hand and listen for fuel sloshing around inside. Another way to check for leakage is by immersing the floats completely in a container of solvent (do not use gasoline) and checking for air bubbles. Replace the floats if necessary.

25. Check the accelerator pump diaphragm and related parts (**Figure 51**). Replace parts as required.

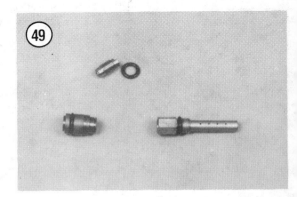

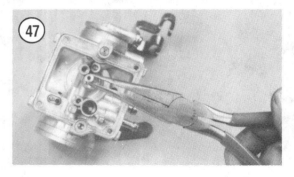

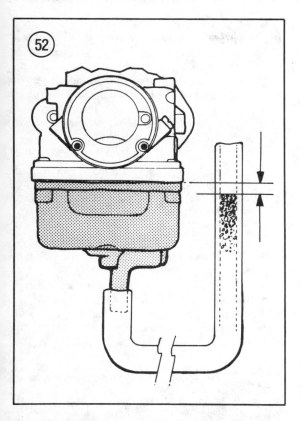

26. Assembly is the reverse of these steps, noting the following.
27. Install a new float bowl gasket if the old one is torn. Make sure the gasket does not cover or block any holes or components.
28. Check the float height and adjust if necessary as described in this chapter.
29. After the carburetor has been assembled adjust the idle speed. Refer to *Idle Speed Adjustment* in this chapter.

CARBURETOR ADJUSTMENTS

Float Level Adjustment

NOTE
Prior to performing this adjustment, remove the float assembly and check the float valve and valve seat (Figure 41); if worn, adjustment will be incorrect. Replace any worn parts.

The bike must be *exactly* level for this measurement to be accurate. Support the bike by wood block(s) or place a suitable size jack under the engine and position the bike so that the carburetor is level.

Use either the Yamaha special level gauge (part No. 90890-01312-00 (**Figure 52**) or a piece of clear vinyl tubing with an inside diameter of 0.24 in. (6 mm). The tubing should be long enough to reach up to the side of the carburetor as shown in **Figure 52**.

WARNING
Before starting any procedure involving gasoline have a class B fire extinguisher rated for gasoline or chemical fires within reach. Do not smoke, allow anyone to smoke or work where there may be open flames. The work area must be well-ventilated.

1. Turn the fuel shutoff valve to the ON position.
2. Place a small container under the carburetor to catch any fuel that may drip from the float bowl.
3. Insert the level gauge adapter and hose into the carburetor drain nozzle. **Figure 52** shows the hose installed. **Figure 53** (XT125 and XT200) and **Figure 54** (XT250) show the drain nozzles for the individual carburetors.
4. Hold the loose end of the tube up above the float bowl level (**Figure 52**) and loosen the drain screw. When the drain screw is loosened fuel will flow into the tube. Make sure to hold the loose end up or the fuel will flow out of the tube.
5. Start the engine and let it run for 2-3 minutes. This is necessary to make sure the fuel level is at the normal operating level in the float bowl.

6. Hold the loose end of the tube up against the carburetor body (**Figure 52**). Measure the fuel level in the tube from the edge of the carburetor body to the fuel level. This is the fuel level measurement. See **Table 1** for specifications. Remove the tube from the carburetor float bowl nozzle. Immediately wipe up any spilled fuel on the engine.

> *WARNING*
> *Do not let any fuel spill on the hot exhaust system.*

7. If the fuel level is incorrect, remove the carburetor.

8. Adjust the float by carefully bending the tang on the float arm. Bend the float tang upward very slightly to lower the fuel level; bend the float tang downward to raise the fuel level. If the float level is set too high, the result will be a rich air-fuel mixture. If it is set too low, the mixture will be too lean.

9. Install the carburetor and repeat this procedure until the fuel level is correct.

Needle Jet Adjustment

The position of the needle jet is fixed. No adjustment is provided.

Idle Speed Adjustment

Before starting this procedure the air cleaner must be clean, otherwise this procedure cannot be done properly.

1. Start the engine and let it reach normal operating temperature.

2. Turn the idle stop screw in or out to achieve the desired idle speed. See **Figure 55** (XT125 and XT200) or **Figure 56** (XT250). **Table 1** lists the correct idle speed for all models.

> *WARNING*
> *With the engine idling, move the handlebar from side to side. If idle speed increases during this movement, the throttle cable needs adjusting or it may be incorrectly routed through the frame. Correct this problem immediately. Do not ride the motorcycle in this unsafe condition.*

High-elevation Adjustment

If the vehicle is going to be operated for any sustained period of time at high elevations (above 5,000 ft or 1,500 m), the main jet should be changed to a one-stop smaller jet. Never change the jet by more than one size at a time without test riding the bike and running a spark plug test. Refer to Chapter Three.

The carburetor is set with the standard jet for normal sea level conditions. If the vehicle is run at higher elevations or under heavy load (deep sand or mud), the main jet should be replaced or it will run too rich and carbon up quickly.

> *CAUTION*
> *If the bike has been rejetted for high elevation operation, it must be changed back to the standard main jet if ridden at elevations below 5,000 ft. (1,500 m); otherwise, engine overheating and piston seizure may occur.*

Refer to **Table 1** (end of chapter) for standard main jet size.

1. Turn the fuel shutoff valve to the OFF position and disconnect the fuel line.

2. Loosen the 2 screws on the clamping bands on each side of the carburetor and pivot the carburetor to one side.

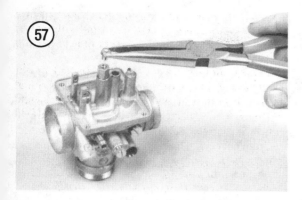

57

58

59

60

3. Loosen the float bowl screw and drain out all fuel in the bowl.

> *WARNING*
> *Place a metal container under the cover to catch the fuel that will flow out. Do not let it drain out onto the engine or the bike's frame as it presents a real fire danger. **Do not** perform this procedure with a hot engine. Dispose of the fuel properly; wipe up any that may have spilled on the bike and the floor.*

4. Remove the float bowl.
5. Remove the main jet and replace it with a different one. Remember, change by only one jet size at a time. Refer to **Figure 57** (XT125 and XT200) or **Figure 58** (XT250).
6. Install the float bowl. Tighten it securely.

> *NOTE*
> *When installing the float bowl on XT250 models, check that the O-ring (**Figure 59**) and main jet washer (**Figure 60**) are positioned properly.*

7. Pivot the carburetor back to its original position. Tighten the clamping band screws and reinstall the carburetor fuel line.

THROTTLE CABLE

Removal

1. Place a milk crate or wood block(s) under the engine to support the bike securely.
2. Remove the side covers and seat.
3. Remove the fuel tank as described in this chapter.
4A. *XT125 and XT200*: Clean the area around the carburetor cap thoroughly so that no dirt will fall into the carburetor. Then unscrew the cap and pull the throttle valve assembly up and out of the carburetor (**Figure 61**). Depress the throttle valve

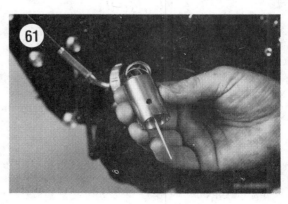

61

6

spring, remove the throttle valve and spring and remove the throttle cable from the throttle valve.

> *NOTE*
> *Place a clean shop rag over the top of the carburetor to keep any foreign matter from falling into the carburetor bore.*

4B. *XT250*: Disconnect the throttle cables at the carburetor. See **Figure 62**.

5. Remove the screws securing the throttle cover and separate the 2 halves of the twist grip assembly. Remove the assembly from the handlebar. See **Figure 63** (XT125 and XT200) or **Figure 64** (XT250).

6. Disconnect the throttle cable at the twist grip.

> *NOTE*
> *XT250 models use 2 throttle cables.*

> *NOTE*
> *The piece of string attached in the next step will be used to pull the new throttle cable(s) back through the frame so it will be routed in the exact same position as the old one. On XT250 models, use the string to pull both cables.*

7. Tie a piece of heavy string or cord (approximately 6-8 ft./2-3 m long) to the carburetor end of the throttle cable(s). Wrap this end with masking or duct tape. Do not use an excessive amount of tape as it will be pulled through the frame loop during removal. Tie the other end of the string to the frame.

8. At the twist grip end of the cable, carefully pull the cable (and attached string) out through the frame loop and from behind the headlight housing. Make sure the attached string follows the same path of the cable through the frame and behind the headlight.

9. Remove the tape and untie the string from the old cable.

Installation

> *NOTE*
> *When purchasing throttle cables for the XT250, note that the cables are different. Have the cables labeled as to their respective mounting position.*

1. Lubricate the new cable(s) as described in Chapter Three.

2. Tie the string (used during *Removal*) to the new throttle cable(s) and wrap them with tape.

3. Carefully pull the string back through the frame, routing the new cable(s) through the same path as the old one(s).

4. Remove the tape and untie the string from the cable(s) and the frame.

5. Reverse Steps 1-6 of *Removal*, noting the following.

6. Apply grease to the sliding surface of the twist grip and install it onto the handlebar.

7. Operate the twist grip and make sure the carburetor throttle linkage is operating correctly and with no binding. If operation is incorrect, carefully check that the cable(s) are attached correctly and there are no tight bends.

8. Adjust the throttle cable(s) as described in Chapter Three.

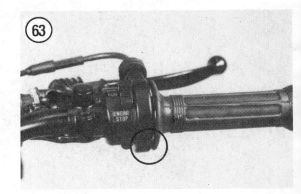

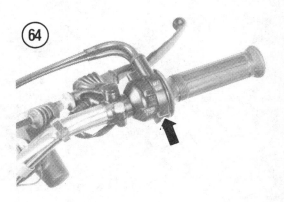

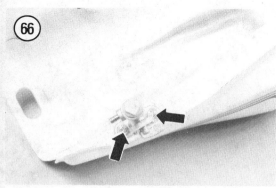

9. Test ride the bike to make sure the throttle is operating correctly.

FUEL SHUTOFF VALVE

Removal/Cleaning/Installation

The integral fuel filter in the fuel shutoff valve removes particles in the fuel which might otherwise enter into the carburetor. This could cause the float needle to stay in the open position or clog one of the jets.

1. Turn the fuel shutoff valve to the OFF position and disconnect the fuel line at the carburetor (**Figure 65**).

> *NOTE*
> *The fuel tank can either be removed or left in place. In either case, drain all fuel from it.*

2. Place the loose end into a clean, sealable metal container. This fuel can be reused if kept clean.
3. Turn the fuel shutoff valve to the RES position and open the fuel filler cap. This will speed up the flow of fuel. Drain the tank completely.
4. Remove the screws securing the fuel shutoff valve to the tank and remove it. See **Figure 66**.
5. After removing the valve, insert a corner of a clean shop rag into the opening in the tank to stop the dribbling of fuel onto the engine and frame.
6. Unscrew the bowl from the bottom of the fuel shutoff valve and disassemble it. Clean all parts in solvent with a medium soft toothbrush, then dry. Check the small O-ring within the valve and the O-ring gasket; replace if they are starting to deteriorate or get hard. Make sure the lever spring is not broken or getting soft; replace if necessary.
7. Reassemble the valve and install it on the tank. Don't forget the O-ring gasket between the valve and bowl. Check for fuel leakage after installation is completed.

FUEL TANK

Removal/Installation

1. Place a milk crate or wood block(s) under the engine to support the bike securely.
2. Turn the fuel shutoff valve to the OFF position and remove the fuel line to the carburetor (**Figure 65**).
3. On all 1983 California models, disconnect the evaporative canister to fuel tank hose at the canister. See **Figure 67** (XT125 and XT200) or **Figure 68** (XT250).

4. Remove the seat.

5. Remove the bolts securing the the fuel tank (**Figure 69**) and remove it.

6. Inspect the rubber cushions on the frame where the fuel tank is held in place. See **Figure 70** (front) and **Figure 71** (rear). Replace as necessary if damaged or starting to deteriorate.

7. Install by reversing these removal steps.

Sealing (Pin-hole Size)

A small pin hole size leak can be sealed with the use of a product called Thextonite Gas Tank Sealer Stock or equivalent. Follow the manufacturer's instructions.

Sealing (Small Hole Size)

This procedure requires the use of a non-petroleum, non-flammable solvent.

If you feel unqualified to seal it, take the tank to a dealer and have them seal it for you.

> *WARNING*
> *Before attempting any service on the fuel tank, be sure to have a fire extinguisher rated for gasoline or chemical fires within reach. Do not smoke or allow anyone to smoke or work where there are any open flames (this includes pilot lights on home gas appliances). The work area must be well-ventilated.*

1. Remove the fuel tank as described in this chapter. Drain the tank of all fuel.

2. On all 1983 California models, remove the roll-over valve from the fuel tank as described in this chapter. Plug the hole to prevent leakage of the sealing compounds.

3. Mark the spot on the tank where the leak is visible with a grease pencil.

4. Open the fuel filler cap and turn the fuel shutoff valve to RES. Use compressed air to blow the interior of the tank dry.

5. Turn the fuel shutoff valve to the OFF position and pour about 1 liter (1 qt.) of non-petroleum solvent into the tank. Close the fuel filler cap and shake the tank vigorously for 1 to 2 minutes. This removes all fuel residue.

6. Drain the solvent solution into a safe storable container. This solution may be reused. Leave the fuel filler cap open and allow the tank to air out overnight before using the sealant.

7. Remove the fuel shutoff valve from the tank. If necessary, plug the tank opening with a cork or tape it closed with duct tape. Thoroughly clean the surrounding area with ignition contact cleaner so the tape will stick securely.

8. Again, blow the tank interior completely dry with compressed air.

9. The following step is best done out-of-doors as the fumes are very strong and flammable. Pour a sealant into the tank (a silicone rubber base sealer such as Pro-Tech, Kreem Super Sealer or equivalent). These are available at most motorcycle supply dealers.

> *CAUTION*
> *Do not spill the sealant onto the painted surface of the tank as it will destroy the finish.*

10. Position the tank so that the point of the leak is at the lowest part of the tank. This will allow the sealant to accumulate at the point of the leak.

11. Keep the tank in this position for at least 48 hours.

12. After the sealant has dried, install the fuel shutoff valve. Install the roll-over valve on 1983 California models as described in this chapter. Turn the shutoff valve to the OFF position and refill the tank with fuel.

13. After the tank has been filled, let it sit for at least 2 hours and recheck the leak area.

14. Install the tank on the motorcycle.

> *NOTE*
> *Motorcycle fuel tanks are relatively maintenance-free. However, a major cause of fuel tank leakage occurs when the fuel tank is not mounted securely and is allowed to rattle when riding. When installing the tank, make sure the front rubber cushions (**Figure 71**) on both sides of the frame and the rear cushion (**Figure 72**) are in position and that the tank is mounted securely at the back with the proper fasteners (**Figure 69**).*

EMISSION CONTROL SYSTEM

All 1983 XT models sold in California are equipped with an evaporative emission control system to reduce the amount of fuel vapors released into the atmosphere. The system consists of a charcoal canister, unvented fuel filler cap, roll-over valve, assorted vacuum lines and a modified carburetor and fuel tank. See **Figure 72** (XT125 and XT200) or **Figure 73** (XT250). A schematic of the emission control system is on a special decal on one of the side covers. See **Figure 74**.

During engine operation, fuel vapors formed in the fuel tank exit the tank through a roll-over valve and enter the charcoal canister (**Figure 75**) through a connecting hose. The vapors are stored in the charcoal canister until the bike is ridden at high speed, when the vapors are then passed through a hose to the carburetor and mixed and burned with the incoming fresh air. During low-speed engine operation or when the bike is parked, the fuel vapors are stored in the charcoal canister.

The roll-over valve is installed in the fuel tank (**Figure 76**). Air and fuel vapor passage through the

6

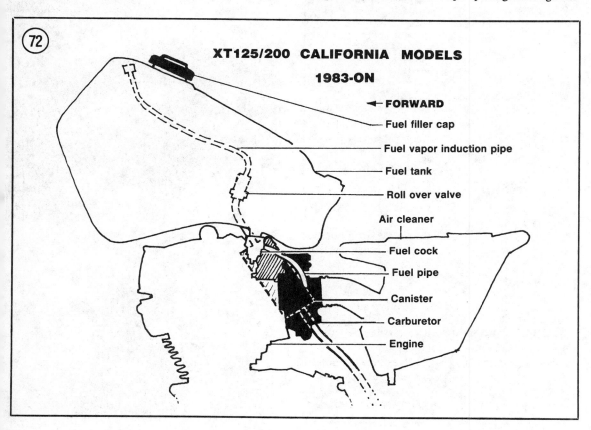

72

XT125/200 CALIFORNIA MODELS
1983-ON

◄ **FORWARD**

— Fuel filler cap

— Fuel vapor induction pipe

— Fuel tank

— Roll over valve

Air cleaner

— Fuel cock

— Fuel pipe

— Canister

— Carburetor

— Engine

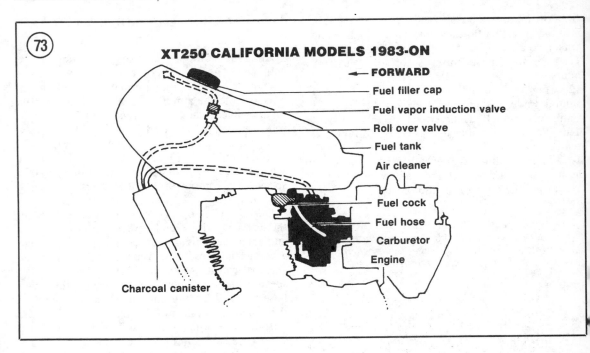

⑦73

XT250 CALIFORNIA MODELS 1983-ON

◄── FORWARD

Fuel filler cap

Fuel vapor induction valve

Roll over valve

Fuel tank

Air cleaner

Fuel cock

Fuel hose

Carburetor

Engine

Charcoal canister

⑦75

Vapor to carburetor
(to purge vent)

From fuel tank

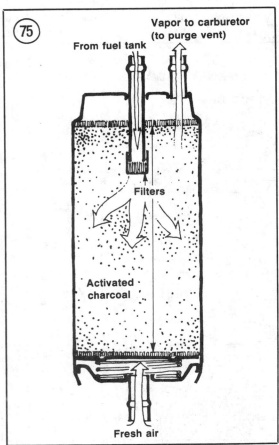

Filters

Activated
charcoal

Fresh air

⑦74

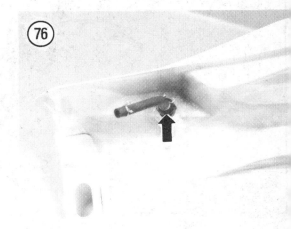

⑦76

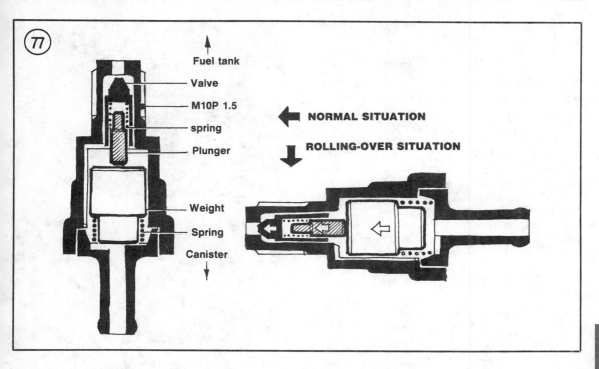

77

Fuel tank
Valve
M10P 1.5
spring
Plunger

NORMAL SITUATION

ROLLING-OVER SITUATION

Weight
Spring
Canister

6

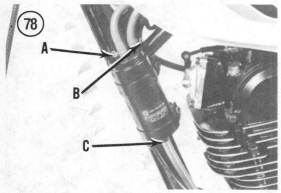

78

A

B

C

valve is controlled by an internal weight (**Figure 77**). During normal riding (or when the fuel tank is properly positioned), the weight is at the bottom of the valve. In this position, the breather passage is open to allow the fuel vapors to flow to the charcoal canister at the correct engine speed. When the bike is rolled or turned over, the weight moves to block off the passage. In this position it is impossible for stored fuel vapors to flow to the charcoal canister. The roll-over valve also prevents fuel from flowing to the carburetor under these conditions, since the fuel filler cap is not vented.

Service to the emission control system is limited to replacement of damaged parts. No attempt should be made to modify or remove the emission control system.

Parts Replacement

When purchasing replacement parts (carburetor, fuel tank, fuel tank cap, etc.), always make sure the parts are for California emission controlled bikes. Parts sold for non-emission controlled bikes will not work with the emission control system.

Charcoal Canister
Removal/Installation

1. Label and disconnect the following hoses at the charcoal canister:
   a. Roll-over valve hose (A, **Figure 78**).
   b. Carburetor valve hose (B, **Figure 78**).
   c. Vent hose (C, **Figure 78**).
2. Disconnect the clamps securing the charcoal canister to the frame and remove it.
3. Installation is the reverse of these steps. During installation, make sure the bottom vent hose (C, **Figure 78**) is not blocked.

Roll-over Valve
Removal/Installation

1. Remove the fuel tank as described in this chapter.
2. Drain the fuel tank of all gasoline. Store the gasoline in a safety approved canister.
3. Remove the roll-over valve (**Figure 76**) with a socket or wrench.
4. Installation is the reverse of these steps. Tighten the roll-over valve to 1.4-2.9 ft.-lb. (2-4 Nm).

5. After filling the fuel tank with gas, check for leaks.

EXHAUST SYSTEM

The exhaust system is a vital performance component and frequently, because of its design, it is a vulnerable piece of equipment. Check the exhaust system for deep dents and fractures and repair them or replace parts immediately. Check the muffler frame mounting flanges for fractures and loose bolts. Check the cylinder head mounting flange for tightness. A loose exhaust pipe connection will not only rob the engine of power, it could also damage the piston and cylinder.

The exhaust system consists of an exhaust pipe, muffler and spark arrestor. On XT125 and XT200 models, the header pipe separates from the exhaust pipe.

Removal/Installation

1. Place a milk crate or wood block(s) under the engine to support the bike securely. Remove the right-hand side cover.
2. Remove the bolts securing the header pipe to the cylinder. See **Figure 79** (XT125 and XT200) or **Figure 80** (XT250).
3A. On XT125 and XT200 models, loosen or remove the following:
    a. Heat shield (**Figure 81**).
    b. Loosen the header to exhaust pipe clamp (**Figure 82**).
    c. Remove the muffler bolts and the muffler (**Figure 83**).
3B. On XT250 models, remove the muffler bolts and the exhaust pipe assembly (**Figure 84**).
4. Inspect the gaskets at all joints; replace as necessary.
5. Install the head pipe gaskets or seals and install the exhaust pipe assembly into position. On XT125 and XT200 models, install the header pipe first. Install the frame bolt and washers only finger-tight at this time until the header pipe bolt and washers are installed. This will minimize an exhaust leak at the cylinder.
6. Tighten all fasteners securely.
7. Make sure the head pipe is correctly seated in the exhaust port.
8. Install the seat and fenders.
9. After installation is complete, start the engine and make sure there are no exhaust leaks.

Carbon Removal

The spark arrester should be cleaned at specified intervals. Refer to Chapter Three for the specified time interval and the complete procedure.

Table 1 CARBURETOR SPECIFICATIONS

Item	XT125	XT200
Type	Y24P	Y24P
I.D. mark	15E00	15A00
Manufacturer	TK	TK
Main jet	118	122
Main air jet	1.4	1.4
Jet needle	4B90	4C96
Needle jet	2,600	2,595
Slide cutaway	2.5	2.5
Pilot jet	40	40
Pilot air jet	1.2	1.2
Air screw	Pre-set	Pre-set
Valve seat	2.0	2.0
Starter jet	GS1 #60	GS1 #60
	GS2 #60	GS2 #60
Fuel level	0.14 in.	0.14 in.
	(3.5 mm)	(3.5 mm)
Float height	0.98 in.	0.98 in.
	(25 mm)	(25 mm)
Idle speed	1,300 rpm	1,250 rpm

Item	XT250G, H, J
Type	VM28SS
I.D. mark	NA*
Manufacturer	Mikuni
Main jet	165
Needle jet	0-9
Pilot jet	17.5
Starter jet	50
Jet needle	5DM67
Fuel level	16 in. (4.0 mm)
Main air jet	70
Pilot air jet	130
Slide cutaway	2.5
Idle speed	1,200 rpm

(continued)

Table 1 CARBURETOR SPECIFICATIONS (continued)

Item	XT250K	XT250KC
Type	VM28SS	VM28SS
I.D. mark	3Y1 00	20T 00
Manufacturer	Mikuni	Mikuni
Main jet	165	165
Main air jet	70	70
Jet needle	5DM65	5DM65
Needle jet	0-8	0-8
Slide cutaway	2.5	2.5
Pilot jet	17.5	17.5
Pilot air jet	130	130
Pilot screw	Pre-set	Pre-set
Valve seat	2.0	2.0
Starter jet	GS1 #50	GS1 #50
	GS2 #0.7	GS2 #0.7
Fuel level	0.16 in.	0.16 in.
	(4.0 mm)	(4.0 mm)
Float height	0.93 in.	0.93 in.
	(23.5 mm)	(23.5 mm)
Idle speed	1,200 rpm	1,200 rpm

* Not available.

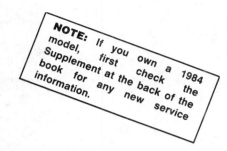

NOTE: If you own a 1984 model, first check the Supplement at the back of the book for any new service information.

CHAPTER SEVEN

ELECTRICAL SYSTEM

This chapter contains operating principles and service procedures for all electrical and ignition components. The XT models are equipped with components approved for street-legal operation. These include the battery, charging systems, headlight, taillight/brakelight, front and rear directional signals and horn.

The electrical systems include:
a. Charging system.
b. Ignition system.
c. Lighting system.
d. Directional signals.
e. Horn.

Refer to Chapter Three for routine ignition system maintenance. Electrical system specifications are in **Table 1**. **Table 1** and **Table 2** are at the end of the chapter. Wiring diagrams are at the end of the book.

CHARGING SYSTEM

The charging system consists of the battery, alternator, a solid-state rectifier and a voltage regulator. See **Figure 1** (XT125 and XT200) or **Figure 2** (XT250).

The alternator generates alternating current (AC) which the rectifier converts to direct current (DC). The regulator maintains the voltage to the battery and load (lights, ignition, etc.) at a constant level regardless of variations in engine speed and load. Refer to Chapter Three for battery service.

Charging System Output Test

Whenever the charging system is suspected of trouble, make sure the battery is fully charged before going any further. Clean and test the battery as described in Chapter Three. If the battery is in good condition, test the charging system as follows.
1. Disconnect the battery wires. Connect a 0-15 DC voltmeter and a 0-10 DC ammeter into the circuit as shown in **Figure 3**.
2. Start the engine and let it idle. Check the output at the different engine speeds described in **Table 1**.
3. If charging voltage is lower than specified, check the alternator, rectifier and a voltage regulator. It is less likely that the charging voltage is too high; however, in that case the regulator is probably faulty. Test the separate charging system components as described in this chapter.

ALTERNATOR

The alternator is a form of electrical generator in which a magnetized field called a rotor revolves near a set of stationary coils called a stator. As the rotor revolves, alternating current is induced in the stator. The current is then rectified to direct current and used to operate the electrical accessories on the

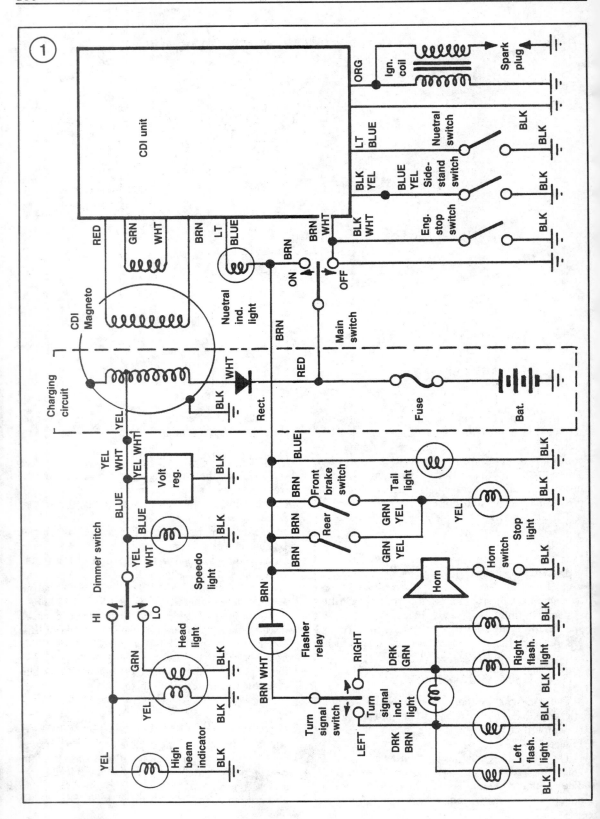

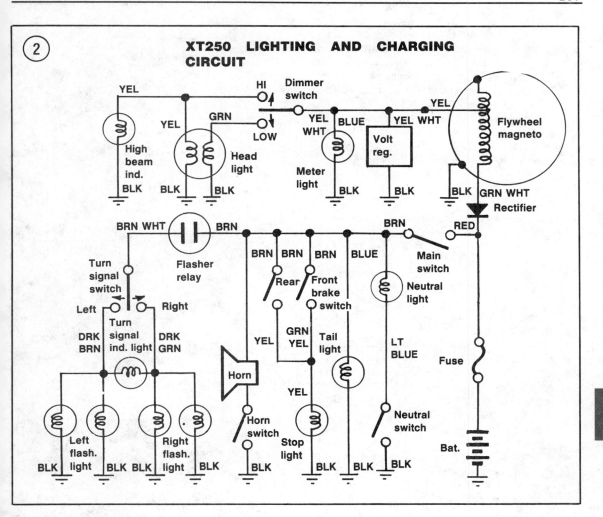

XT250 LIGHTING AND CHARGING CIRCUIT

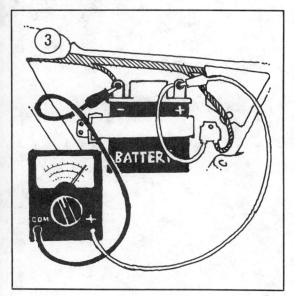

motorcycle and to charge the battery. The rotor is a permanent magnet.

Stator Coil Testing

It is not necessary to remove the stator assembly to perform the following tests. It is shown removed in the following procedures for clarity.

In order to get accurate resistance measurements the stator assembly must be warm (minimum temperature is 68° F/20° C). If necessary, start the engine and let it warm up to normal operating temperature.

1. Raise the seat and remove the left-hand side cover.

2. Disconnect the alternator connector (**Figure 4**).

3. Using an ohmmeter, measure the resistance as follows:

    a. To check the charge coil, connect the ohmmeter between the white and black wires (XT125 and XT200) or between the brown and red wires (XT250). See **Figure 5**. The specified resistance is listed in **Table 1**.

   b. To check the lighting coil, connect the ohmmeter between the yellow and black wires. See **Figure 5**. The specified resistance is listed in **Table 1**.

4. If the values are not within the specified range, check the· electrical wires to and within the connector. If they are okay, remove and inspect the stator and rotor as described in this chapter.

Removal/Installation
(XT125 and XT200)

Alternator cover/coil assembly

1. Place a milk crate or wood block(s) under the engine to support the bike securely.
2. Disconnect the negative battery cable.
3. Drain the engine oil as described in Chapter Three.
4. Remove the left-hand side cover and disconnect the alternator connector.
5. Remove the screws securing the alternator cover/coil assembly (**Figure 6**).
6. Remove the alternator cover/coil assembly and electrical cables (**Figure 7**).
7. To replace the charge and lighting coils (if necessary), perform the following:

   a. Remove the cover screw (A, **Figure 8**) and remove the cover.

   b. Remove the 4 screws (B, **Figure 8**) securing the coils to the cover.

   c. Remove the rubber oil plugs (**Figure 9**) and remove the charge and lighting coils from the cover.

   d. Install new coils by reversing these steps.

8. Install the alternator cover/coil assembly by reversing these removal steps, noting the following.
9. Fill the engine with the recommended type and quantity of oil as described in Chapter Three.

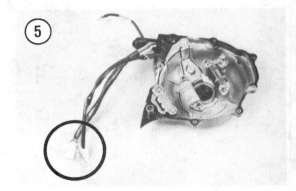

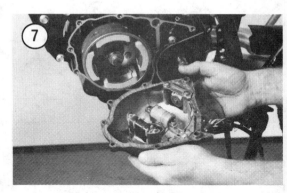

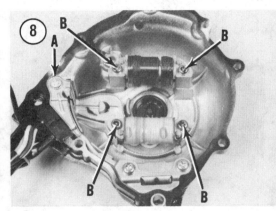

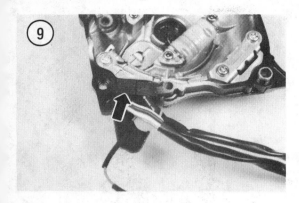

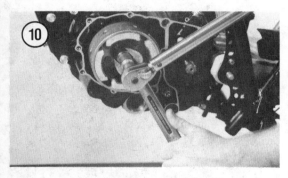

Rotor

1. Remove the alternator cover/coil assembly as described in this chapter.

2. Remove the bolt and washer securing the alternator rotor.

> *NOTE*
> *If necessary, hold a wrench across the flats on the end of the rotor when loosening the bolt. See **Figure 10**.*

3. Screw in a flywheel puller (**Figure 11**) until it stops. Use a wrench on the puller (**Figure 10**) and hold the rotor with a wrench to keep it from turning. Gradually tighten the puller until the rotor disengages from the crankshaft.

> *NOTE*
> *If the rotor is difficult to remove, strike the end of the puller with a hammer a few times. This will usually break it loose. Do not hit the rotor.*

> *CAUTION*
> *If normal rotor removal attempts fail, do not force the puller as the threads may be stripped out of the rotor causing expensive damage. Take it to a dealer and have them remove it.*

4. Remove the puller and rotor. Don't lose the Woodruff key on the crankshaft.

> *CAUTION*
> *Carefully inspect the inside of the rotor (**Figure 12**) for small bolts, washers or other metal debris that may have been picked up by the magnets. These small metal bits can cause severe damage to the stator plate.*

5. Install by reversing these removal steps, noting the following.

6. Make sure the Woodruff key (**Figure 13**) is in place on the crankshaft and align the keyway in the

7

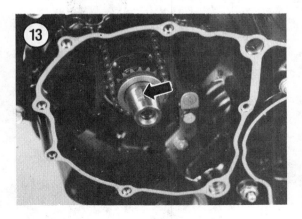

rotor (**Figure 14**) with the key when installing the rotor.

7. Be sure to install the washer prior to installing the rotor bolt. Install the rotor bolt.

8. To keep the rotor from turning, hold it with the same tool setup used in Step 2.

9. Tighten the rotor bolt to 36 ft.-lb. (50 Nm).

Removal/Installation (XT250)

Rotor

1. Place a milk crate or wood block(s) under the engine to support the bike securely.

2. Disconnect the negative battery cable.

3. Drain the engine oil as described in Chapter Three.

4. Remove the left-hand side cover and disconnect the alternator connector.

5. Remove the screws securing the alternator cover (**Figure 15**) and remove it.

6. Remove the nut and washer securing the alternator rotor.

> *NOTE*
> *If necessary, hold the rotor with a holding tool as shown in **Figure 16** when loosening the nut.*

7. Screw in a flywheel puller (**Figure 17**) until it stops. Use a wrench on the puller (**Figure 16**) and hold the rotor to keep it from turning. Gradually tighten the puller until the rotor disengages from the crankshaft.

> *NOTE*
> *If the rotor is difficult to remove, strike the end of the puller with a hammer a few times. This will usually break it loose. Do not hit the rotor.*

> *CAUTION*
> *If normal rotor removal attempts fail, do not force the puller as the threads may be stripped out of the rotor causing expensive damage. Take it to a dealer and have them remove it.*

8. Remove the puller and rotor. Don't lose the Woodruff key on the crankshaft.

> *CAUTION*
> *Carefully inspect the inside of the rotor (**Figure 12**) for small bolts, washers or other metal debris that may have been picked up by the magnets. These small metal bits can cause severe damage to the stator plate.*

9. Install by reversing these removal steps, noting the following.

10. Make sure the Woodruff key (**Figure 13**) is in place on the crankshaft and align the keyway in the rotor (**Figure 14**) with the key when installing the rotor.

11. Be sure to install the washer prior to installing the rotor nut. Install the rotor nut.

12. To keep the rotor from turning, hold it with the same tool setup used in Step 6.

13. Tighten the rotor bolt to 57 ft.-lb. (80 Nm).

14. Fill the engine with the recommended type and quantity of oil as described in Chapter Three.

Stator assembly

1. Drain the engine oil as described in Chapter Three.

2. Remove the rotor as described in this section.

3. Disconnect the stator coil electrical connectors (**Figure 18**).

4. Remove the 2 stator plate mounting screws (**Figure 19**) and pull the rubber plug (**Figure 20**) out of the engine case.

5. Thread 2 M8 bolts into the threads provided in the stator plate (**Figure 21**). Then pull on the 2 bolts and remove the stator plate from the engine case.

6. If necessary, remove the screws securing the charge and lighting coils to the stator plate and replace them.

7. Install by reversing these removal steps, noting the following.

8. Check the oil seal (**Figure 22**) and O-ring (**Figure 23**) in the stator plate. Replace them as required to prevent oil leakage during engine operation.

9. Lightly grease the oil seal (**Figure 22**) and O-ring (**Figure 23**). Then install the stator plate by pushing it into the engine case. After installing the rotor, check that the pulser coil (A, **Figure 24**) and the rotor (B, **Figure 24**) are parallel. Realign the stator plate as required.

7

10. Fill the engine with the recommended type and quantity of oil as described in Chapter Three.

RECTIFIER

Removal/Installation

1. Remove the fuel tank as described in Chapter Six.
2. Disconnect the battery negative lead.
3. Disconnect the electrical connector from the rectifier and remove the rectifier. See **Figure 25** (XT125 and XT200) or **Figure 26** (XT250).
4. Install by reversing these removal steps. Make sure all electrical connections are clean and tight.

Testing

1. Disconnect the electrical connector from the rectifier. See **Figure 25** (XT125 and XT200) or **Figure 26** (XT250). The rectifier connector contains 2 wires (one red and one white).
2. Connect the ohmmeter positive lead to the red wire and the negative lead to the white wire. The ohmmeter should show continuity.
3. Reverse the ohmmeter leads and repeat Step 2. This time the ohmmeter should show no continuity.
4. If the rectifier fails to pass the tests in Step 2 and Step 3, the unit is defective and must be replaced.

VOLTAGE REGULATOR

Removal/Installation

1. Remove the seat and left-hand side cover on XT125 and XT200 models or remove the fuel tank on XT250 models.
2. Disconnect the battery negative lead.
3. Disconnect the electrical connector from the voltage regulator and remove it. See **Figure 27** (XT125 and XT200) or **Figure 28** (XT250).
4. Install by reversing these removal steps. Make sure all electrical connections are clean and tight.

Testing

Testing the voltage regulator on all XT models requires the use of a special Yamaha tester. Refer all testing to your dealer.

IGNITION SYSTEM

All models are equipped with a capacitor discharge ignition (CDI) system which is a solid-state system that uses no breaker points. Refer to **Figure 29**, **Figure 30** or **Figure 31** for the ignition circuit for your model.

Alternating current from the alternator is rectified to direct current and is used to charge the

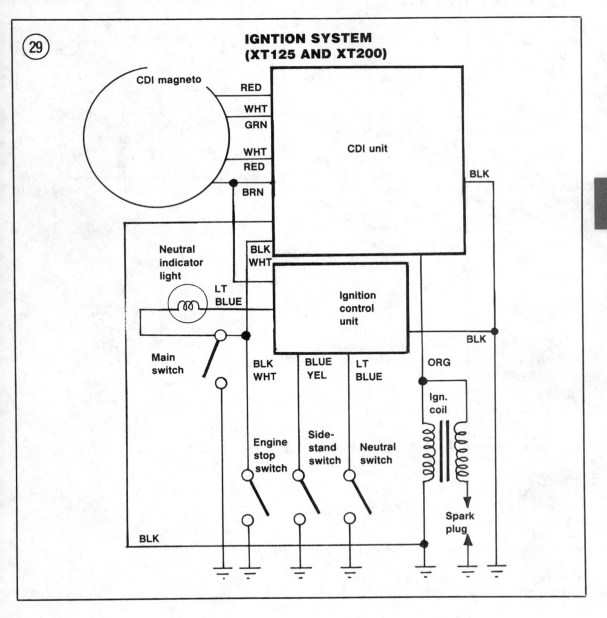

**IGNITION SYSTEM
(XT125 AND XT200)**

CDI magneto

RED
WHT
GRN
WHT
RED
BRN

CDI unit

BLK

Neutral
indicator
light

BLK
WHT

LT
BLUE

Ignition
control
unit

BLK

Main
switch

BLK
WHT

BLUE
YEL

LT
BLUE

ORG

Ign.
coil

Engine
stop
switch

Side-
stand
switch

Neutral
switch

Spark
plug

BLK

7

capacitor. As the piston approaches the firing position, a pulse from the exciter coil is used to trigger the silicone controlled rectifier. The rectifier in turn allows the capacitor to discharge quickly into the primary circuit of the ignition coil, where the voltage is stepped up in the secondary circuit to a value sufficient to fire the spark plug.

On 1982 and later models, the ignition system will not work unless the sidestand is up or the transmission is in NEUTRAL. This is controlled by the neutral switch and the sidestand switch. On 125-200 cc models, these 2 switches are wired directly to the CDI unit. On 250 cc models, the 2 switches are wired to an additional ignition control unit which in turn is wired to the CDI unit.

Precautions

Certain measures must be taken to protect the capacitor discharge system. Instantaneous damage to the semiconductors in the system will occur if the following are not observed.

1. Never connect the battery backwards. If the battery polarity is wrong, damage will occur to the voltage regulator, alternator and CDI unit.
2. Do not disconnect the battery while the engine is running. A voltage surge will occur which will damage the voltage regulator and possibly burn out the lights.
3. Keep all connections between the various units clean and tight. Be sure that the wiring connectors are pushed together firmly.
4. Each solid state unit is mounted on a rubber vibration isolator. Always be sure that the isolators are in place when replacing any units.

Troubleshooting

Problems with the capacitor discharge ignition system are usually limited to the production of a weak spark or no spark at all.

> *NOTE*
> *If your bike is a 1982 or later model, a no-spark condition may be caused by a problem in the neutral switch, the sidestand switch or (on XT250 models) the ignition control unit. Test ignition control unit. Test procedures for these parts appear separately in this chapter.*

Test procedures for troubleshooting the ignition system are found in **Figure 32**. A volt/ohm/ammeter, described in Chapter One, is required to perform the test procedures. When using the procedures in **Figure 32** to troubleshoot the ignition system, keep in mind that the procedures cannot accurately determine ignition

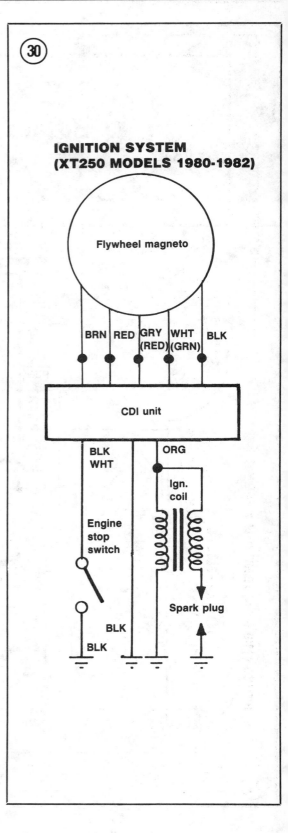

IGNITION SYSTEM (XT250 MODELS 1980-1982)

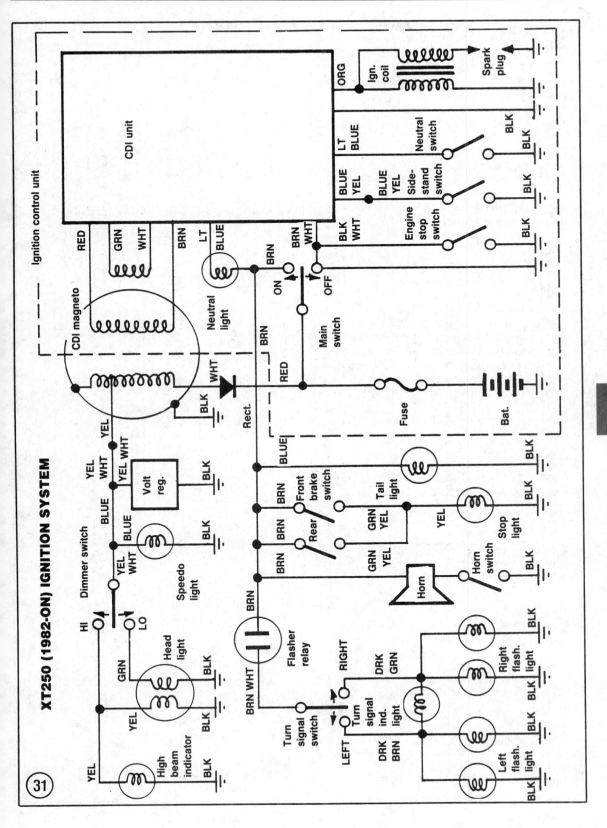

XT250 (1982-ON) IGNITION SYSTEM

7

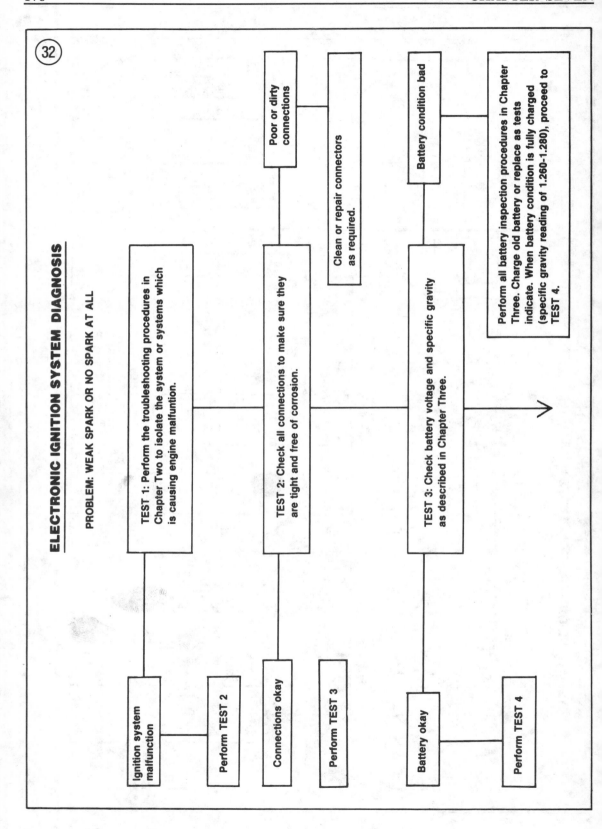

ELECTRONIC IGNITION SYSTEM DIAGNOSIS

PROBLEM: WEAK SPARK OR NO SPARK AT ALL

TEST 1: Perform the troubleshooting procedures in Chapter Two to isolate the system or systems which is causing engine malfuntion.

Ignition system malfunction

Perform TEST 2

TEST 2: Check all connections to make sure they are tight and free of corrosion.

Poor or dirty connections

Clean or repair connectors as required.

Connections okay

Perform TEST 3

TEST 3: Check battery voltage and specific gravity as described in Chapter Three.

Battery condition bad

Perform all battery inspection procedures in Chapter Three. Charge old battery or replace as tests indicate. When battery condition is fully charged (specific gravity reading of 1.260-1.280), proceed to TEST 4.

Battery okay

Perform TEST 4

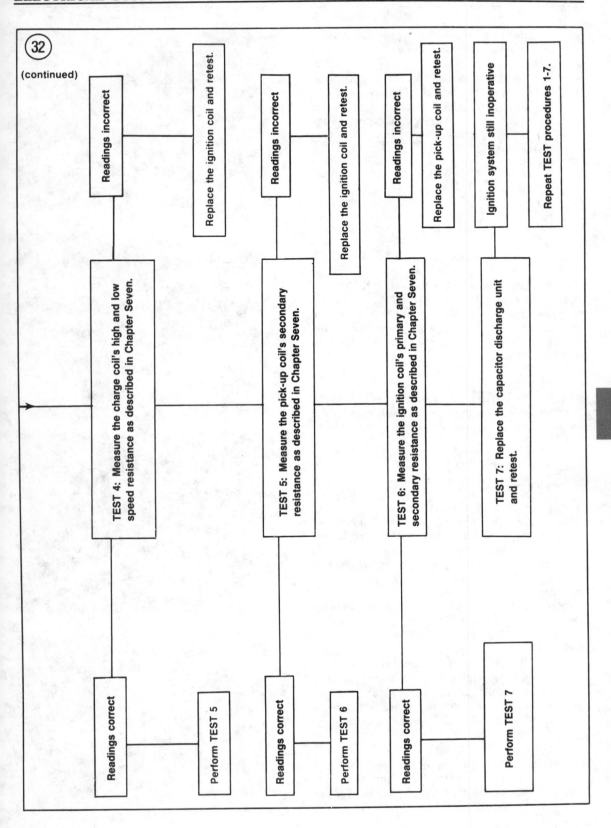

32 (continued)

TEST 4: Measure the charge coil's high and low speed resistance as described in Chapter Seven.

Readings incorrect → Replace the ignition coil and retest.

Readings correct → Perform TEST 5

TEST 5: Measure the pick-up coil's secondary resistance as described in Chapter Seven.

Readings incorrect → Replace the ignition coil and retest.

Readings correct → Perform TEST 6

TEST 6: Measure the ignition coil's primary and secondary resistance as described in Chapter Seven.

Readings incorrect → Replace the pick-up coil and retest.

Readings correct → Perform TEST 7

TEST 7: Replace the capacitor discharge unit and retest.

Ignition system still inoperative → Repeat TEST procedures 1-7.

7

problems due to vibration or detect marginal units that only malfunction when the engine is under a load or hot.

Before beginning actual troubleshooting, read the entire test procedure (**Figure 32**). The diagnostic chart will refer you to a certain chapter and procedure for service information when required. Basic ignition system and spark plug troubleshooting information can be found in Chapter Two.

IGNITION UNIT

Replacement

1. Remove the fuel tank as described in Chapter Six.
2. Disconnect the battery negative lead.
3. Disconnect the electrical connectors from the CDI unit and remove it. See **Figure 33** (XT125 and XT200) or **Figure 34** (XT250).
4. Install by reversing these removal steps. Before connecting the electrical wire connectors at the CDI unit, make sure the connectors are clean of any dirt or moisture.

Testing

The CDI unit should be tested by a Yamaha mechanic familar with capacitor discharge ignition testing. Improper testing of a good unit can damage it.

IGNITION COIL

Removal/Installation

1. Support the bike by its sidestand.
2. Disconnect the negative lead from the battery.
3. Remove the fuel tank as described in Chapter Six.
4. Disconnect the spark plug lead (**Figure 35**) and the coil primary electrical wires at the electrical connector.
5. Remove the 2 nuts and lockwashers securing the coil to the frame and remove the coil. See A, **Figure 36** (XT125 and XT200) or A, **Figure 37** (XT250).
6. Install by reversing these removal steps. Make sure to correctly connect the primary electrical wires to the coils. In addition, make sure the ground wire is attached correctly. See B, **Figure 36** (XT125 and XT200) or B, **Figure 37** (XT250).

Testing

The ignition coil is a transformer which develops the high voltage required to jump the spark plug gap. The only maintenance required is keeping the electrical connections clean and tight and

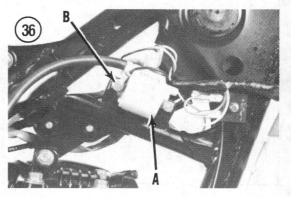

occasionally checking to see that the coils are mounted securely.

If the coil condition is doubtful, there are several checks which may be made.

First, as a quick check of coil condition, disconnect the high voltage lead from the spark plug. Remove the spark plug from the cylinder head. Connect a new or known good spark plug to the high voltage lead and place the spark plug base on a good ground such as the engine cylinder head (**Figure 38**). Position the spark plug so you can see the electrodes.

> *WARNING*
> *Do not hold the high voltage lead by hand. The high voltage generated by the CDI could produce serious or fatal shocks.*

Turn the engine over with the kickstarter. If a fat blue spark occurs, the coil is in good condition; if not, proceed as follows. Make sure that you are using a known good spark plug for this test. If the spark plug used is defective the test results will be incorrect.

Reinstall the spark plug in the cylinder head.

Refer to **Figure 39** for this procedure. Disconnect all ignition coil wires before testing.

7

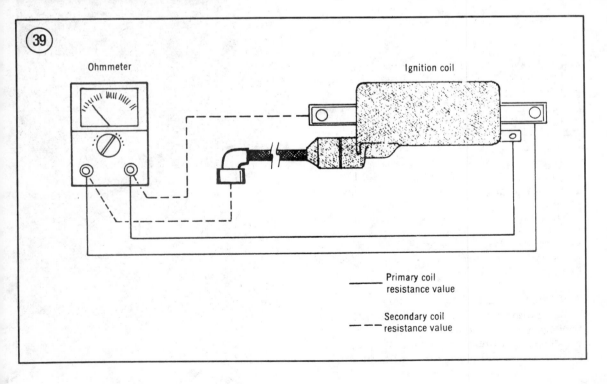

Ohmmeter

Ignition coil

———— Primary coil resistance value

– – – – Secondary coil resistance value

NOTE
In order to get accurate resistance measurements the coil must be warm (approximately 60° F/20° C).

1. Measure the coil primary resistance using an ohmmeter set at R×1. Measure between the primary terminal (orange wire) and ground. Resistance is specified in **Table 1**.

2. Measure the secondary resistance using an ohmmeter set at R×100. Measure between the secondary lead (spark plug lead) and the orange wire. Resistance is specified in **Table 1**.

3. Replace the coil if the spark plug lead shows visible damage or if it does not test within the specifications in Step 1 or Step 2.

PICK-UP COIL

Removal/Installation

Remove the alternator coil assembly as described in this chapter. Replace the pick-up coil as follows.

XT125 and XT200

To replace the pick-up coil on XT125 and XT200 models, remove the 2 mounting screws (A, **Figure 40**) and the guide (B, **Figure 40**). Then replace the pick-up coil assembly (C, **Figure 40**). During installation, make sure the grommet (D, **Figure 40**) is positioned correctly in the cover.

XT250

The pick-up coil is shown in **Figure 41**. Refer to **Figure 42** when performing this procedure.

1. Remove the 2 screws securing the pick-up coil to the stator plate.

2. Slide the wire protector away from the wire connection at the pick-up coil to expose the solder connection.

3. Using a suitable soldering gun, melt the solder at the pick-up coil and disconnect the wire connection. Remove the old pick-up coil.

4. Place the new pick-up coil in position and re-solder the connection.

NOTE
Rosin core solder must be used when soldering the pick-up coil connection—never use acid core solder on electrical connections.

5. Tighten the 2 pick-up coil mounting screws lightly. Install the rotor so that the projection (A, **Figure 43**) faces up to the pick-up coil. Referring to **Figure 44**, measure the clearance between the pick-up coil and the rotor projection. The

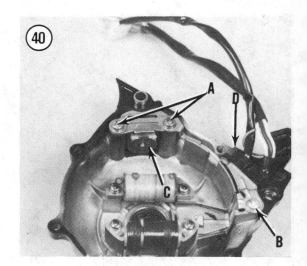

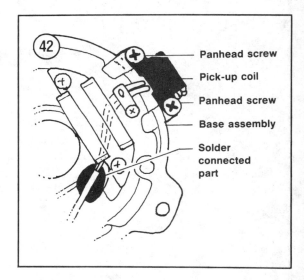

- Panhead screw
- Pick-up coil
- Panhead screw
- Base assembly
- Solder connected part

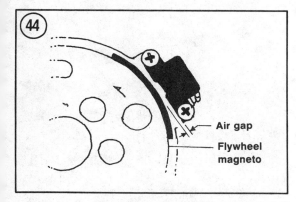

Air gap

Flywheel
magneto

clearance should be approximately 0.03 in. (0.8 mm). Adjust the clearance by repositioning the pick-up coil. When the clearance is correct, tighten the 2 pick-up coil screws securely and recheck the clearance.

Testing

If the pick-up coil condition is doubtful, perform the following test.

1. Disconnect the pick-up coil wire connector.
2. Use an ohmmeter to measure the pick-up coil resistance between the white and green terminals (XT125 and XT200) or between the white/red and white/green terminals (XT250). Resistance is specified in **Table 1**.
3. Replace the pick-up coil if it does not meet the test specification.

SPARK PLUGS

The spark plugs recommended by the factory are usually the most suitable for your machine. If riding conditions are mild, it may be advisable to go to spark plugs one step hotter than normal. Unusually severe riding conditions may require slightly colder plugs. See Chapter Two and Chapter Three for details.

IGNITION CONTROL UNIT
(1982-ON XT250)

Testing

1. Rest the motorcycle on its sidestand.
2. Locate the ignition control unit brown wire underneath the left-hand side of the fuel tank and disconnect it.
3. Try to start the engine by operating the kickstarter. The engine should not start with the ignition control unit wire disconnected. If the engine starts, the unit is damaged and must be replaced.

Replacement

1. Remove the fuel tank as described in Chapter Six.
2. Disconnect the 4-pin wire connector at the ignition control unit (**Figure 45**). Also disconnect the single brown wire.
3. Remove the screws securing the ignition control unit to the frame and remove it.
4. Installation is the reverse of these steps. Make sure the connectors are clean and secured tightly.

LIGHTING SYSTEM

The lighting system consists of the headlight and taillight/brakelight combination, directional signals and speedometer and tachometer illumination lights. In the event of trouble with any light, the first thing to check is the bulb itself. If the bulb is good, check all wiring and connections with a testlight. **Table 2** lists the replacement bulbs for these components.

Headlight Replacement

1. Remove the mounting screws from the bottom of the headlight housing. See **Figure 46**.

2. Pull the trim bezel and headlight unit out and disconnect the electrical connector (**Figure 47**) from the bulb.

> *WARNING*
> *If the headlight has just burned out or turned off it will be **hot**. Don't touch the bulb until it cools off.*

3. Remove the sealed beam unit from the bezel.
4. Install by reversing these steps.
5. Adjust the headlight as described in this chapter.

Headlight Adjustment

Adjust the headlight vertically according to the Department of Motor Vehicles regulations in your area. To adjust, loosen the bolts (**Figure 48**) on both sides of the headlight and tilt the headlight up or down with your hands until the proper adjustment is achieved. Tighten the bolts after making the adjustment.

Taillight Replacement

Remove the screws securing the lens (**Figure 49**) and remove it. Wash the inside and outside of the lens with a mild detergent, rinse thoroughly and wipe dry. Wipe off the reflective base surrounding the bulb with a soft cloth. Replace the bulb (**Figure 50**) and install the lens; do not overtighten the screws or the lens may crack.

Directional Signal
Light Replacement

Remove the two screws securing the lens (**Figure 51**) and remove it. Wash out the inside and outside of it with a mild detergent. Replace the bulb (**Figure 52**). Install the lens; do not overtighten the screws or the lens may crack.

Speedometer/Instrument Panel Illumination Bulb Replacement

1. Disconnect the speedometer drive cable (**Figure 53**) from the backside of the meter housing.
2. Remove the clips and washers securing the bottom of the instrument panel to the panel housing.
3. Remove the bolts (**Figure 54**) securing the instrument panel assembly to the steering crown and move it up and forward slightly to gain access to the bulb sockets.
4. Replace the defective bulb(s).
5. Reverse these steps for reassembly.

SWITCHES

Switches can be tested with an ohmmeter like the one described in Chapter One or a battery operated test light. Follow the manufacturer's instructions when using their test equipment.

> *CAUTION*
> *When testing switch continuity, the negative battery cable must be disconnected if the switch connector is not unplugged. When performing resistance checks, battery power can only be provided by the test instrument. If the battery is left connected and the switch turned ON during testing, the test instrument will be ruined.*

Use the color wiring diagrams at the end of this book to help in locating and identifying the following switch wiring and terminal connectors.

Front Brake Light Switch Testing/Replacement

The front brake light switch is incorporated into a sealed unit. Pull the rubber protective cap back from the switch and disconnect the switch electrical connectors. Check the switch by testing its continuity in the off and on operating conditions. Continuity should be recorded when the brake lever is pulled by hand. If the switch is faulty, disconnect the switch from the front brake lever housing (**Figure 55**). Install a new switch and connect the wires.

Rear Brake Light Switch Testing/Replacement

> *NOTE*
> *This procedure is shown on an XT125 model; adjustment procedures for other models are similar.*

1. On XT250 models, remove the right-hand side cover.

2. Unhook the spring from the brake arm (A, **Figure 56**) and disconnect the electrical wires.

3. Check the switch (B, **Figure 56**) by testing its continuity in each of its operating conditions. Continuity should be recorded when the spring attached to the switch arm is pulled down. If the switch is faulty, replace it as follows.

4. Unscrew the switch housing and locknut from the bracket.

5. Replace the switch; adjust as described in this chapter.

Rear Brake Light
Switch Adjustment

1. Turn the ignition switch ON.

2. Depress the brake pedal. The light should come on just as the brake begins to work.

3. To make the light come on earlier, hold the switch body and turn the adjusting nut as required.

Sidestand Switch
Testing/Replacement

1. Support the bike by wood block(s) or a milk crate.

2. Remove the left-hand side cover and locate the blue/yellow and black sidestand switch wire connector. Disconnect the wire connector.

3. Connect an ohmmeter to the switch (**Figure 57**), turn the ohmmeter to×1. Interpret results as follows:

    a. With the sidestand up, the reading should be 0 ohms.

    b. With the sidestand down (A, **Figure 58**) the reading should be infinite.

4. If the sidestand switch failed the test procedure in Step 3, it must be replaced by removing the 2 mounting screws (B, **Figure 58**) and pulling the switch away from the frame. Reverse to install.

Neutral Switch
Testing/Replacement

1. Support the bike by wood block(s) or a milk crate.

2. Remove the left-hand side cover and locate the sky blue wire connector (with the magneto wires) and disconnect it. See **Figure 57**.

3. Connect an ohmmeter to the sky blue wire connector and ground. Turn the ohmmeter to×1. Interpret results as follows:

    a. With the transmission in NEUTRAL, the reading should be 0 ohms.

    b. With the transmission in gear, the reading should be infinite.

4. If the neutral switch failed the test procedure in Step 3, it must be replaced by removing the

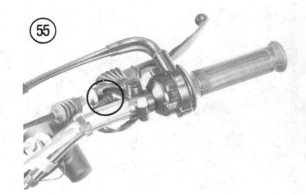

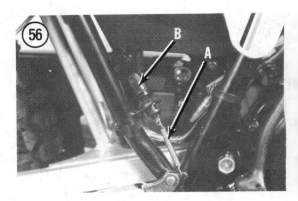

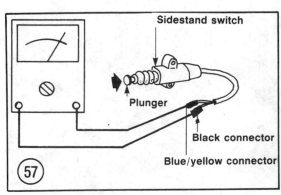

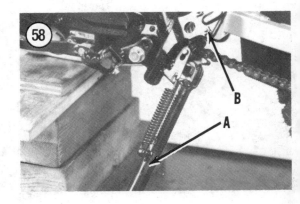

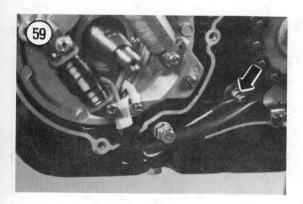

sprocket cover and disconnecting the wire at the neutral switch (**Figure 59**). Have an assistant lay the bike over to the right side and remove the neutral switch with a wrench or socket. Reverse to install.

HORN

Removal/Installation

1. Disconnect the horn electrical connectors.
2. Remove the bolts securing the horn (**Figure 60**).
3. Installation is the reverse of these steps.

Testing

1. Disconnect horn wires from harness.
2. Connect horn wires to 12 volt battery (pink wire to negative terminal). If it is good, it will sound.

CIRCUIT BREAKER (XT250)

All XT250 models have a circuit breaker that opens the electrical circuit to prevent damage to the electrical and wiring systems if a short circuit should occur anywhere in the electrical system. If the current is shut off when riding the bike, turn off all switches. Wait 30 seconds and depress the knob on top of the circuit breaker (**Figure 61**). If the circuit breaker opens again, there is a short in the wiring or in an electrical component.

> *NOTE*
> *Always wait 30 seconds before depressing the knob on the circuit breaker.*

FUSE (XT125 AND XT200)

There is only one fuse used on the XT125 and XT200 models. It is the 10 amp main fuse located under the left-hand side cover. See **Figure 62**.

> *NOTE*
> *Always carry a spare fuse.*

Whenever a fuse blows, find out the reason for the failure before replacing the fuse. Usually, the trouble is a short circuit in the wiring. This may be caused by worn-through insulation or a disconnected wire shorting to ground.

> *CAUTION*
> *Never substitute metal foil or wire for a fuse. Never use a higher amperage fuse than specified. An overload could result in fire and complete loss of the bike.*

7

Table 1 IGNITION SYSTEM SPECIFICATIONS

Magneto system	
Pickup coil resistance	
XT125 and XT200	265 ohms ±10%*
XT250	215 ohms ±10%*
Pickup coil test wires	
XT125 and XT200	White to green
XT250	Grey/red to white/green
Charging coil resistance	
XT125 and XT200	450 ohms ±10%*
XT250	490 ohms ±10%*
Charging coil test wires	Red to brown
Ignition coil	
Primary winding resistance	
XT125 and XT200	1.6 ±10%*
XT250	1.0 ±15%*
Secondary winding resistance	
XT125 and XT200	6.6 K ohms ±20%*
XT250	5.9 K ohms ±15%*
Charging/lighting system specifications	
Charging current	
XT125	1.4 amps or more @ 4,100 rpm
	2.7 amps or less @ 8,000 rpm
XT200	1.2 amps or more @ 4,100 rpm
	3.0 amps or more @ 8,000 rpm
XT250	1.0-1.6 amps @ 2,500 rpm
	1.2-1.8 amps @ 8,000 rpm
Charging coil resistance	
XT125 and XT200	0.35 ohms ±20%*
XT250	0.34 ohms ±10%*
Charging coil test wires	
XT125 and XT200	White to black
XT250	Green to black
Lighting coil resistance	0.21 ohms ±20%*
Lighting coil test wires	Yellow to black
Lighting voltage	
XT125 and XT200	7.1 volts or more @ 3,200 rpm
XT250	6.5 volts or more @ 2,500 rpm

* Measurements made @ 68° F (20° C).

Table 2 REPLACEMENT BULBS

Item	Voltage/wattage
Headlight	6V 35/35W
Tail/brake light	6V 5.3/25W
Flasher light	6V 17W
Indicator lights	
Meter light	6V 3W
Neutral light	6V 3W
High beam light	6V 3W
Turn light	6V 3W

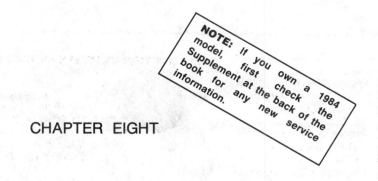

NOTE: If you own a 1984 model, first check the Supplement at the back of the book for any new service information.

CHAPTER EIGHT

FRONT SUSPENSION AND STEERING

This chapter discusses service operations on suspension components, steering, wheels and related items. Specifications are listed in **Table 1**. **Tables 1-3** are at the end of the chapter.

Because the XT models are dual purpose street/dirt bikes, care and attention to the suspension components are vital to the overall safe operation of the bike. If the XT has been ridden hard off-road, the entire suspension system should be inspected carefully for signs of loose nuts and bolts or damaged parts. Chapter Nine describes service to the rear suspension.

FRONT WHEEL

Refer to **Figure 1** when performing these procedures.

Removal/Installation

1. Place a milk crate or wood block(s) under the crankcase to lift the front wheel off the ground.
2. Remove the axle nut cotter pin, nut and washer. Discard the cotter pin.
3. To remove the speedometer cable, squeeze the cable wire clamp with a pair of pliers and pull the wire clamp out of the hub. Then pull the cable out of the hub (**Figure 2**).

4. Loosen the front brake cable adjusters at the handlebar (**Figure 3**) and at the front brake hub (A, **Figure 4**). Then remove the cable from the brake arm (B, **Figure 4**) and remove the cable adjustment bolt (C, **Figure 4**) from the hub.
5. Pull the axle out from the right-hand side (**Figure 5**) and remove the right-hand side axle spacer (**Figure 6**).
6. Remove the wheel.
7. Install the axle spacer, washers and axle nut on the axle to prevent their loss when servicing the wheel or brake hub. See **Figure 7**.

Inspection

1. Remove any corrosion on the front axle with a piece of fine emery cloth.
2. Clean the rim of all rust and dirt. Measure the axial and radial runout of the wheel rim with a dial indicator as shown in **Figure 8**. The maximum runout is 0.08 in. (2.0 mm). Some runout can be corrected by either tightening or replacing any loose or bent spokes as described in this chapter. If runout cannot be corrected by performing these procedures, check the condition of the front wheel bearings. See *Front Hub* in this chapter.
3. Check the axle runout as described under *Front Hub Inspection* in this chapter.

8

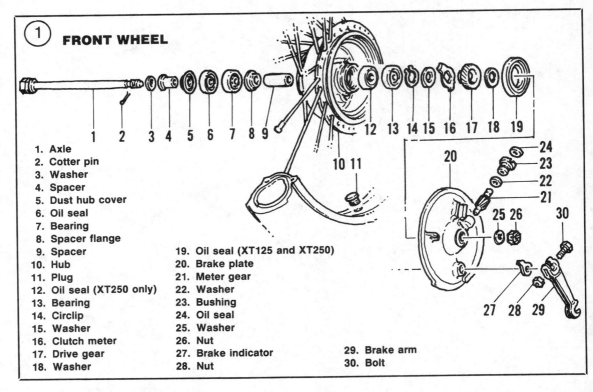

① **FRONT WHEEL**

1. Axle
2. Cotter pin
3. Washer
4. Spacer
5. Dust hub cover
6. Oil seal
7. Bearing
8. Spacer flange
9. Spacer
10. Hub
11. Plug
12. Oil seal (XT250 only)
13. Bearing
14. Circlip
15. Washer
16. Clutch meter
17. Drive gear
18. Washer
19. Oil seal (XT125 and XT250)
20. Brake plate
21. Meter gear
22. Washer
23. Bushing
24. Oil seal
25. Washer
26. Nut
27. Brake indicator
28. Nut
29. Brake arm
30. Bolt

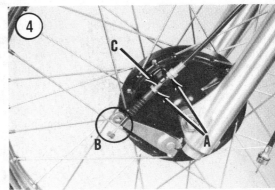

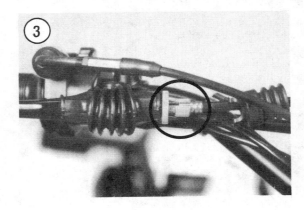

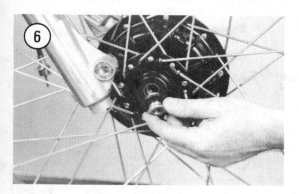

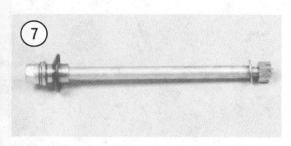

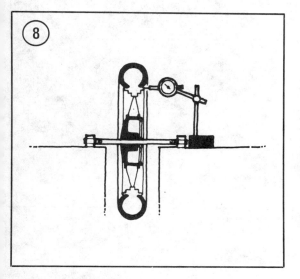

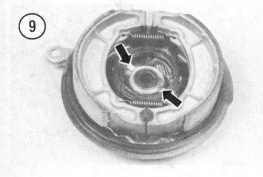

Installation

1. Check the fork slider axle bearing surfaces to make sure they are free from burrs or nicks. This condition can be repaired with fine grit sand paper or careful work with hand files.

2. Clean the axle in solvent and thoroughly dry. Make sure all axle contact surfaces are clean and free of road dirt and old grease prior to installation. If these surfaces are not cleaned, the axle may be difficult to remove later.

3. Align the tangs on the speedometer drive (**Figure 9**) with the slots (**Figure 10**) in the hub and install the brake panel.

4. Install the right-hand side axle spacer (**Figure 6**) onto the wheel.

5. Position the wheel in place, carefully inserting the boss on the left-hand fork slider into the locating groove on the brake panel (**Figure 11**). This is necessary for correct front brake operation.

6. Install the axle from the right-hand side through the wheel hub. Install the washer and axle nut. Tighten the nut to specifications in **Table 2**. Install a new cotter pin.

7. Slowly rotate the front wheel and install the speedometer cable into the brake hub. Secure it with the wire clamp.

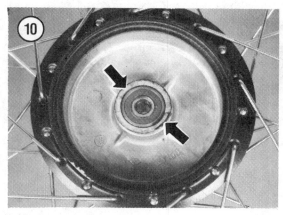

8

8. Install the front brake cable adjustment bolt into the brake panel and install the end of the brake cable into the brake arm. Adjust the front brake as described in Chapter Three.

> *NOTE*
> *Check the front brake (A, **Figure 12**) and speedometer (B, **Figure 12**) cables. If a cable is twisted in its clamp, loosen the clamp and reposition the cable.*

9. After the wheel is completely installed and the front brake adjusted, rotate the front wheel and apply the brake. Do this a couple of times to make sure the front wheel and brake are operating correctly.

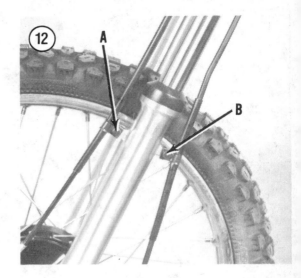

FRONT HUB

Refer to **Figure 1** for this procedure.

Disassembly

Oil seals have two sealing lips to help ensure proper bearing operation. The main lip on the inside of the seal prevents bearing grease or other lubrication from leaking out of the hub. The dust lip on the outside of the seal prevents water or dust from leaking into the hub and damaging the hub bearings. Whenever the wheels are removed, the dust seals should be inspected for any wear or hardening condition that would allow lubricants to leak out or debris to enter the hub. If a seal is bad, the bearing should be inspected carefully and replaced if required.

1. Remove the front wheel as described in this chapter.
2. Remove the spacer (**Figure 6**) from the right-hand side.
3. Remove the right-hand side oil seal (**Figure 13**) by prying it out of the wheel with a screwdriver. Remove the left-hand oil seal in the same manner.

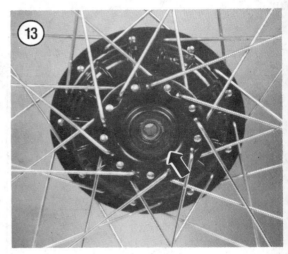

> *CAUTION*
> *Excessive force used to remove the oil seals could damage the hub. If the seals are difficult to remove, work the screwdriver around the seal until it pops out.*

4. The wheel hubs use two factory installed sealed bearings which are filled with grease. The bearings are press-fit into the hub. Turn the bearings by hand and check for excessive play in the inner bearing race or excessive noise when rotating the

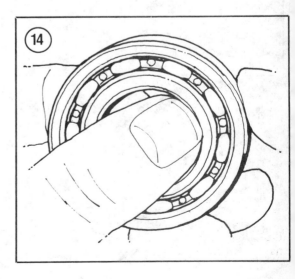

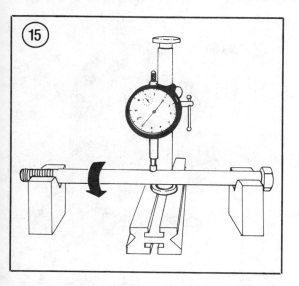

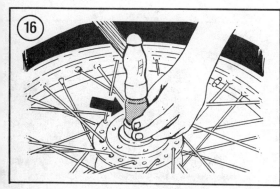

bearing. If these or other problems are detected, the bearings should be replaced.

> *CAUTION*
> *Tapping the bearing on its inner race destroys the bearing. Bearings removed by this method must be replaced.*

5. To remove the right- and left-hand bearings and the 2 spacers, insert a soft aluminum or brass drift into one side of the hub. Push the spacers over to one side and place the drift on the inner race of the lower bearing. Tap the bearing out of the hub with a hammer working around the perimeter of the inner race.

6. Remove the spacers and tap out the opposite bearing in the same manner.

Inspection

1. Clean the hub thoroughly in solvent.
2. Inspect the hub carefully for signs of damage in the spoke head and bearing areas. The hub will have to be replaced if any such damage is found.

3. Clean all non-sealed bearings thoroughly in solvent and dry with compressed air. Sealed bearings should not be cleaned in any way other than wiping dirt from the outside of the bearing.

> *WARNING*
> *Do not spin bearings with the air jet while drying. Instead hold the inner race with your hand. Because the air jet can spin the bearing race at higher speeds than it was designed for, the bearing may disintegrate and cause severe injury.*

4. Turn each bearing by hand (**Figure 14**), making sure it turns smoothly. Check balls for evidence of wear, pitting or excessive heat (bluish tint). Replace bearings if necessary; always replace as a complete set.

> *NOTE*
> *On sealed bearings, it is impossible to visually inspect the balls for the conditions described in Step 4; replace them if they do not turn smoothly by hand.*

5. On all non-sealed bearings that check out okay, lubricate and wrap them in a clean, lint-free cloth until reassembly.
6. Check the axle for wear and straightness. Use V-blocks and a dial indicator as shown in **Figure 15**. If the runout is 0.008 in. (0.2 mm) or greater, the axle must be replaced.

Assembly

1. Pack all non-sealed bearings thoroughly with multipurpose grease. Work the grease between the balls thoroughly.
2. Pack the wheel hub and axle spacer with multipurpose grease.

> *NOTE*
> *When installing the bearings, make sure to apply even pressure all the way around the outside bearing race. If pressure is given to one side only, the bearing may be damaged as it is driven in. A good tool to use when installing the bearings is a large socket with a diameter the same as that of the outside bearing race. See **Figure 16**.*

3. Install the right-hand wheel bearing.
4. Install the bearing spacers from the left-hand side.
5. Install the left-hand wheel bearing.
6. Install the oil seals and lubricate the outside lip.
7. Install the front wheel as described in this chapter.

8

WHEELS

Wheel Balance

An unbalanced wheel is unsafe. Depending on the degree of unbalance and the speed of the bike, the rider may experience anything from a mild vibration to a violent shimmy and loss of control.

Balance weights are applied to the spokes on the light side of the wheel to correct the condition.

NOTE
Be sure to balance the rear wheel with the driven sprocket assembly attached as it will affect the balance.

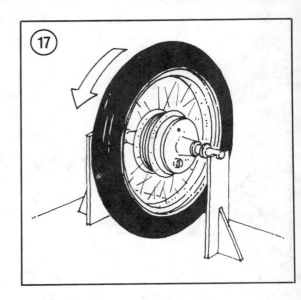

Before attempting to balance the wheels, check to be sure that the wheel bearings are in good condition and properly lubricated. The wheel must rotate freely.

1. Remove the wheel as described in this chapter or Chapter Nine.
2. Mount the wheel on a fixture such as the one shown in **Figure 17** so it can rotate freely.
3. Give the wheel a spin and let it coast to a stop. Mark the tire at the lowest point.
4. Spin the wheel several more times. If the wheel keeps coming to rest at the same point, it is out of balance.
5. Attach a weight to the upper (or light) side of the wheel on the spoke. Weights come in various sizes. Crimp the weights onto the spoke with pliers. See **Figure 18**.
6. Experiment with different weights until the wheel, when spun, comes to rest at a different position each time. When this happens, the wheel is balanced. Tighten the weights so they can't be thrown off.

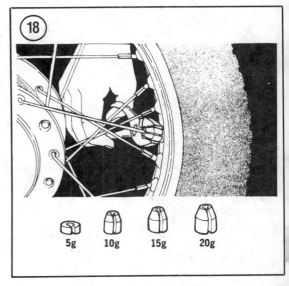

Spoke Inspection and Replacement

Spokes loosen with use and should be checked periodically. The "tuning fork" method for checking spoke tightness is simple and works well. Tap the center of each spoke with a spoke wrench (**Figure 19**) or the shank of a screwdriver and listen for a tone. A tightened spoke will emit a clear, ringing tone and a loose spoke will sound flat or dull. All the spokes in a correctly tightened wheel will emit tones of similar pitch but not necessarily the same precise pitch. The tension of the spokes does not determine wheel balance.

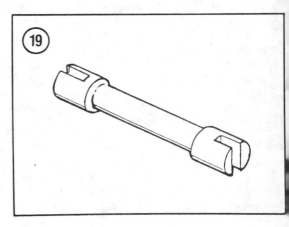

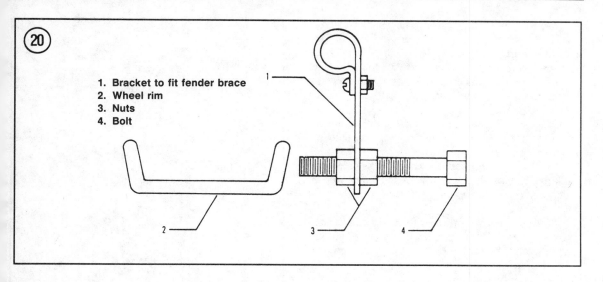

1. Bracket to fit fender brace
2. Wheel rim
3. Nuts
4. Bolt

Bent, stripped or broken spokes should be replaced as soon as they are detected, as they can destroy an expensive hub.

NOTE
If you are riding off-road and one or more spokes break, tie the broken spokes to an undamaged spoke with wire or string until you can replace it. This will prevent the spoke from dangling and eventually damaging the fork tubes or the rear sprocket and drive chain.

Unscrew the nipple from the spoke and depress the nipple into the rim far enough to free the end of the spoke; take care not to push the nipple all the way in. Remove the damaged spoke from the hub and use it to match a new spoke of identical length. If necessary, trim the new spoke to match the original and dress the end of the thread with a thread die. Install the new spoke in the hub and screw on the nipple; tighten it until the spoke's tone is similar to the tone of the other spokes in the wheel. Periodically check the new spoke; it will stretch and must be retightened several times before it takes a final set.

Spoke Adjustment

If all spokes appear loose, tighten all on one side of the hub, then tighten all on the other side. One-half to one turn should be sufficient; do not overtighten.

After tightening the spokes, check rim runout to be sure you haven't pulled the rim out of shape.

One way to check rim runout is to mount a dial indicator on the front fork or swing arm so that it bears against the rim.

If you don't have a dial indicator, improvise one as shown in **Figure 20**. Adjust the position of the bolt until it just clears the rim. Rotate the rim and note whether the clearance increases or decreases. Mark the tire with chalk or light crayon at areas that produce significantly large or small clearances. Clearance must not change by more than 2 mm (0.08 in.).

To pull the rim out, tighten spokes which terminate on the same side of the hub and loosen spokes which terminate on the opposite side of the hub (**Figure 21**). In most cases, only a slight amount of adjustment is necessary to true a rim. After adjustment, rotate the rim and make sure another area has not been pulled out of true. Continue adjustment and checking until runout is less than 2.0 mm (0.08 in.).

Rim Replacement

During hard off-road riding, the rim can be bent. If this should happen, the rim should be replaced before the bike is ridden back on the street. A bent or dented wheel creates very dangerous handling.

If the spokes are not bent or damaged also, they may be reused. This procedures describes how to replace the rim without removing the spokes.
1. Remove the tire as described in this chapter.
2. Securely fasten the spokes together with wire, string or tape at each point where they cross (**Figure 22**).
3. Place the replacement rim on top of the old rim and align the nipple holes of both rims. This is to make sure the replacement rim is the correct one. When the rims are aligned correctly, mark one spoke and its corresponding nipple hole on the new rim.

8

4. Remove the nipples from the spokes using a spoke wrench. If they are coated with dirt or rust, clean them in solvent and allow to dry. Then check the nipples for signs of cracking or other damage. Spoke nipples in this condition can strip when the wheel is later trued. Replace all nipples as necessary.

5. Lift the hub and spokes out of the old rim, making sure not to knock the spokes out of alignment.

6. Position the hub and spokes into the new rim, making sure to align the marks made in Step 3. Then insert the spokes into the rim until they are all in place.

7. Place a drop of oil onto the threaded end of each spoke and install the nipples. Thread the nipples halfway onto the spokes (before they make contact with the rim).

8. Lift the wheel and stand it up on the workbench. Check the hub to make sure it is centered in the rim. If not, reposition it by hand.

9. With the hub centered in the rim, thread the nipples until they just seat against the rim. True the wheel as described under *Spoke Adjustment* in this chapter.

Seating Spokes

When spokes loosen or when installing new spokes, the head of the spoke should be checked for proper seating in the hub. If it is not seated correctly, it can loosen further and may cause severe damage to the hub when riding off-road. If one or spokes require reseating, hit the head of the spoke as shown in **Figure 23** with a punch. True the wheel as described under *Spoke Adjustment* in this chapter.

TIRE CHANGING

Removal

1. Remove the valve core to deflate the tire.
2. Loosen the rim lock nut (**Figure 24**).
3. Press the entire bead on both sides of the tire into the center of the rim.
4. Lubricate the beads with soapy water.
5. Insert the tire iron under the bead next to the valve (**Figure 25**). Force the bead on the opposite side of the tire into the center of the rim and pry the bead over the rim with the tire iron.
6. Insert a second tire iron next to the first to hold the bead over the rim. Then work around the tire with the first tool, prying the bead over the rim. Be careful not to pinch the inner tube with the tire irons.

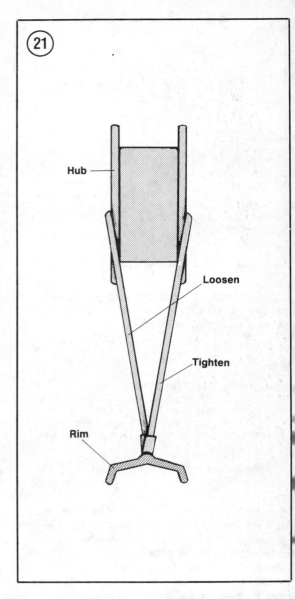

Hub

Loosen

Tighten

Rim

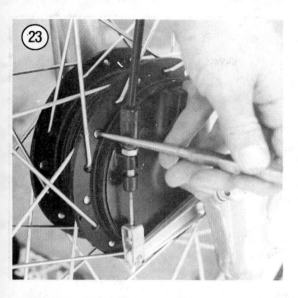

7. Remove the valve from the hole in the rim and remove the tube from the tire.

> *NOTE*
> *Step 8 is required only if it is necessary to completely remove the tire from the rim, such as for tire replacement or rim replacement.*

8. Stand the tire upright. Insert a tire tool between the second bead and the same side of the rim that the first bead was pried over (**Figure 26**). Force the bead on the opposite side from the tool into the center of the rim. Pry the second bead off the rim, working around the wheel with 2 tire irons as with the first.

Installation

1. Carefully inspect the tire for any damage, especially inside.
2. A new tire may have balancing rubbers inside. These are not patches and should not be disturbed. A colored spot near the bead indicates a lighter point on the tire. This spot should be placed next to the valve stem.
3. Check that the spoke ends do not protrude through the nipples into the center of the rim where they can puncture the tube. File off any protruding spoke ends. Be sure the rim rubber band is in place with the rough side toward the rim.
4. Inflate the tube until its shape rounds out. Check it for leaks.

> *NOTE*
> *Perform Step 4 when installing a new tube also. This will help to shape the tube for installation.*

5. Deflate the tube just enough to barely round it out. Too much air will make installation difficult.

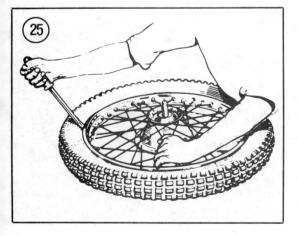

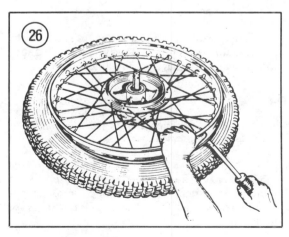

6. Dust the outside of the tube with talcum power to prevent it from sticking to the tire. Then place the tube inside the tire.

7. Lubricate both beads of the tire with soapy water.

8. Place the backside of the tire into the center of the rim and insert the valve stem through the stem hole in the wheel. The lower bead should go into the center of the rim and the upper bead outside. Work around the tire in both directions (**Figure 27**). Use a tire iron for the last few inches of bead (**Figure 28**). When the lower bead is in position, make sure it slipped over the rim lock also. If not, use a tire iron while pulling on the rim lock.

9. Press the upper bead into the rim opposite the valve (**Figure 29**). Pry the bead into the rim on both sides of the initial point with a tire tool, working around the rim to the valve (**Figure 30**).

10. Wiggle the valve to be sure the tube is not trapped under the bead. Set the valve stem squarely in its hole before screwing on the valve nut to hold it against the rim.

11. Check the bead on both sides of the tire for an even fit around the rim. Make sure also that the rim lock is in position inside the tire.

12. Inflate the tire slowly to seat the beads in the rim. It may be necessary to bounce the tire to complete the seating.

13. Inflate the tire to the required pressure. See **Table 3**. Tighten the valve stem locks and screw on the cover cap.

14. Tighten the rim lock nut securely.

15. Balance the wheel assembly as described in this chapter.

TIRE REPAIRS

Every rider will eventually experience trouble with a tire or tube. Repairs and replacement are fairly simple and every rider should know the techniques.

Patching a motorcycle tube is only a temporary fix. A motorcycle tire flexes too much and the patch could rub right off. However, a patched tube will get you far enough to buy a new tube.

> *NOTE*
> *A can of a pressurized tire sealant can be carried in your tool box or tow vehicle. It may be able to seal the hole as a temporary fix.*

Tire Repair Kits

The repair kits can be purchased from motorcycle dealers and some auto supply stores. When buying, specify that the kit you want is for motorcycles.

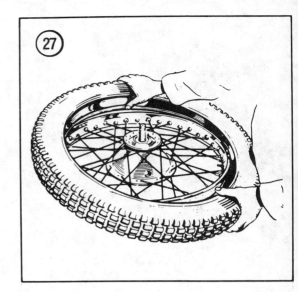

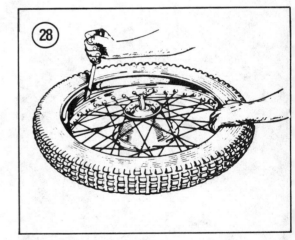

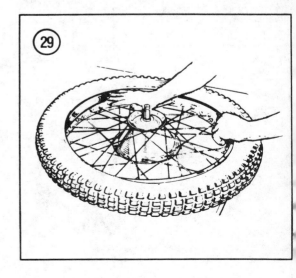

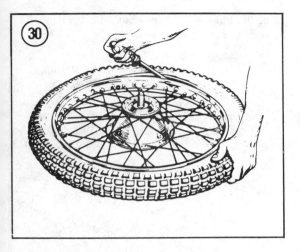

There are 2 types of tire repair kits:
a. Hot patch.
b. Cold patch.

Hot patches are stronger because they actually vulcanize to the tube, becoming part of it. However, they are far too bulky to carry for roadside repairs and the strength is unnecessary for a temporary repair.

Cold patches are not vulcanized to the tube; they are simply glued to it. Though not as strong as hot patches, cold patches are still very durable. Cold patch kits are less bulky than hot and more easily applied under adverse conditions. A cold patch kit contains everything necessary and tucks easily in with your emergency tool kit.

Tube Inspection

1. Remove the inner tube as described under *Tire Changing*.
2. Install the valve core into the valve stem (**Figure 31**) and inflate the tube slightly. Do not overinflate.
3. Immerse the tube in water a section at a time (**Figure 32**). Look carefully for bubbles indicating a hole. Mark each hole and continue checking until you are certain that all holes are discovered and marked. Also make sure that the valve core is not leaking; tighten it if necessary.

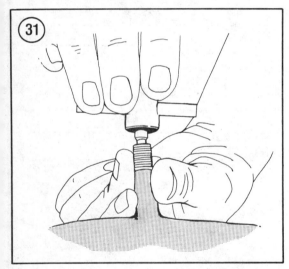

> *NOTE*
> *If you do not have enough water to immerse sections of the tube, try running your hand over the tube slowly and very close to the surface. If your hand is damp, it works even better. If you suspect a hole anywhere, apply some saliva to the area to verify it (**Figure 33**).*

4. Apply a cold patch using the techniques described under *Cold Patch Repair* in this chapter.

8

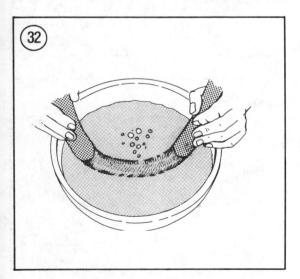

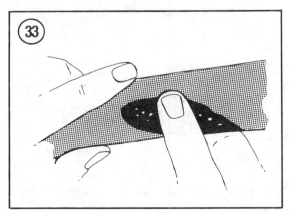

5. Dust the patch area with talcum powder to prevent it from sticking to the tire.

6. Carefully check the inside of the tire casing for small rocks or sand which may have damaged the tube. If the inside of the tire is split, apply a patch to the area to prevent it from pinching and damaging the tube again.

7. Check the inside of the rim.

8. Deflate the tube prior to installation in the tire.

Cold Patch Repair

1. Roughen an area around the hole slightly larger than the patch, using the cap from the tire repair kit or a pocket knife (**Figure 34**). Do not scrape too vigorously or you may cause additional damage.

2. Apply a small quantity of special cement to the puncture and spread it evenly with your finger (**Figure 35**).

3. Allow the cement to dry until tacky—usually thirty seconds or so is sufficient.

4. Remove the backing from the patch.

> *CAUTION*
> *Do not touch the newly exposed rubber with your fingers or the patch will not stick firmly.*

5. Center the patch over the hole. Hold the patch firmly in place for about 30 seconds to allow the cement to set (**Figure 36**).

6. Dust the patched area with talcum powder to prevent sticking.

HANDLEBAR

Removal

1. Remove the rear view mirrors.

2. Slacken the front brake cable adjuster (**Figure 37**) and remove the cable from the bracket. Remove the clutch cable in the same manner.

3. Remove the wire clamps (A, **Figure 38**) from the handlebar.

4. Remove the screws securing the left-hand switch assembly (**Figure 39**) and allow it to hang down.

5. The throttle housing/engine stop switch are combined into the same unit (**Figure 40**). If it is necessary to separate the unit, remove the screws and pull the throttle housing away from the switch one or two inches. Then disconnect the throttle cable from the twist grip and remove all parts. If it is not necessary to separate the unit, simply loosen the screws securing the unit to the handlebar and

slide the unit off the handlebar once the handlebar is removed from the bike.

> *CAUTION*
> *Do not bend the throttle cable during removal or it may be damaged.*

6. Loosen the handlebar holder bolts (B, **Figure 38**) and remove the holders and handlebar.

7. To maintain a good grip on the handlebar and to prevent it from slipping down, clean the knurled

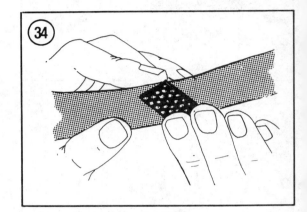

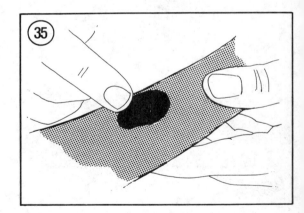

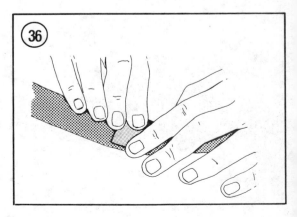

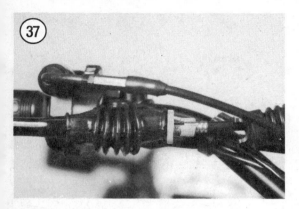

section of the handlebar with solvent. It should be kept clean so it will be held securely by the holders. The upper and lower holders should also be kept clean and free of any metal that may have been gouged loose by handlebar slippage.

> *WARNING*
> *Always replace a bent handlebar, no matter how slight the damage may be. Because a handlebar flexes slightly during riding, a bent handlebar may slip in the holders, causing an accident.*

8. Install by reversing these removal steps, noting the following:
   a. Install the handlebar and handlebar holders. Install the bolts and tighten lightly.
   b. Sit on the seat and position the handlebars to best suit your riding position. Tighten the front bolts first, then the rear to specifications in **Table 2**.
   c. Adjust the clutch, brake and throttle cables as described in Chapter Three.

STEERING HEAD

Disassembly

Refer to **Figure 41** for this procedure.
1. Remove the fuel tank as described in Chapter Six.

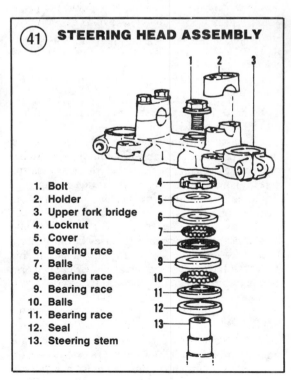

STEERING HEAD ASSEMBLY

1. Bolt
2. Holder
3. Upper fork bridge
4. Locknut
5. Cover
6. Bearing race
7. Balls
8. Bearing race
9. Bearing race
10. Balls
11. Bearing race
12. Seal
13. Steering stem

2. Remove the front wheel as described in this chapter.

3. Remove the handlebar as described in this chapter.

4. Remove the headlight assembly as described in Chapter Seven.

5. Remove the instrument panel as described in Chapter Seven.

6. Remove the bolts securing the front fender and remove the fender.

7. Remove the front forks as described in this chapter.

8. Loosen the steering stem bolt and remove the upper fork bridge.

9. Remove the upper adjusting nut (**Figure 42**) with a spanner wrench (**Figure 43**).

> *NOTE*
> *Have an assistant hold a large pan underneath the steering head assembly to catch the loose balls as they fall out.*

10. Remove the upper bearing cover and then pull the steering stem out of the frame (**Figure 44**). The upper and lower bearings are loose ball bearings so be ready to catch them as they fall out.

> *NOTE*
> *There are a total of 41 ball bearings used—22 in the top and 19 in the bottom. The bearings should not be intermixed because if worn or damaged, they must be replaced in sets.*

11. Remove the ball bearings that did not fall out of the upper or lower race.

Inspection

1. Clean the bearing races in the steering head and all ball bearings with solvent.

2. Check for broken welds on the frame around the steering head. If any are found, have them repaired by a competent frame shop or welding service familar with motorcycle frame repair.

3. Check the balls for pitting, scratches or discoloration indicating wear or corrosion. Replace them in sets if any are bad.

4. Check the upper and lower races in the steering head. See *Bearing Race Replacement* in this chapter if races are pitted, scratched or badly worn.

5. Check steering stem for cracks.

Bearing Race Replacement

The headset and steering stem bearing races are pressed into place. Because they are easily bent, do not remove them unless they are worn and require

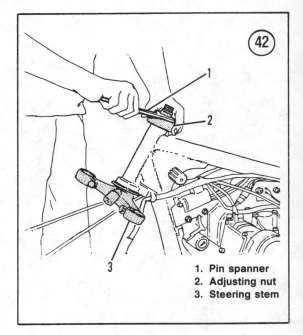

1. Pin spanner
2. Adjusting nut
3. Steering stem

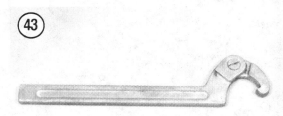

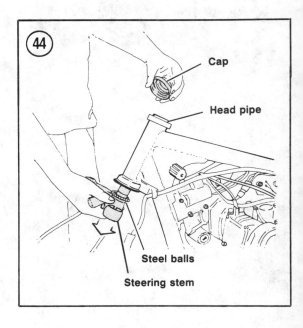

Cap

Head pipe

Steel balls

Steering stem

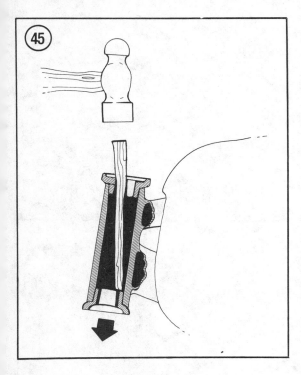

replacement. Take old races to the dealer to ensure exact replacement.

To remove a headset race, insert a hardwood stick into the head tube and carefully tap the race out from the inside (**Figure 45**). Tap all around the race so that neither the race nor the head tube are bent. To install a race, fit it into the end of the head tube. Tap it slowly and squarely with a block of wood (**Figure 46**).

Assembly

Refer to **Figure 41** for this procedure.
1. Make sure the steering head bearing races are properly seated.
2. Apply a coat of wheel bearing grease to the lower bearing race cone and fit 19 ball bearings around it (**Figure 47**).
3. Apply a coat of wheel bearing grease to the upper bearing race cone and fit 22 ball bearings around it (**Figure 48**).
4. Insert the steering stem into the head tube. Hold it firmly in place.

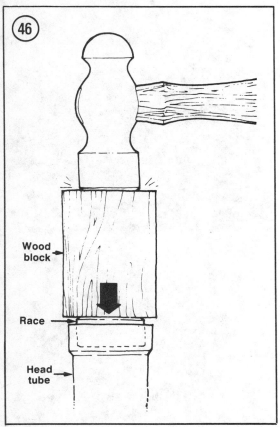

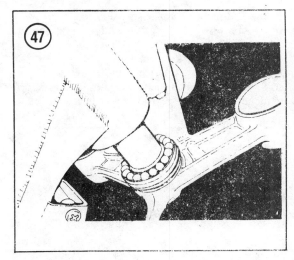

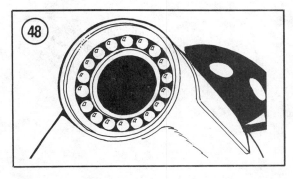

5. Install the upper bearing race and upper bearing cover.

6. Install the adjusting nut and tighten it (**Figure 49**) to approximately 18 ft.-lb. (25 N•m). Then loosen it 1/4 turn.

> *NOTE*
> *The adjusting nut should be tight enough to remove play, both horizontal and vertical (**Figure 50**), yet loose enough so that the assembly will turn to both lock positions under its own weight after a light push.*

7. Continue assembly by reversing *Removal* Steps 1-8. Torque the bolts to the specifications in **Table 2**.

8. After the total assembly is installed, check the stem for looseness or binding; readjust if necessary.

Steering Stem Adjustment

If play develops in the steering system, it may only require adjustment. However, don't take a chance on it. Disassemble the stem as described in this chapter and check for damaged parts.

FRONT FORKS

The Yamaha front suspension consists of a spring-controlled, hydraulically dampened telescopic fork. Before suspecting major trouble, drain the front fork oil and refill with the proper type and quantity; refer to Chapter Three. If you still have trouble, such as poor damping, a tendency to bottom or top out or leakage around

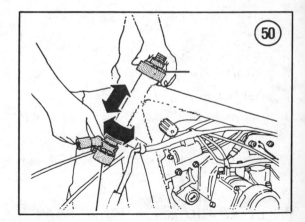

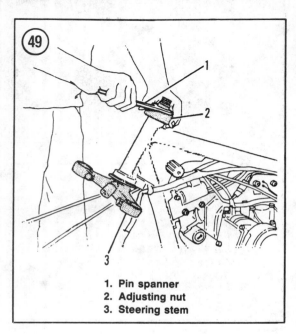

1. Pin spanner
2. Adjusting nut
3. Steering stem

the rubber seals, follow the service procedures in this section.

To simplify fork service and to prevent the mixing of parts, the legs should be removed, serviced and installed individually.

Removal/Installation

1. Remove the front wheel as described in this chapter.
2. Disconnect the front brake and speedometer cables from the left-hand side fork tube. See **Figure 51**.

3. Loosen the pinch bolts (**Figure 52**) on the upper fork bridge bolts.
4. Loosen the lower fork bridge bolts (**Figure 53**).
5. Withdraw the fork tube. It may be necessary to slightly rotate the tube while removing it.
6. Install by reversing these removal steps. Torque the bolts to the specifications in **Table 2**.

Disassembly

Refer to **Figure 54** (XT125 and XT200) or **Figure 55** (XT250) for this procedure.

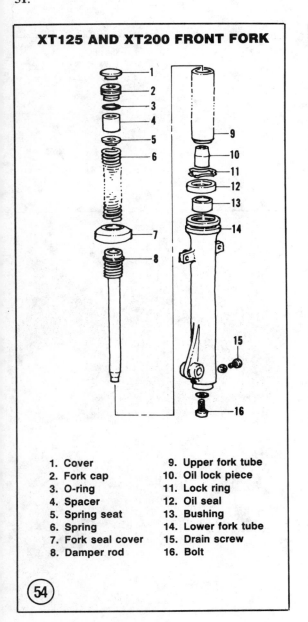

XT125 AND XT200 FRONT FORK

1. Cover	9. Upper fork tube
2. Fork cap	10. Oil lock piece
3. O-ring	11. Lock ring
4. Spacer	12. Oil seal
5. Spring seat	13. Bushing
6. Spring	14. Lower fork tube
7. Fork seal cover	15. Drain screw
8. Damper rod	16. Bolt

(54)

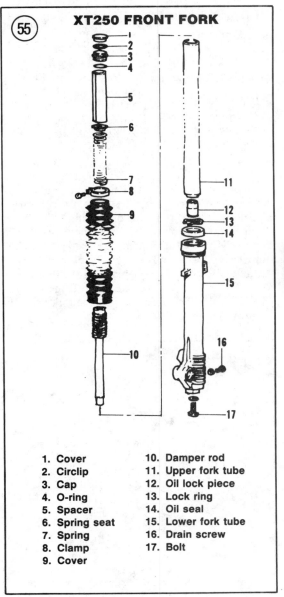

XT250 FRONT FORK

(55)

1. Cover	10. Damper rod
2. Circlip	11. Upper fork tube
3. Cap	12. Oil lock piece
4. O-ring	13. Lock ring
5. Spacer	14. Oil seal
6. Spring seat	15. Lower fork tube
7. Spring	16. Drain screw
8. Clamp	17. Bolt
9. Cover	

8

1. Hold the upper fork tube in a vise with soft jaws (**Figure 56**).

2. On XT250 models, remove the fork boot.

3A. *XT125 and XT200*; Remove the fork cap using a 17 mm Allen wrench or a 17 mm bolt head and Vise Grips as shown in **Figure 57**.

3B. *XT250*; The fork cap and spring are held in position by a spring wire ring. To remove the wire ring, it is necessary to have an assistant depress the fork cap (**Figure 58**) using a suitable size drift. Then pry the wire ring out of its groove in the fork with a small screwdriver. When the wire ring is removed, release tension from the fork cap and remove it.

4. Remove the spacer (**Figure 59**) and the spring seat (**Figure 60**).

5. Withdraw the fork spring (**Figure 61**).

6. Remove the fork from the vise, pour the oil out and discard it. Pump the fork several times by hand to expel most of the remaining oil.

7. On XT125 and XT200 models, remove the rubber boot out of the notch in the lower fork tube and slide it off of the upper fork tube (**Figure 62**).

8. Clamp the slider in a vise with soft jaws.

9A. *XT125 and XT200*: Insert the correct damper rod holding tool into the upper fork tube to prevent the damper rod from turning. Then remove the Allen bolt (**Figure 63**) at the bottom of the slider and pull the fork tube out of the slider. The part number for the damper rod holder for XT125 models is YM-33466. The number for XT200 models is YM-33256. A typical holder is shown connected to a ratchet extension in **Figure 64**.

9B. *XT250*: Remove the Allen bolt (**Figure 63**) at the bottom of the slider and pull the fork tube out of the slider.

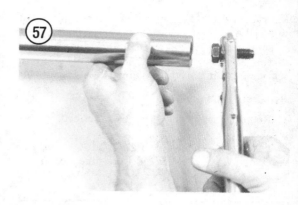

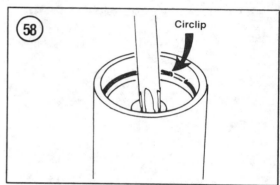

Circlip

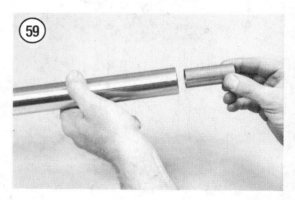

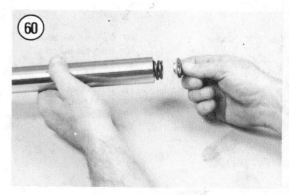

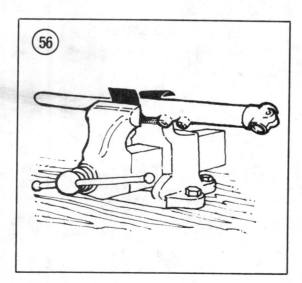

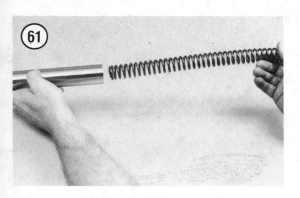

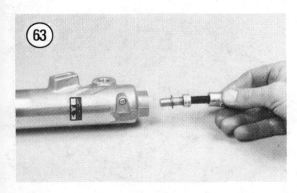

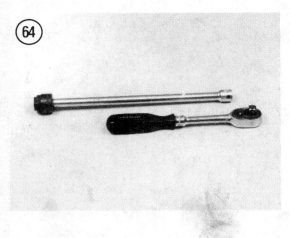

10. Remove the oil lock piece, damper rod and rebound spring.

> *NOTE*
> *If the oil seal has been leaking, it can be removed as described in Step 11.*

11. Remove snap ring and oil seal from the lower fork tube.

> *CAUTION*
> *Use a dull screwdriver blade to remove the oil seal as shown in **Figure 65**. Do not damage the outer edge or inner surface of the slider.*

Inspection

1. Thoroughly·clean all parts in solvent and dry them.

2. Check the damper rod for straightness. **Figure 66** shows one method. The rod should be replaced if the runout is 0.008 in. (0.2 mm) or greater.

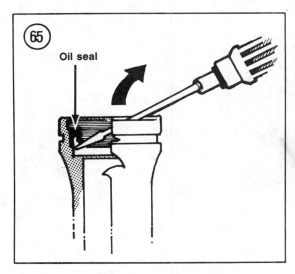

Oil seal

3. Carefully check the damper valve and the piston ring (**Figure 67**) for wear or damage.

4. Check upper fork tube exterior for scratches and straightness. If bent or scratched, it should be replaced.

5. Check the lower fork tube for dents or exterior damage that may cause the upper fork tube to hang up during riding conditions. Replace if necessary.

6. Measure the uncompressed length of the fork spring. Replace the spring if it is too short. See **Table 1** for specifications.

7. Check the O-ring seal (**Figure 68**) on the fork cap. Replace if necessary.

8. Any parts that are worn or damaged should be replaced. Simply cleaning and reinstalling unserviceable components will not improve performance of the front suspension.

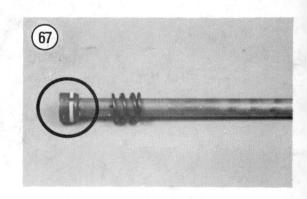

Assembly

1. Install the oil seal and snap ring in the lower fork tube.

> *NOTE*
> *Make sure the seal seats squarely and fully in the bore of the tube.*

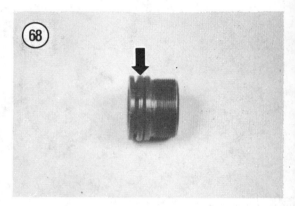

2. Insert the damper rod into the fork tube (**Figure 69**) and install the oil lock piece.

3. Apply a light coat of oil to the outside of the fork tube and install it into the slider (**Figure 70**). Apply Loctite Lock N' Seal to the threads of the Allen bolt and install it (**Figure 63**).

> *NOTE*
> *On XT125 and XT200 models, use the damper rod holder tool used during disassembly to hold the damper rod when tightening the Allen bolt.*

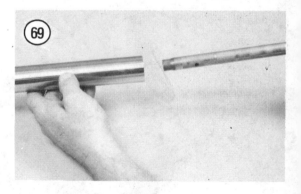

4. On XT-125 and XT200 models, slide the rubber boot into place on the lower fork tube.

5. Fill fork tube with fresh fork oil. Capacity for each fork tube is listed in **Table 1**.

> *NOTE*
> *In order to measure the correct amount of fluid, use a plastic baby bottle. These have measurements in fluid ounces (oz.) and cubic centimeters (cc) on the side. Many fork oil containers have a semi-transparent strip on the side of the bottle to aid in measuring.*

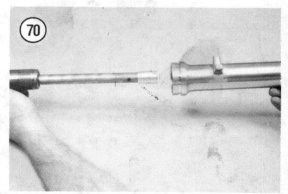

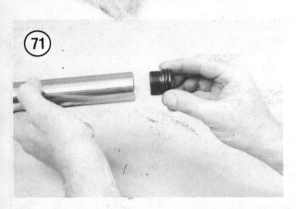

6. Insert the spring with the small coil diameter facing down toward the axle. See **Figure 61**.

7. Install the spring seat (**Figure 60**) and spacer (**Figure 59**).

8A. *XT125 and XT200*: Install the fork cap (**Figure 71**) and tighten it with an Allen wrench or a bolt and Vise Grips (**Figure 57**).

8B. *XT250*: Place the fork cap in position in the top of the fork tube. Then have an assistant compress the fork cap and install a new spring wire spring. Make sure the fork cap seats fully in the groove in the fork tube.

9. Install the fork as described in this chapter.

Table 1 FRONT SUSPENSION SPECIFICATIONS

Steering system	
Number/size of steel balls	
Upper	22 balls; 3/16 in.
Lower	19 balls; 1/4 in.
Front suspension	
Front fork travel	
XT125	7.09 in. (180 mm)
XT200	8.07 in. (205 mm)
XT250	8.07 in. (205 mm)
Fork spring free length	
XT125	15.06 in. (382.5 mm)
XT200	19.55 in. (496.5 mm)
XT250	17.97 in. (456.5 mm)
Front fork oil capacity (each leg)	
XT125	6.49 oz. (192 cc)
XT200	8.42 oz. (249 cc)
XT250	9.10 oz. (269 cc)
Oil weight	SAE 10
Front wheel	
Runout limit	0.08 in. (2.0 mm)

8

Table 2 FRONT SUSPENSION TIGHTENING SPECIFICATIONS

Item	ft.-lb.	N•m
Front axle nut		
XT125 and XT200	28	39
XT250	75	105
Fork bridge bolts		
Upper	14	20
Lower	27	38
Handlebar	14	20
Front fork cap nut		
(XT125 and XT200)	16	22
Steering stem nut		
XT125 and XT200	40	55
XT250	38	53

Table 3 TIRE INFLATION PRESSURE

Tire size	Air pressure
Front tire	
2.75 x 21—4 PR	
Cold	18 psi (1.3 kg/cm^2)
Maximum load limit*	18 psi (1.3 kg/cm^2)
Off-road	14 psi (1.0 kg/cm^2)
3.00 x 21—4PR	
Cold	18 psi (1.3 kg/cm^2)
Maximum load limit**	22 psi (1.5 kg/cm^2)
High-speed riding	22 psi (1.5 kg/cm^2)
Rear tire	
100/80 x 17—52P	
Cold	22 psi (1.5 kg/cm^2)
Maximum load limit*	26 psi (1.8 kg/cm^2)
Off-road	14 psi (1.0 kg/cm^2)
4.60 x 17—4PR	
Cold	22 psi (1.5 kg/cm^2)
Maximum load limit**	26 psi (1.8 kg/cm^2)
High-speed riding	26 psi (1.8 kg/cm^2)

* Maximum load limit: 201-351 lb. (91-159 kg).
** Maximum load limit: 198-353 lb. (90-160 kg).

NOTE: If you own a 1984 model, first check the Supplement at the back of the book for any new service information.

CHAPTER NINE

REAR SUSPENSION

The monoshock rear suspension is basically the same on all models. The rear swing arm is steel and the monoshock is nestled up in the frame backbone.

This chapter contains repair and replacement procedures for the rear wheel and hub and the rear suspension components. Service to the rear suspension consists of periodically checking bolt tightness, replacing swing arm bushings, checking the spring/gas monoshock unit and replacing it if necessary.

Tire changing and wheel service procedures are described in Chapter Eight.

Refer to **Table 1** for rear suspension service specifications. **Tables 1-3** are at the end of chapter.

REAR WHEEL

Refer to **Figure 1** or **Figure 2** when performing these procedures.

Removal/Installation

1. Place a milk crate or wood block(s) under the frame so the rear wheel is off the ground.
2. Compress the spring and remove the brake rod adjusting wing nut (A, **Figure 3**). Then remove spring and disconnect the brake rod.

NOTE
*Mark the position of the chain adjuster in relation to the locator pin on the swing arm (**Figure 4**) so the wheel can be reinstalled in the same location with the same amount of drive chain slack.*

3. Remove the cotter pin and remove the axle nut (B, **Figure 3**) and chain adjuster. Discard the old cotter pin.
4. Push the rear wheel forward to allow drive chain slack.
5. Pull the drive chain up and off the sprocket and withdraw the rear axle from the left-hand side (**Figure 5**).
6. Slide the wheel back and remove the spacers from the left- (**Figure 6**) and right-hand (**Figure 7**) sides.
7. Install by reversing these steps, noting the following.
8. Make sure the arm on the swing arm is positioned in the slot in the brake backing plate (**Figure 8**). This assures correct rear wheel brake action.
9. Locate the drive chain adjusters in the original positions as noted in Step 2.
10. If the drive chain master link was removed, be sure to install a new clip with the closed end facing in the direction of chain travel (**Figure 9**).

9

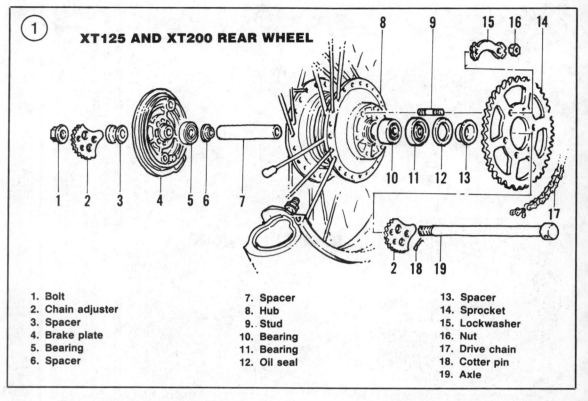

XT125 AND XT200 REAR WHEEL

1. Bolt
2. Chain adjuster
3. Spacer
4. Brake plate
5. Bearing
6. Spacer
7. Spacer
8. Hub
9. Stud
10. Bearing
11. Bearing
12. Oil seal
13. Spacer
14. Sprocket
15. Lockwasher
16. Nut
17. Drive chain
18. Cotter pin
19. Axle

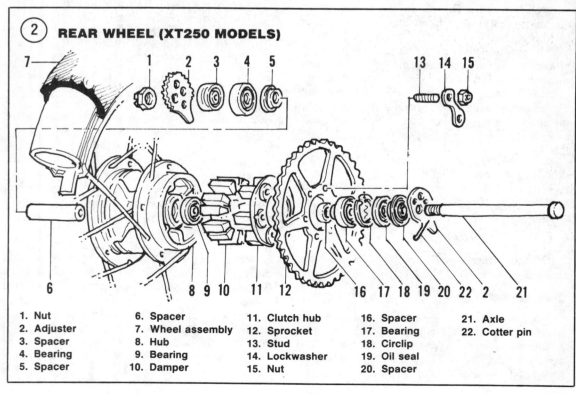

REAR WHEEL (XT250 MODELS)

1. Nut
2. Adjuster
3. Spacer
4. Bearing
5. Spacer
6. Spacer
7. Wheel assembly
8. Hub
9. Bearing
10. Damper
11. Clutch hub
12. Sprocket
13. Stud
14. Lockwasher
15. Nut
16. Spacer
17. Bearing
18. Circlip
19. Oil seal
20. Spacer
21. Axle
22. Cotter pin

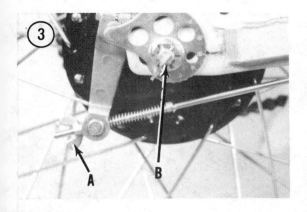

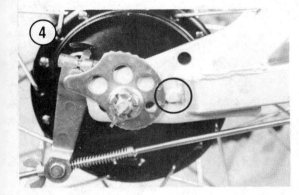

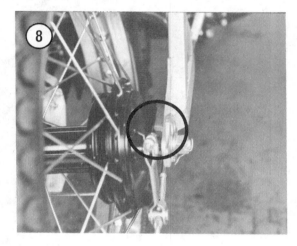

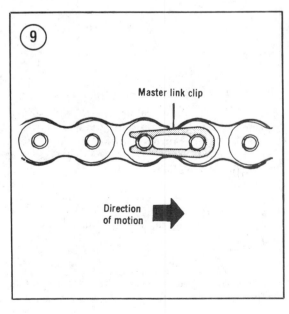

Master link clip

Direction
of motion

9

11. Clean the axle in solvent and thoroughly dry. Make sure all axle contact surfaces are clean and free of road dirt and old grease prior to installation. If these surfaces are not cleaned, the axle may be difficult to remove later.

12. Install the axle from the drive sprocket side.

13. Adjust the drive chain tension as described in Chapter Three.

14. Tighten the axle nut to the torque values in **Table 1**. Install a new cotter pin in the axle—never reuse an old cotter pin. Bend the cotter pin over completely.

15. After the wheel is completely installed, rotate it several times to make sure it rotates smoothly. Apply the brake several times to make sure it operates correctly.

16. Adjust the rear brake as described in Chapter Three.

Inspection

1. Remove any corrosion on the front axle with a piece of fine emery cloth.

2. Clean the rim of all rust and dirt. Then measure the axial and radial runout of the wheel rim with a dial indicator as shown in **Figure 10**. The maximum runout is 0.08 in. (2.0 mm). Some of this condition can be corrected by either tightening or replacing any loose or bent spokes. Refer to Chapter Eight. If this condition cannot be corrected by performing these procedures, check the rear wheel bearings. See *Rear Hub* in this chapter.

3. Check the axle runout as described under *Rear Hub Inspection* in this chapter.

REAR HUB

Refer to **Figure 1** or **Figure 2** for this procedure.

Disassembly

Oil seals have two sealing lips to help ensure proper bearing operation. The main lip on the inside of the seal prevents bearing grease or other lubrication from leaking out of the hub. The dust lip on the outside of the seal prevents water or dust from entering the hub and damaging the hub bearings. Whenever the wheels are removed, the dust seals should be inspected for any wear or hardening condition that would allow lubricants to leak out of or debris to enter the hub. If a seal is bad, the bearing should be inspected carefully and replaced if required.

1. Remove the rear wheel as described in this chapter.

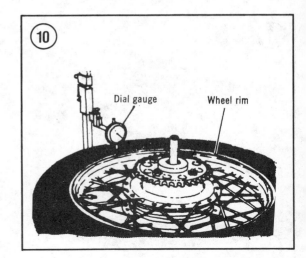

Dial gauge   Wheel rim

2. Remove the left-hand side oil seal (**Figure 11**) by prying it out of the wheel with a screwdriver.

> *CAUTION*
> *Do not use excessive force to remove the oil seal as this could damage the hub. If the seal is difficult to remove, work the screwdriver around the seal until it pops out.*

3. The wheel hub uses two factory installed sealed bearings which are filled with grease. The bearings are press-fit into the hub. Turn the bearings by hand and check for excessive play in the inner bearing race or excessive noise when rotating the bearing. If these or other problems are detected, the bearings should be replaced.

> *CAUTION*
> *Tapping the bearings on the inner race destroys the bearing. Bearings removed by this method must be replaced.*

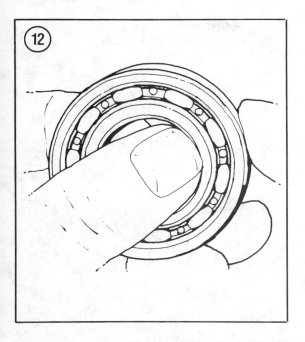

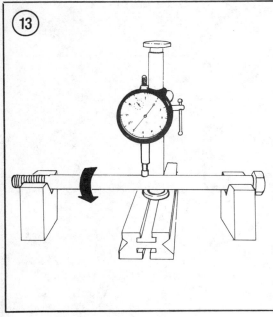

Inspection

1. Clean the hub thoroughly in solvent.

2. Inspect the hub carefully for signs of damage in the spoke head and bearing areas. The hub will have to be replaced if any such damage is found.

3. Clean all non-sealed bearings thoroughly in solvent and dry with compressed air. Sealed bearings should not be cleaned in any way other than wiping dirt from the outside of the bearing.

> *WARNING*
> *Do not spin non-sealed bearings with the air jet while drying. Instead hold the inner race with your hand. Because the air jet can spin the bearing race at higher speeds than it was designed for, the bearing may disintegrate and cause severe injury.*

4. Turn each bearing by hand (**Figure 12**), making sure it turns smoothly. Check balls for evidence of wear, pitting or excessive heat (bluish tint). Replace bearings if necessary; always replace as a complete set.

> *NOTE*
> *On sealed bearings, it is impossible to visually inspect the balls for the conditions described in Step 4. On these bearings, replace them if they do not turn smoothly by hand.*

5. On all non-sealed bearings that check out okay, lubricate and wrap them in a clean, lint-free cloth until reassembly.

6. Check the axle for wear and straightness. Use V-blocks and a dial indicator as shown in **Figure 13**. If the runout is 0.008 in. (0.2 mm) or greater, the axle must be replaced.

Assembly

1. Pack all non-sealed bearings thoroughly with multipurpose grease. Work the grease between the balls thoroughly.

2. Pack the wheel hub and axle spacer with multipurpose grease.

> *NOTE*
> *When installing the bearings, make sure to apply even pressure all the way around the outside bearing race. If pressure is given to one side only, the bearing may be damaged as it is driven in. A good tool to use when installing the bearings is a large socket with a diameter the same as that of the outside bearing race. See **Figure 14**.*

3. Install the right-hand wheel bearing.

4. To remove the right- and left-hand bearings and the 2 spacers, inset a soft aluminum or brass drift into one side of the hub. Push the distance spacer over to one side and place the drift on the inner race of the lower bearing. Tap the bearing out of the hub with a hammer working around the perimeter of the inner race.

5. Remove the spacers and tap out the opposite bearing in the same manner.

9

4. Install the bearing spacers from the left-hand side.

5. Install the left-hand wheel bearing.

6. Install the oil seal and lubricate the outside lip.

7. Install the rear wheel as described under in this chapter.

DRIVE SPROCKET
(XT125 AND XT200)

The drive sprocket on XT125 and XT200 models is attached directly to the rear wheel hub. See **Figure 1**.

Disassembly/Assembly

1. Remove the rear wheel as described in this chapter.

2. Straighten the locking tabs on the lockwashers and remove the bolts and lockwashers (**Figure 15**). Remove the drive sprocket.

3. Assemble by reversing these disassembly steps, noting the following.

4. Tighten the bolts to the torque values given in **Table 2** at the end of this chapter.

5. Install new lockwashers.

Inspection

Inspect the teeth on the sprocket. If they are visibly worn as shown in **Figure 16**, replace the sprocket.

If the sprocket requires replacement, the drive chain is probably worn also and should be replaced. Refer to Chapter Three for inspection procedures.

DRIVE SPROCKET
ASSEMBLY (XT250)

On all XT250 models, the drive sprocket is attached to the drive sprocket hub assembly, which is equipped with rubber dampers. See **Figure 2**.

Removal/Disassembly

1. Remove the rear wheel as described in this chapter.

2. If the drive sprocket is going to be removed, straighten the locking tabs on the lockwashers and loosen the bolts prior to removing the drive sprocket assembly.

3. Remove the drive sprocket assembly by pulling it straight up and out of the wheel hub assembly.

NOTE
If the drive sprocket assembly is difficult to remove from the hub, tap around the perimeter of the sprocket with a plastic mallet to break it loose.

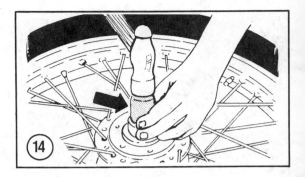

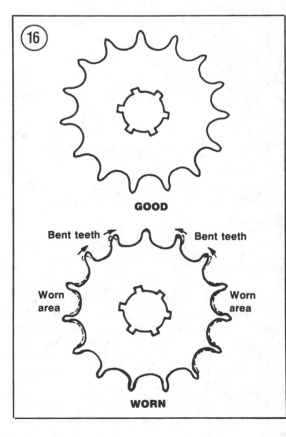

GOOD

Bent teeth — Bent teeth

Worn area — Worn area

WORN

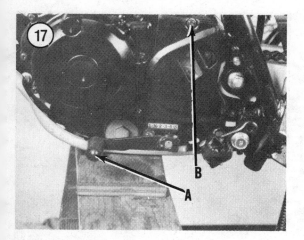

4. Remove the sprocket bolts, lockwashers and sprocket.
5. Remove the oil seal and circlip from the sprocket hub.
6. Remove the sprocket hub bearing as described under *Rear Hub Disassembly* in this chapter.

Inspection

1. Thoroughly clean out the inside of the sprocket hub with solvent and dry with comprssed air.
2. Inspect the teeth on the sprocket. If they are visibly worn as shown in **Figure 16**, replace the sprocket. If the sprocket requires replacement, the drive chain is probably worn also and should be replaced. See Chapter Three.
3. Inspect the rubber dampers. If they are worn or damaged, replace them as a set.
4. Inspect the sprocket hub circlip and replace it if necessary.
5. Inspect the sprocket hub bearing as described under *Rear Hub Inspection* in this chapter.

Assembly/Installation

1. Install the sprocket hub spacer and bearing as described under *Rear Hub Assembly* in this chapter.
2. Install the circlip and oil seal.

NOTE
Lubricate the lip of the new oil seal with grease after installation.

3. Install the damper rubbers into the sprocket hub.
4. Install the sprocket hub into the rear wheel hub.
5. If removed, install the drive sprocket and new lockwashers. Tighten the bolts to the torque values given in **Table 2**. Bend the lockwasher locking tabs up.
6. Install the rear wheel as described in this chapter.

DRIVE CHAIN

For service and inspection of the drive chain, refer to Chapter Three.

Removal/Installation

1. Place a milk crate or wood block(s) under the frame so the rear wheel is off the ground.
2. Remove the shift lever (A, **Figure 17**) and the drive sprocket cover (B, **Figure 17**).
3. Turn the rear wheel and drive chain until the master link is stopped on the drive sprocket. This makes removal of the master link clip easier.
4. Remove the master link clip (**Figure 18**) and remove the master link. On XT250 models, it may be necessary to use a universal chain link removal tool to push the master link out of the chain.
5. Slowly rotate the rear wheel and pull the drive chain off the drive sprocket.
6. Install by reversing these removal steps.
7. Install a new master link assembly. Install the clip on the master link so that the closed end of the clip is facing the direction of chain travel (**Figure 19**).

SWING ARM

The swing arm is steel. Removal and installation are the same for all models.

In time the bushings will wear beyond service limits and must be replaced. The condition of the bushings can greatly affect handling performance and if not replaced they can produce erratic and dangerous handling. Common symptoms are wheel hop, pulling to one side under acceleration and pulling to the other side during braking.

Refer to **Figure 20** or **Figure 21** when performing procedures in this section.

9

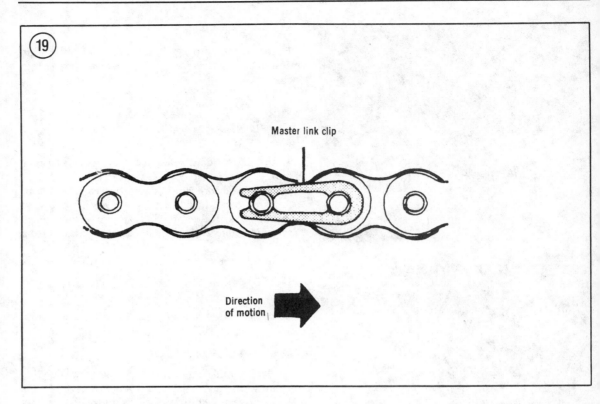

Master link clip

Direction
of motion

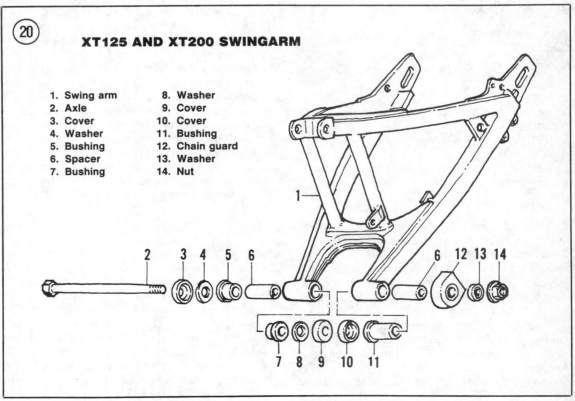

XT125 AND XT200 SWINGARM

1. Swing arm
2. Axle
3. Cover
4. Washer
5. Bushing
6. Spacer
7. Bushing
8. Washer
9. Cover
10. Cover
11. Bushing
12. Chain guard
13. Washer
14. Nut

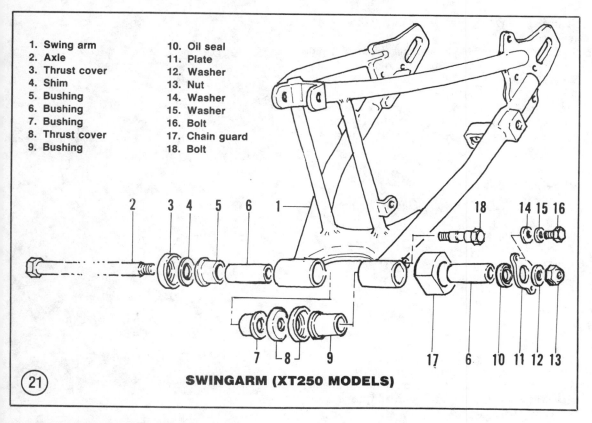

1. Swing arm
2. Axle
3. Thrust cover
4. Shim
5. Bushing
6. Bushing
7. Bushing
8. Thrust cover
9. Bushing
10. Oil seal
11. Plate
12. Washer
13. Nut
14. Washer
15. Washer
16. Bolt
17. Chain guard
18. Bolt

SWINGARM (XT250 MODELS)

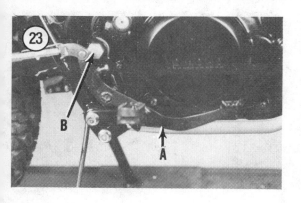

Removal

1. Place a milk crate or wood block(s) under the frame so the rear wheel is off the ground.

2. Remove the seat.

3. Remove the rear wheel and drive chain as described in this chapter.

4. Disconnect the brake rod spring from the swing arm (A, **Figure 22**).

5. On XT250 models, remove the rear brake pedal assembly. See A, **Figure 23**.

6. Remove the cotter pin and flat washer (**Figure 24**) from the lower monoshock-to-swing arm mount.

7. Slide out the pivot pin and gently let the swing arm pivot down (**Figure 25**).

NOTE
Do not lose the shock cover washers on either side of the monoshock when the swing arm is pivoted down. See Figure 26.

8. After the upper 'end of the swing arm is disconnected, grasp the rear end of it and try to move it from side-to-side in a horizontal arc. Maximum allowable side play is specified in **Table 1**. If play is greater than this and the pivot shaft is

tightened correctly, the bushings should be replaced.

9. Remove the nut and lockwasher (**Figure 27**) and withdraw the pivot shaft from the right-hand side. See B, **Figure 22** (XT125 and XT200) and B, **Figure 23** (XT250). It is not necessary to remove the engine to remove the swing arm.

10. Slide the swing arm back out of the frame.

11. Remove the chain guide from the swing arm if necessary.

Disassembly/Inspection/Assembly

Refer to **Figure 20** or **Figure 21** for this procedure.

1. Remove the swing arm.

2. Secure the swing arm in a vise with soft jaws.

3. Remove the chain guard seal from the left-hand side of the swing arm.

4. Remove the thrust covers from the swing arm.

> *NOTE*
> *Do not lose the shim behind the right-hand thrust cover.*

5. Inspect the inner and outer bushings. If they are worn or damaged they must be replaced.

6. If necessary, tap out the bushings. Use a suitable size drift or socket and extension and drive them out with a hammer.

> *CAUTION*
> *Do not remove the bushings just for inspection as they are usually damaged during removal.*

7. Wash all parts, including the inside of the swing arm pivot area, in solvent and thoroughly dry.

8. Apply a light coat of waterproof grease to all parts prior to installation.

9. Install all parts in the reverse order of disassembly. Tap the new bushings into place slowly and *squarely* with a block of wood and hammer (**Figure 28**). If the bushings seem to be cocked sideways, stop and realign them before installing any further. Make sure they are completely seated.

> *CAUTION*
> *Never install a bushing that has been removed. During removal it becomes slightly damaged and is no longer true to alignment. If installed, it will create an unsafe riding condition.*

Installation

1. Install the chain guard if removed.

2. Install the thrust covers in the correct position on the swing arm. See **Figure 20** or **Figure 21**.

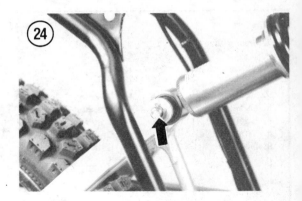

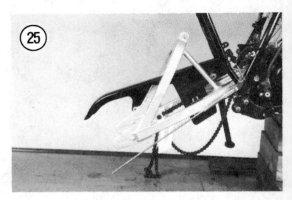

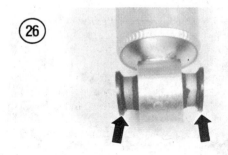

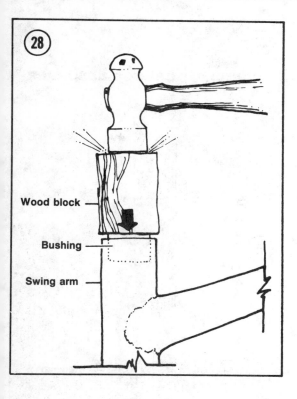

Wood block

Bushing

Swing arm

Make sure to install the shim before installing the right-hand side thrust cover.

3. Position the swing arm into the lower mounting area. Align the holes in the swing arm with the hole in the frame. Insert a drift in from the left-hand side and align the holes.

4. Insert the pivot bolt from the right-hand side removing the drift used in Step 3. Install the washer and nut. Tighten the nut to the specifications in **Table 2**.

5. Install the cover washers on each side of the monoshock (**Figure 26**).

6. Apply a light coat of grease to the upper mounting pin and install it from the left-hand side.

7. Install the flat washer and a new cotter pin—never reuse a cotter pin as it may break and fall out. Bend over the end of the cotter pin completely.

NOTE
Make sure that both monoshock-to-swing arm cover washers are installed. They are used to maintain the proper clearance between the monoshock and the swing arm. If they are slightly flattened out, replace them as a set.

8. Install the rear brake pedal assembly on XT250 models.

9. Connect the rear brake rod spring to the swing arm.

10. Install the rear wheel as described in this chapter.

11. Install the seat.

REAR SUSPENSION
(DECARBON MONOCROSS SYSTEM)

The rear suspension on all XT models is basically the same. The monoshock unit is tucked into the upper section of the frame.

System Operation

The monoshock unit is a nitrogen-charged, free-piston shock constructed of a single cylinder (**Figure 29**).

Basically the monoshock unit works as follows: in the stretch stroke, the oil is forced downward by the change in gas pressure. As the piston speed increases, the floating valve allows the oil to flow faster, creating friction and damping the stretch of the suspension. The damping amount is automatically controlled according to the speed of the piston movement.

In the compression stroke, the oil stored under the piston moves upward, compressing the nitrogen in the gas chamber. Again, as the piston moves faster, the floating valve reacts, allowing the oil to move faster, thus creating a damping force. The damping is controlled automatically by the speed of the piston.

WARNING
The monoshock unit contains highly compressed nitrogen gas. Do not tamper with or attempt to open the damper/cylinder assembly. See the warning label on your monoshock (Figure 30). Do not place it near an open flame or other extreme heat. Do not weld on the frame near it. Do not dispose of the damper subassembly yourself. Take it to a Yamaha dealer where it can be deactivated and disposed of properly.

Spring Adjustment

The spring preload can be adjusted to suit riding conditions:

a. Increase in spring length: Spring preload is decreased. This softens the shock and slows the rebound action.

b. Decrease in spring length: Spring preload is increased. This stiffens the shock and quickens the rebound action.

9

1. Remove the monoshock as described in this chapter.

2. Loosen the monoshock locknut (A, **Figure 31**). Turn the adjustment nut clockwise to increase the preload or counterclockwise to decrease the preload. See **Figure 32**. Do not exceed specifications in **Table 3** when adjusting shock spring length.

NOTE
One complete turn of the adjustment nut will change the preload approximately 1/32 in. (1 mm). Make changes in increments of 3/32 in. (2 mm).

3. Install the monoshock unit as described in this chapter and test ride the bike after each adjustment. Select the adjustment that offers you the best riding condition and comfort.

Monoshock Removal/Installation

1. Place a milk crate or wood block(s) under the frame to lift the rear wheel off the ground at least 10-12 inches.

2. Remove the seat.

3. Remove the fuel tank. See Chapter Six.

4. Remove the nut and flat washer (**Figure 33**) securing the monoshock to the frame. Remove the pivot pin.

5. Remove the cotter pin and flat washer (**Figure 34**) securing the monoshock to the swing arm. Remove the pivot pin and discard the cotter pin.

6. Pivot down the rear wheel and swing arm. Do not lose the 2 cover washers on each side of the lower monoshock mount.

7. Carefully withdraw the monoshock assembly through the rear of the frame over the rear wheel.

NOTE
If you cannot withdraw the monoshock over the rear wheel, either block up the frame higher (make sure it is stable) or remove the rear wheel.

8. Install by reversing these removal steps, noting the following.

9. Insert the monoshock with the spring locknut facing toward the front of the bike.

10. Install the cover washers (**Figure 35**) on each side of the monoshock at the lower end.

11. Apply a light coat of grease to each pivot pin prior to installing it. Insert the upper pivot pin from the left-hand side and the lower pivot pin from the right-hand side.

12. Install the washer and nut on the upper pivot pin and tighten it to specifications in **Table 2**.

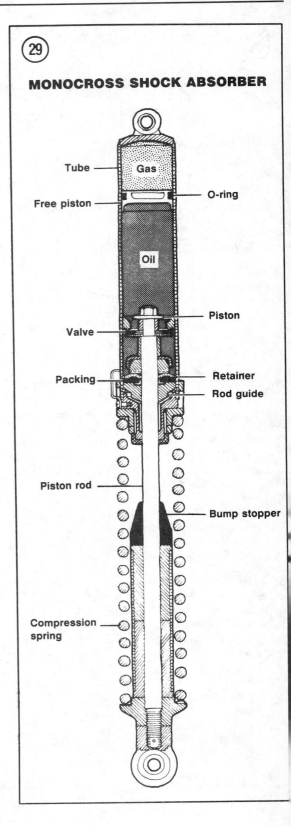

(29)

MONOCROSS SHOCK ABSORBER

Tube — Gas

Free piston — O-ring

Oil

Piston

Valve

Packing — Retainer

Rod guide

Piston rod — Bump stopper

Compression spring

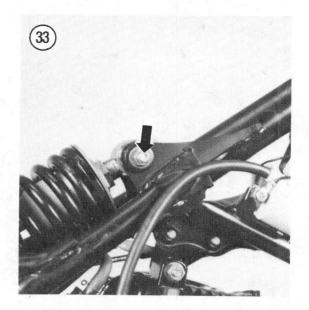

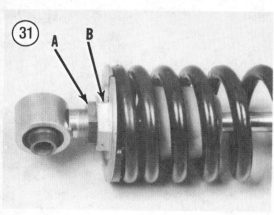

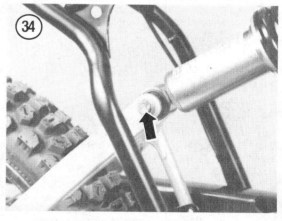

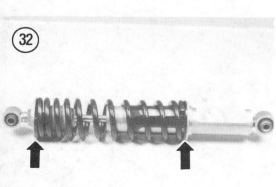

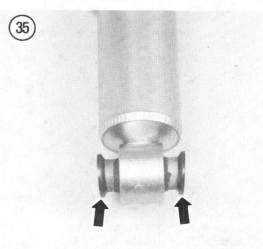

9

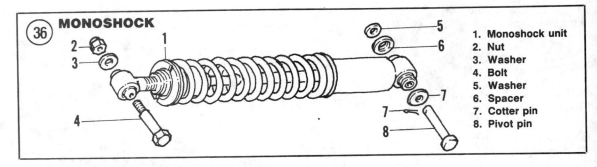

MONOSHOCK

36

1. Monoshock unit
2. Nut
3. Washer
4. Bolt
5. Washer
6. Spacer
7. Cotter pin
8. Pivot pin

Install a *new* cotter pin on the lower pivot pin—never reuse a cotter pin as it may break and fall out. Bend over the end of the cotter pin completely.

> *NOTE*
> *Make sure that both cover washers are installed. They are necessary to maintain the proper clearance between the monoshock and the swing arm. If they are slightly flattened out, replace them as a set.*

Monoshock Disassembly/Inspection/Assembly

Refer to **Figure 36** for this procedure. The spring on the monoshock unit is not under the same amount of pressure as those used on a dual-shock rear suspension. Therefore a spring compression tool is not needed for disassembly.

> *NOTE*
> *This procedure describes disassembly for all models. However, replacement parts are available for the XT250 monoshock units only. If any part (other than bushings) is damaged on the XT125 or XT200 monoshock unit, the entire shock must be replaced.*

1. Remove the monoshock as described in this chapter.

> *NOTE*
> *In order to maintain the same spring pre-load adjustment, measure the spring length prior to disassembly.*

2. Loosen the locknut (A, **Figure 31**) as far as possible.
3. Loosen the spring locknut (B, **Figure 31**) as far as possible. Then push down on the spring (from the top) with your hands and the spring seats

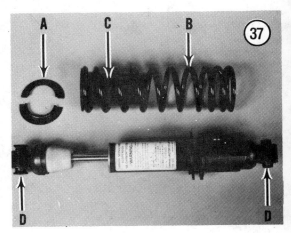

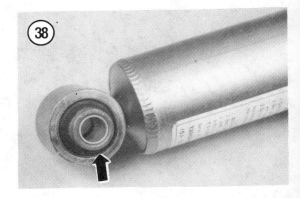

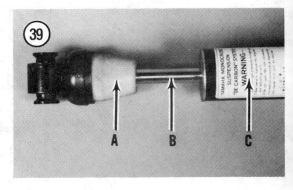

(keepers) will become loose; remove them (A, **Figure 37**) if they do not fall out by themselves.

4. Slide off the spring (B, **Figure 37**) and spring guide (C, **Figure 37**).

5. Inspect the upper and lower mounting bushings (**Figure 38**). Replace if necessary.

6. Inspect the rubber stopper (A, **Figure 39**). Replace if necessary.

7. Check the damper unit for leakage and make sure the damper rod (B, **Figure 39**) is straight.

NOTE
If the damper unit is leaking it must be replaced as a unit; it cannot be rebuilt.

WARNING
*The monoshock unit contains highly compressed nitrogen gas. Do not tamper with or attempt to open the damper/cylinder assembly. See C, **Figure 39**. Do not place it near an open flame or other extreme heat. Do not dispose of the damper subassembly yourself. Take it to a Yamaha dealer where it can be deactivated and disposed of properly.*

8. Install the spring, making sure all parts are in their correct position; refer to **Figure 36**.

9. Install the spring seats (keepers) and adjust the spring length to the installed length before disassembly. See *Spring Adjustment* in this chapter.

10. Install the monoshock as described in this chapter.

9

Table 1 REAR SUSPENSION SPECIFICATIONS

Shock absorber travel	
XT125	3.23 in. (82 mm)
XT200	3.62 in. (92 mm)
XT250	4.06 in. (103 mm)
Shock absorber spring length	
XT125	8.86 in. (225 mm)
XT200	10.43 in. (265 mm)
XT250	11.8 in. (300 mm)
Swing arm free play limit	0.04 in. (1.0 mm)
Rear wheel runout limit	0.08 in. (2.0 mm)

Table 2 REAR SUSPENSION TIGHTENING TORQUES

Item	ft.-lb.	N•m
Rear axle nut		
XT125 and XT200	61	85
XT250	75	105
Swing arm pivot shaft		
XT125 and XT200	58	80
XT250	47	65
Rear sprocket bolts	22	30
Rear shock unit		
XT125 and XT200		
Mounting bolts	18	25
Locknut	40	55
XT250		
Mounting bolts	18	25

Table 3 MONOSHOCK SPRING ADJUSTMENT SPECIFICATIONS

	in.	mm
XT125		
Standard length	9.72	247
Adjustment range	9.84-9.25	250-235
XT200		
Standard length	10.16	258
Adjustment range	10.24-9.65	260-245
XT250		
Standard length	11.3	287
Adjustment range	11.0-11.6	280-295

CHAPTER TEN

BRAKES

Both the front and rear brake are drum type. The brake system consists of a brake drum, camshaft, pivot post, brake shoes and linings. See **Figure 1**. Activating the brake hand lever or foot pedal pulls the cable or rod which in turn rotates the camshaft. This forces the brake shoes out into contact with the brake drum.

Lever and pedal free play must be maintained on both brakes to minimize brake drag and premature brake wear and to compensate for brake lining wear. Refer to in Chapter Three for complete adjustment procedures.

The front brake cable on all models must be inspected and replaced periodically as it stretches with use until it can no longer be properly adjusted. To increase cable life, it should be periodically lubricated as described in Chapter Three.

Brake specifications are found in **Table 1**, located at the end of this chapter.

FRONT AND REAR BRAKE

The front and rear brake assemblies are almost identical and both are covered in the same procedure. Where differences occur they are identified.

Disassembly

Refer to **Figure 2**.
1. Remove the front or rear wheel as described in Chapter Eight or Chapter Nine.
2. Pull the brake assembly straight up and out of the brake drum. See **Figure 3**.

> *NOTE*
> *Do not touch the brake linings (**Figure 4**) during removal. Instead place a clean shop rag on the linings to protect them from oil and grease.*

> *NOTE*
> *Prior to removing the brake shoes from the backing plate, measure them as described under **Inspection** in this chapter.*

3. Examine the brake shoes for identification marks "L" or "R." See **Figure 5**. These markings represent left- and right-hand brake shoes. If the

10

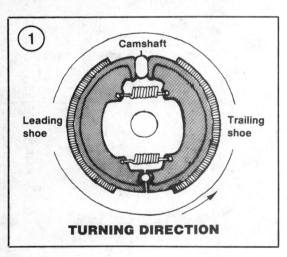

① Camshaft

Leading shoe

Trailing shoe

TURNING DIRECTION

brake shoes on your bike are not identified, mark them with a grease pencil to represent alignment. The brake shoes must be returned to their original position during installation.

4. Remove the brake shoes from the backing plate by firmly pulling up on the center of each shoe as shown in **Figure 6**.

5. Remove the return springs and separate the shoes.

6. Loosen the bolt (A, **Figure 7**) securing the brake lever to the cam. Remove the lever, dust seal (if present), wear indicator and camshaft.

Inspection

1. Thoroughly clean and dry all parts except the linings.

2. Check the contact surface of the drum (**Figure 8**) for scoring. If there are grooves deep enough to snag a fingernail, the drum should be reground and new shoes fitted. This type of wear can be avoided to a great extent if the brakes are disassembled and thoroughly cleaned after riding the bike in water, mud or deep sand.

> *NOTE*
> *Oil and grease on the drum surface should be cleaned with a clean rag soaked in lacquer thinner—do not use any solvent that may leave an oil residue.*

3. Check the bearing seal (**Figure 9**) for damage that could allow axle grease to contaminate the

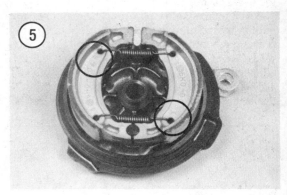

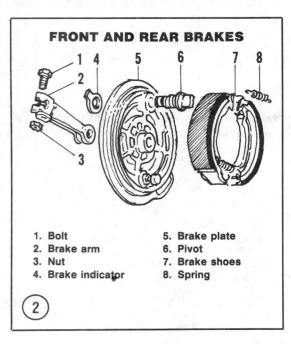

FRONT AND REAR BRAKES

1. Bolt
2. Brake arm
3. Nut
4. Brake indicator
5. Brake plate
6. Pivot
7. Brake shoes
8. Spring

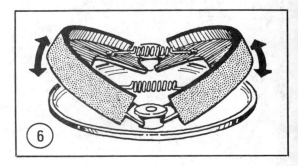

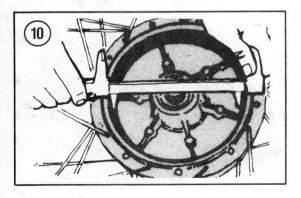

brake linings. If the seal is damaged, it must be replaced. Refer to Chapter Eight or Chapter Nine for front or rear wheel bearing removal.

4. Use vernier calipers and check the inside diameter of the drum for out-of-roundness or excessive wear (**Figure 10**). Replace the drum if worn beyond specifications (**Table 1**).

5. Inspect the linings for imbedded foreign material. Dirt can be removed with a stiff wire brush. Check for traces of oil or grease; if contaminated, they must be replaced.

6. Measure the brake linings with vernier calipers (**Figure 11**). They should be replaced as a set if worn beyond specifications (**Table 1**).

7. Inspect the cam lobe (A, **Figure 12**) and the pivot pin area on the shaft (B, **Figure 12**) for wear and corrosion. Minor roughness can be removed with fine emery cloth.

8. Inspect the backing plate bearing surface (C, **Figure 12**). If worn or damaged, the backing plate must be replaced. The camshaft should also be replaced at the same time.

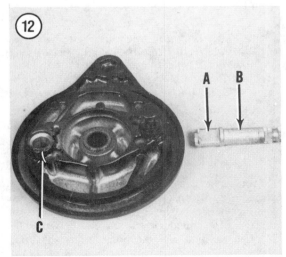

10

9. Inspect the brake shoe return springs (**Figure 13**) for wear. If they are stretched, they will not fully retract the brake shoes from the drum, resulting in a power-robbing drag on the drums and premature wear of the linings. Also check springs for rust. Replace as necessary; always replace as a pair.

Assembly

1. Assemble the brakes by reversing the disassembly steps, noting the following.
2. Grease the shaft, cam and pivot post with a light coat of multipurpose brake grease (**Figure 14**); avoid getting any grease on the brake plate where the linings come in contact with it.

> *CAUTION*
> *Make sure to use a grease that can withstand high braking temperatures without thinning. A lightweight grease will run onto the brake drum area and contaminate the brake linings.*

3. Install the cam into the backing plate from the backside. From the outside of the backing plate install the dust seal (if so equipped). Install the wear indicator and push it down onto the backing plate.
4. When installing the brake lever onto the brake camshaft, be sure to align the punch marks on the two parts (B, **Figure 7**).
5. Hold the brake shoes in a "V" formation with the return springs attached and snap them in place on the brake backing plate. Make sure they are firmly seated between the camshaft and pivot post. See **Figure 15**.
6. Install the brake panel assembly onto the brake drum.
7. Install the front or rear wheel as described in Chapter Eight or Chapter Nine.

> *NOTE*
> *When installing the front or rear wheels, be sure that the locating slot in the brake panel is engaged with the boss on the front fork (**Figure 16**) or swing arm (**Figure 17**).*

8. Adjust the front brake as described in Chapter Three. Adjust the rear brake as described in Chapter Three.

FRONT BRAKE CABLE

Front brake cable adjustment should be checked periodically because the cable stretches with use and increases brake lever free play. Free play is the distance the brake lever travels between the released position and the point where the brake shoes come in contact with the brake drum.

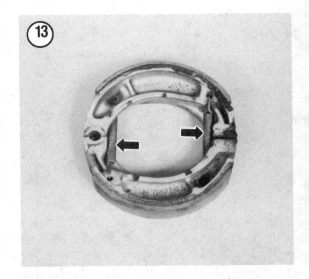

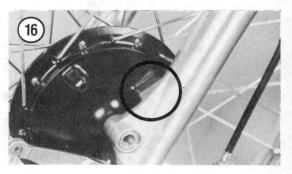

If brake adjustment (as described in Chapter Three) can no longer be achieved and the brake linings are not worn excessively, the cable must be replaced.

Replacement

1. At the hand lever, slide back the protective cover. Loosen the locknut and turn the adjusting barrel (**Figure 18**) all the way toward the cable sheath.

2. At the brake assembly, loosen the locknut (A, **Figure 19**) and screw it all the way toward the cable sheath. Unhook the cable end from the end of the brake lever (B, **Figure 19**) and pull the cable out of the receptacle on the backing plate (C, **Figure 19**).

3. Pull the hand lever all the way to the grip, remove the cable nipple from the lever and remove the cable.

4. Disconnect the cable at the fork tube. See **Figure 20**.

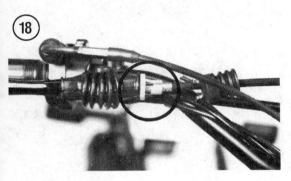

> *NOTE*
> *Prior to removing the cable, make a drawing of the cable routing through the frame. It is very easy to forget once it has been removed. Replace it exactly as it was, avoiding any sharp turns.*

5. Withdraw the cable from the holders on the front fork.

6. Install by reversing these removal steps.

7. Adjust the brake as described in Chapter Three.

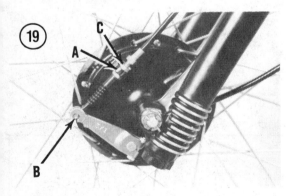

REAR BRAKE
PEDAL ASSEMBLY

Removal/Installation

1. Place a milk crate or wood block(s) under the frame to hold the bike securely in place.

2. Completely unscrew the adjustment screw (**Figure 21**) from the brake rod.

10

3. Unhook the tension spring (A, **Figure 22**) and rear brake light switch spring (B, **Figure 22**) from the brake rod.

4. On XT125 and XT200 models, remove the right-hand side foot pegs (A, **Figure 23**) and remove the brake pedal assembly. On XT250 models, remove the spring clip from the backside (**Figure 24**) of the brake pedal and slide the brake pedal assembly out of the frame. On all models remove the brake pedal with the brake rod.

5. Install by reversing these removal steps, noting the following.

6. Apply grease to the brake arm pivot shaft and the shaft receptacle in the frame prior to installing the brake pedal assembly. Make sure that all springs are properly attached.

7. Adjust the rear brake pedal as described in Chapter Three.

Table 1 BRAKE SPECIFICATIONS

Item	Standard	Wear limit
Front drum inside diameter	5.12 in. (130 mm)	5.16 in. (131 mm)
Rear drum inside diameter		
XT125 and XT200	4.33 in. (110 mm)	4.37 in. (111 mm)
XT250	NA*	5.12 in. (130 mm)
Brake lining thickness (front and rear)	0.16 in. (4 mm)	0.08 in. (2 mm)
* Not available.		

CHAPTER ELEVEN

FRAME AND REPAINTING

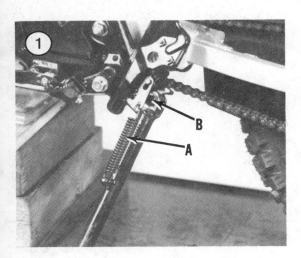

The frame does not require routine maintenance. However, it should be inspected immediately after any accident or spill.

This chapter describes procedures for completely stripping the frame. In addition, recommendations are provided for repainting the stripped frame.

This chapter also includes procedures for the sidestand and the footpegs.

SIDESTAND

Removal/Installation

1. Place a milk crate or wood block(s) under the frame to support the bike securely.
2. Raise the sidestand and disconnect the return spring (A, **Figure 1**) from the frame with Vise Grips.
3. Unbolt the sidestand from the frame (B, **Figure 1**).
4. Install by reversing these removal steps. Apply a light coat of multipurpose grease to the pivot surfaces of the frame tab and the sidestand prior to installation.

FOOTPEGS

Replacement

Remove the bolt(s) securing the front footpegs (**Figure 2**) to the frame.

Make sure the spring and pivot pin are in good conditon and not broken. Replace as necessary.

FRAME

The frame does not require periodic maintenance. However, all welds should be

11

examined immediately after any accident, even a slight one.

Component Removal/Installation

1. Remove the seat, side cover panels and fuel tank.
2. Remove the engine as described in Chapter Four.
3. Remove the front wheel, steering and suspension components as described in Chapter Eight.
4. Remove the rear wheel, fender, monoshock and swing arm as described in Chapter Nine.
5. Remove the battery, lighting and other electrical equipment. Remove the wiring harness. See Chapter Seven.
6. Remove the sidestand and footpegs as described in this chapter.
7. Remove the bearing races from the steering head tube as described in Chapter Eight.
8. Check the frame for bends, cracks or other damage, especially around welded joints and areas which are used as mounting points.
9. Assemble by reversing the removal steps.

Stripping and Painting

Remove all components from the frame. Thoroughly strip off all old paint. The best way is to have it sandblasted or dipped down to bare metal. If this is not possible, you can use a liquid paint remover and steel wool and a fine, hard wire brush.

NOTE
Some shops have chemical stripping tanks capable of stripping entire automobiles in one operation.

CAUTION
The side covers, fenders, air box and instrument cluster are molded plastic. If you wish to change the color of these parts, consult an automotive paint supplier for the proper procedure. Do not use any liquid paint remover on these components as it will damage the surface. The color is an integral part of some of these components and cannot be removed.

When the frame is down to bare metal, have it inspected for hairline and internal cracks. Magnafluxing is the most common and complete process.

Make sure that the primer is compatible with the type of paint you are going to use for the final coat. Spray on one or two coats of primer as smoothly as possible. Let it dry thoroughly and use a fine grade of wet sandpaper (400-600 grit) to remove any flaws. Carefully wipe the surface clean and then spray the final coat. Use either lacquer or enamel and follow the manufacturer's instructions.

A shop specializing in painting will probably do the best job. However, you can do a surprisingly good job with a good grade of spray paint. Spend a few extra bucks and get a good grade of paint as it will make a difference in how well it looks and how long it will stand up. One trick in using spray paints is to first shake the can thoroughly—make sure the ball inside the can is loose; if not, return it and get a good one. Shake the can as long as is stated on the can. Then immerse the can *upright* in a pot or bucket of *warm* water (not over 120° F).

WARNING
*Higher temperatures could cause the can to burst. Do **not** place the can in direct contact with any flame or heat source.*

Leave the can in for several minutes. When thoroughly warmed, shake the can again and spray the frame. Several light mist coats are better than one heavy coat. Spray painting is best done at temperatures of 70-80° F; any temperature above or below this will give you problems.

After the final coat has dried completely, at least 48 hours, any overspray or orange peel may be removed with a *light* application of rubbing compound and finished with polishing compound. Be careful not to rub too hard and go through the finish.

Finish off with a couple of good coats of wax prior to reassembling all the components.

SUPPLEMENT

1984 SERVICE INFORMATION

The following supplement provides additional information for servicing the 1984 Yamaha XT250L and LC models. Other service procedures remain the same as described in the basic book, Chapters One through Eleven.

The chapter headings in this supplement correspond to those in the main portion of this book. If a chapter is not referenced in this supplement, there are no changes affecting that chapter.

If your bike is covered by this supplement, carefully read the appropriate chapter in the basic book before beginning any work.

CHAPTER THREE

LUBRICATION, MAINTENANCE AND TUNE-UP

ROUTINE CHECKS

Table 1 is a suggested factory maintenance schedule for 1984 models.

Tire Pressure

Tire pressure must be checked with the tires cold. Correct pressure depends a lot on the load you are carrying. See **Table 2**.

PERIODIC LUBRICATION

Changing Engine Oil and Filter

Regular oil changes will contribute more to engine longevity than any other maintenance operation performed. The factory recommended oil change interval and the interval for cleaning the oil filter screen and changing the oil filter are found in **Table 1**.

> *NOTE*
> *Refer to Chapter Three in the main book for general information on oil and filter changing.*

1. Start the engine and let it reach operating temperature.

2. Shut it off and place a drip pan under the engine.

3. Remove the skid plate (**Figure 1**).

4. Remove the oil filler cap (**Figure 2**), drain plug (**Figure 3**) and oil strainer (**Figure 4**).

5. Remove the air bleed screw (A, **Figure 5**). Allow the oil to completely drain.

6. Remove the oil filter cover (B, **Figure 5**) and oil filter (**Figure 6**).

NOTE
*If it is not necessary to replace the oil filter, remove only the lower oil filter cover bolt (C, **Figure 5**). This will allow complete draining of the oil filter cavity.*

7. Inspect sealing washers on all plugs, bolts and covers. See **Figure 7** and **Figure 8**. Replace if condition is in doubt.

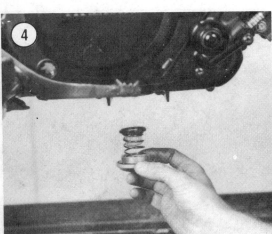

12

8. Clean the oil strainer screen, spring and plug in solvent and thoroughly dry with compressed air. Inspect the filter screen for holes or defects; replace as necessary. Thoroughly clean out the drain plug area in the crankcase with a shop rag and solvent.

9. Install the oil strainer screen, spring and plug. Tighten the plug securely. See **Figure 9**.

NOTE
Make sure the O-ring is installed on the oil strainer plug.

10. Install the drain screw with its washer (**Figure 3**).

11. Install a new oil filter. Install the oil filter cover and tighten the bolts securely (B, **Figure 5**).

12. Install the air bleed screw (A, **Figure 5**).

13. Insert a funnel into the oil fill hole and fill the engine with the correct viscosity and quantity of oil. See **Table 3**.

14. Screw in the oil filler cap securely.

15. Check the oil level. It should be above the minimum mark in the oil check window. See **Figure 10**.

16. To check the engine oil pressure, remove the oil check bolt in the cylinder head (**Figure 11**) and the air bleed screw from the oil filter cover (A, **Figure 5**). Start the engine and allow it to idle. Do not increase engine rpm. Oil should flow out of both holes within one minute. If not, immediately stop the engine and check for the cause.

17. If oil did not flow as described in Step 16, do not run the engine until the problem is located and repaired. Incorrect engine oil pressure will cause engine seizure.

18. Reinstall all parts.

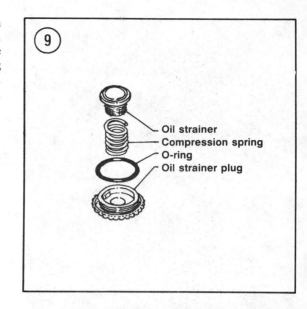

Front Fork Oil Specifications

New front fork oil replacement specifications are in **Table 3**. When changing the fork oil, first remove the handlebar as described in Chapter Eight of the main book. Then remove the air valve cap (**Figure 12**) and depress the air valve to release all air pressure from the fork. Remove the fork cap, spacer and spring seat. See **Figure 13**. After filling the forks with the correct amount of oil, refill the front fork air pressure as described in this chapter.

SUSPENSION ADJUSTMENT

Front Fork Air Pressure

The air pressure in the front forks must be adjusted within the minimum and maximum specifications. See **Table 4**.

1. Place the bike on wooden blocks and raise the front wheel off the ground.
2. Attach an air pressure tool to the air fitting (**Figure 14**).
3. Inflate to the desired pressure.

> *CAUTION*
> *Never exceed the maximum allowable air pressure of 17 psi (1.2 kg/cm²) as the oil seal will be damaged. The pressure difference between the two forks should be 1.4 psi (0.1 kg/cm²) or less.*

Rear Shock Absorber Adjustment

Spring pre-load can be adjusted on 1984 models.

1. Using the 32 mm wrench provided in the bike's tool kit, loosen the locknut and turn the adjuster. See **Figure 15**. To increase the spring pre-load, turn the adjuster clockwise. To decrease the spring

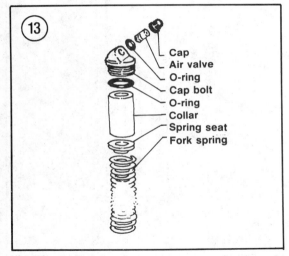

Cap
Air valve
O-ring
Cap bolt
O-ring
Collar
Spring seat
Fork spring

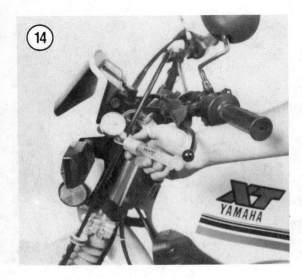

12

pre-load, turn the adjuster counterclockwise. See **Figure 16**.

NOTE
Turning the adjuster one complete turn
changes the preload 0.04 in. (1 mm).

2. The installed spring length (**Figure 17**) must be within the following specifications:
   a. Standard: 8.88 in. (225.5 mm).
   b. Minimum: 8.41 in. (213.5 mm).
   c. Maximum: 9.23 in. (234.5 mm).
3. After making the adjustment, tighten the locknut to 40 ft.-lb. (55 N•m).

PERIODIC MAINTENANCE

Decompression Cable Adjustment

This procedure must be performed after valve adjustment or whatever the the decompression cable is disconnected.
1. Place the bike on the sidestand.
2. Remove the spark plug. This will make it easier to rotate the engine.
3. Remove the fuel tank.
4. Remove the air scoop (**Figure 18**) and valve cover (**Figure 19**).
5. Remove the gearshift lever and the left-hand cover. See **Figure 20**.
6. Turn the rotor counterclockwise to align the "T" mark on the rotor with the crankcase stationary pointer. See **Figure 21**. This places the engine at top dead center (TDC). The cable

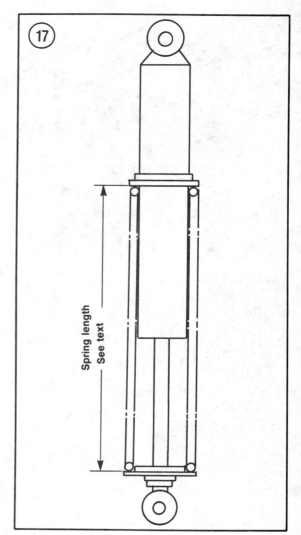

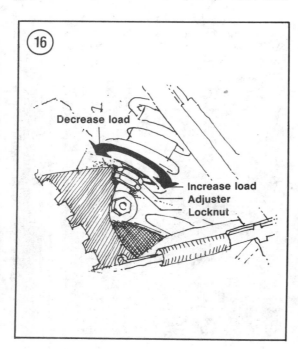

adjustment must be made with the piston at top dead center on the compression stroke.

NOTE
*A piston at TDC will have all of the exhaust and intake valves closed. Check by the camshaft lobe positions. See **Figure 22**. If any valve is open (cam lobe contacting shim), turn the crankshaft an additional 180°.*

7. Loosen the decompression cable locknut (**Figure 23**) and turn the cable adjuster (**Figure 23**)

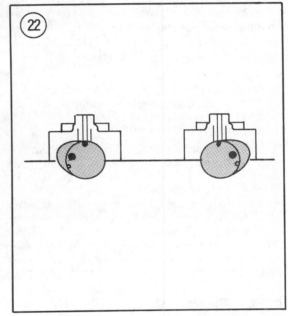

12

to obtain 1/8-3/16 in. (3-5 mm) free play at the lever (**Figure 24**).

8. Tighten the cable locknut (**Figure 23**) and recheck the free play adjustment.

9. Install all parts previously removed.

Air Cleaner
Removal/Cleaning/Installation

1. Place the bike on the sidestand.

2. Remove the right-hand side cover.

3. Remove the air filter cover (**Figure 25**).

4. Remove the air filter from the filter case (**Figure 26**).

5. Slide the air filter off of the guide (**Figure 27**).

6. Wipe out the air box with a shop rag and cleaning solvent. Remove any foreign matter that may have passed through a broken filter. Make sure the screen (**Figure 28**) is clean of all debris.

CAUTION
Inspect the filter; if it is torn or broken in any area it should be replaced. Do not run with a damaged element as it will allow dirt to enter the engine.

7. Pour a small amount of foam air filter oil into the filter and work it into the porous foam material. Do not oversaturate the filter as to much oil will restrict air flow. The filter will be discolored by the oil and should have an even color indicating that the oil is distributed evenly. Let the filter dry for another hour prior to installation. If installed too soon, the chemical carrier in the foam air filter oil will be drawn into the engine and may cause damage.

8. Slide the air filter over the guide.

9. Coat all 4 edges of the filter with grease.

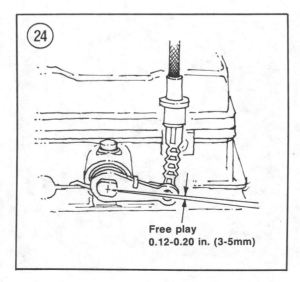

Free play
0.12-0.20 in. (3-5mm)

10. Install the filter assembly into the air box. Make sure it seats completely (**Figure 29**).

> *CAUTION*
> *An improperly installed air cleaner element will allow dirt and grit to enter the carburetor and engine, causing expensive engine damage.*

11. Install the air filter cover and the side cover.

TUNE-UP

New tune-up specifications for 1984 models are in **Table 5**. Tune-up specifications for your bike are also listed on the Vehicle Emission Control Information decal on the backside of one of the side covers. See **Figure 30**.

Cylinder Head Fasteners

An 8 mm Allen wrench (fixed to a socket) is required to torque the cylinder head flange bolts.
1. Remove the valve cover.
2. Disconnect the spark plug cap and remove the spark plug. This will make it easier to turn the engine over by hand.
3. Remove the gearshift lever and the left-hand crankcase cover (**Figure 20**).
4. Remove the oil plug (**Figure 31**) from each camshaft cap.
5. Turn the rotor counterclockwise to align the "T" mark on the rotor with the crankcase stationary pointer. See **Figure 21**. This places the piston at top dead center (TDC).

> *NOTE*
> *The piston must be at TDC to align the 2 holes in each camshaft with the cylinder head flange bolts.*

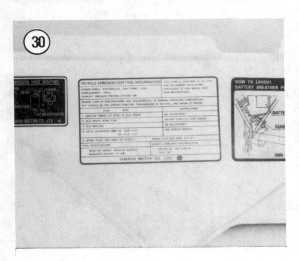

12

6. Tighten the 4 flange bolts in a crisscross pattern (**Figure 32**) to the torque specifications in **Table 5**. Then tighten the 2 nuts (**Figure 33**) to specifications (**Table 5**).

> *NOTE*
> ***Figure 34*** *shows the Allen socket needed to correctly torque the cylinder head flange bolts.*

7. Reinstall the oil plug in each camshaft cap.

> *CAUTION*
> *The oil plugs must be reinstalled in the camshaft caps to prevent an unequal distribution of oil to the camshafts.*

8. Install the valve cover.

Valve Clearance Measurement

Valve clearance measurement must be made with the engine cool.
1. Remove the valve cover and the left-hand crankcase cover.
2. Remove the spark plug.
3. Turn the rotor counterclockwise to align the "T" mark on the flywheel with the crankcase stationary pointer. See **Figure 21**. This places the piston at top dead center (TDC).
4. Insert a feeler gauge between the cam and the lifter surface (**Figure 35**). The clearance is correct when there is a slight drag on the feeler gauge when it is inserted and withdrawn. The correct valve clearance is listed in **Table 5**. Measure the valve clearance with a metric feeler gauge as it will be easier to calculate pad replacement.

> *NOTE*
> *To obtain a correct measurement, the lobe must be directly opposite the lifter surface. See **Figure 36**.*

5. Measure all valves and record the clearance. They must be measured very accurately. If any are out of specification, correct the clearance as described under *Valve Clearance Adjustment* in this supplement.
6. Install the valve cover.

Valve Clearance Adjustment

To correct the clearance, the shim on top of the valve lifter must be replaced with one of the correct thickness. These shims are available from Yamaha dealers in 25 different thicknesses from No. 200 (2.00 mm) to No. 320 (3.20 mm) in increments of 0.05 mm. These are available from Yamaha dealers. The thickness is marked on the face that contacts the lifter body.

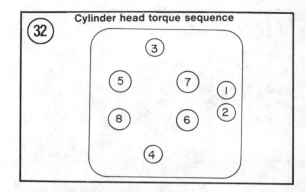

Cylinder head torque sequence

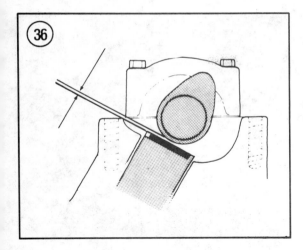

A special Yamaha tool, valve adjusting tool part No. YM-4106 (**Figure 37**), is necessary for this procedure. It is inserted underneath the cam, next to the valve being adjusted. This tool holds the valve lifter down so the adjusting shim can be removed and replaced.

1. The top of each valve lifter has 2 slots. These slots must be turned away from each other on the intake and exhaust side prior to installing the valve adjusting tool.

2. Place a shop rag in the cam chain cavity to prevent a valve shim from falling into the crankcase.

3. If necessary, remove the decompression lever stopper bolt (**Figure 38**) and pull the lever out of the cylinder head.

4. Place the valve adjusting tool onto the camshaft as shown in **Figure 39**. Make sure the tool blade touches only the lifter body (**Figure 40**), not the shim.

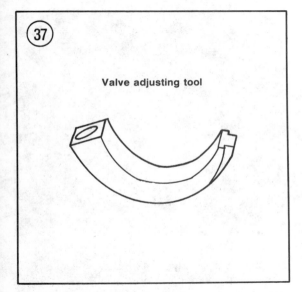

Valve adjusting tool

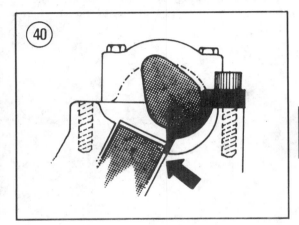

12

5. Remove the shim from the lifter with a small screwdriver and needlenose pliers (**Figure 41**). Turn the shim over and note the number. Confirm the marking with a micrometer measurement.

6. For correct shim selection, proceed as follows:

NOTE
The following numbers are examples only. Use the actual measured clearance, correct clearance specification and existing shim number from your engine.

Actual measured clearance—0.50 mm.
Minus specified clearance—0.19 mm.
Equals excess clearance—0.31 mm.
Existing shim number—220.
Plus excess clearance—31.
Equals new shim number—251.
Round off to the nearest pad number—250.

7. Install the new shim into the lifter with the number facing down. Make sure the shim is positioned correctly into the lifter.

8. Carefully rotate the cam until the lobe comes in contact with the new shim and lifter. Remove the adjusting tool.

9. Rotate the engine a couple of times to make sure the shim has properly seated into the lifter.

10. Recheck valve clearance as described under *Valve Clearance Measurement*. If clearance is incorrect, repeat these steps until proper clearance is obtained.

11. Adjust all valves as necessary, repeating these steps.

12. Reinstall the decompression lever. Adjust the decompression cable as described in this supplement.

Carburetor Idle Speed Adjustment

Procedures used to check and adjust the carburetor idle speed are the same as for 1983 and earlier models, except that the throttle stop screw

has changed. See **Figure 42**. Refer to **Table 5** for new idle speed specifications.

General Specifications

General information and specifications that differ from 1983 models are listed in **Table 6**.

Tables are on the following pages.

Table 1 MAINTENANCE SCHEDULE*

Every 300 miles (500 km) **or as needed**	• Lubricate and adjust drive chain
First 600 miles (1,000 km) **or 1 month**	• Check and adjust valve clearance
Every 3,800 miles (6,000 km) **or 7 months**	• Check and adjust engine idle speed; adjust throttle cable free play if necessary • Check and adjust valve clearance • Check and adjust decompression cable free play • Change engine oil and replace filter • Clean oil strainer • Clean and re-oil air filter • Change fork oil • Adjust brake free play • Adjust clutch free play • Check cables for fraying and lubricate • Check exhaust system for leakage; repair as necessary • Lubricate brake pedal shaft • Lubricate clutch and brake lever pivot shafts • Lubricate kick starter crank boss and sidestand pivot shaft • Check steering for looseness • Check wheel bearings for proper operation; replace if necessary • Check battery specific gravity; fill as necessary
First 3,800 miles (6,000 km) **or 7 months; then every** **6,900 miles (11,000 km)** **or 13 months**	• Check crankcase ventilation hose for cracks or damage; replace hose if necessary • Check emission control system (California models) • Check fuel line for damage; replace if necessary
Every 6,000 miles (10,000 km) **or 12 months**	• Replace spark plug • Lubricate rear swing arm pivot shaft • Replace steering bearings

* This Yamaha factory maintenance schedule should be considered as a guide to general maintenance and lubrication intervals. Harder than normal use and exposure to mud, water, sand, high humidity, etc. will naturally dictate more frequent attention to most maintenance items.

Table 2 TIRE INFLATION PRESSURE

Tire size	Air pressure
Front tire 3.00×21 (4PR)	
Cold	18 psi (1.3 kg/cm²)
Maximum load limit*	22 psi (1.5 kg/cm²)
High speed riding	22 psi (1.5 kg/cm²)
Rear tire 4.10×18 (4PR)	
Cold	22 psi (1.5 kg/cm²)
Maximum load limit*	26 psi (1.8 kg/cm²)
High speed riding	26 psi (1.8 kg/cm²)

* Maximum load limit: 201 lb. (91 kg)

12

Table 3 APPROXIMATE REFILL CAPACITIES

Front forks	10.9 oz. (323 cc)
Engine oil	
Oil change	1.34 qt. (1300 cc)
Engine rebuild	1.7 qt. (1600 cc)

Table 4 FRONT FORK AIR PRESSURE

Standard	0 psi (0 kg/cm²)
Maximum	17 psi (1.2 kg/cm²)

Table 5 TUNE-UP SPECIFICATIONS

Valve clearance	
Intake	0.003-0.005 in. (0.08-0.12 mm)
Exhaust	0.005-0.007 in. (0.12-0.17 mm)
Compression pressure	
Standard	156 psi (11 kg/cm²)
Minimum	128 psi (9 kg/cm²)
Maximum	171 psi (12 kg/cm²)
Spark plug	
Type	NGK D8EA, ND X24ES-U
Gap	0.024-0.028 in. (0.6-0.8 mm)
Torque specification	14 ft.-lb. (20 N•m)
Ignition timing	Fixed
Idle speed	1,350 ±50 rpm
Cylinder head torque	
Flange bolt (M10)	29 ft.-lb. (40 N•m)
Nut (M8)	14 ft.-lb. (20 N•m)
Bolt (M6)	7 ft.-lb. (10 N•m)

Table 6 GENERAL SPECIFICATIONS

Engine type	4-stroke, air-cooled, DOHC
Bore and stroke	2.87×2.35 in. (73.0×59.6 mm)
Displacement	249 cc
Compression ratio	9.5:1
Lubrication	Wet sump
Carburetion	
Type	TK-Kikaki
Model	Y22PV
Ignition	Capacitor discharge ignition (CDI)
Clutch	Wet, multiple-disc
Transmission type	6-speed constant mesh
Transmission ratios	
1st	2.923
2nd	1.889
3rd	1.364
4th	1.080
5th	0.889
6th	0.759
Final reduction ratio	3.200
Starting system	Kickstarter only
Battery capacity	12V 3AH

CHAPTER FOUR

ENGINE

The engine for all 1984 models is a dual-overhead cam design. The crankcase design and service procedures are the same as for 1983 models. Engine specifications are listed in **Table 7** and tightening torques in **Table 8**.

SERVICING ENGINE IN FRAME

The cylinder head, cylinder and piston can be removed with the engine in the frame.

ENGINE

Removal/Installation

1. Drain the engine oil as described in the Chapter Three section of this supplement.
2. Remove the side covers and seat.
3. Remove the fuel tank as described in Chapter Six of the main book.
4. Remove the exhaust system and carburetor as described in the Chapter Six section of this supplement.
5. Remove the bolts securing the skid plate (**Figure 1**) and remove the skid plate.
6. Disconnect the spark plug lead and tie it up out of the way.
7. Remove the alternator as described in the Chapter Seven section of this supplement.
8. Remove the drive chain master link and remove the bolts securing the drive sprocket (**Figure 43**). Remove the sprocket holder and the drive sprocket.
9. Disconnect the tachometer cable at the clutch cover. See **Figure 44**.
10. Remove the right-hand footpeg assembly (**Figure 45**).
11. Remove the following parts as described in this supplement:
    a. Camshafts.
    b. Cylinder head.
    c. Cylinder.
    d. Piston.

12

12. Disconnect the decompression cable bracket at the clutch cover (**Figure 46**).

13. Remove the clutch assembly as described in Chapter Five of the main book.

14. Remove the balancer gear assembly as described in this supplement.

15. Take a final look all over the engine to make sure everything has been disconnected.

16. Remove the bolts and nuts securing the front engine hanger bolts and remove the engine hanger. See **Figure 47**.

17. Remove the lower rear engine mount bolt (**Figure 48**).

> *WARNING*
> *The top rear engine mount and the swing arm use the same bolt. Thus, when performing Step 18, make sure that the bolt is pulled out only as far as required to allow engine removal. Complete removal will cause separation of the swing arm from the frame; the bike would then fall to the floor.*

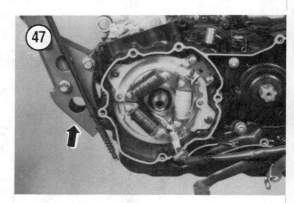

18. With an assistant steadying the engine, pull out the rear engine mounting bolt (**Figure 49**) from the right-hand side. Pull the engine slightly forward and remove it. Take the engine to a workbench for further disassembly.

19. Install bolts through the frame and swing arm so that the bike can be safely moved out of the way.

20. While the engine is removed, check all frame-to-engine mount areas for cracks or other damage.

21. Install by reversing these removal steps, noting the following.

22. Tighten the engine mount bolts to the following torque specifications:
    a. Front engine bracket bolts: 24 ft.-lb. (33 N•m).
    b. Rear engine mount bolt: 24 ft.-lb. (33 N•m).
    c. Rear pivot shaft mount bolt: 61 ft.-lb. (85 N•m).

23. If the engine was installed as a complete unit, tighten the upper engine mount bolts to 24 ft.-lb. (33 ft.-lb.).

24. Fill the engine with the recommended type and quantity of oil; refer to the Chapter Three section of this supplement.

25. Adjust the clutch, drive chain and rear brake pedal as described in Chapter Three of the main book.

26. Adjust the decompression cable as described in Chapter Three section of this supplement.

27. Start the engine and check for leaks.

CYLINDER HEAD AND CAMSHAFTS

This section describes removal, inspection and installation procedures for the cylinder head and camshaft components. Valve and valve component service in described in a separate section. Refer to **Figure 50** when performing these procedures.

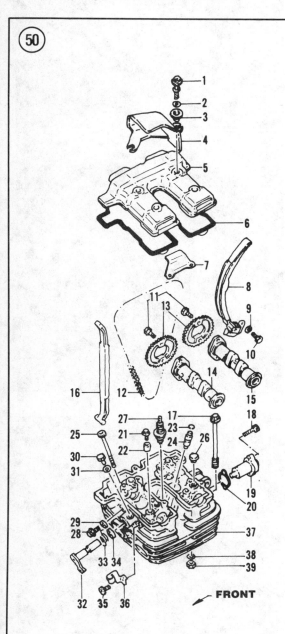

CAMSHAFT/CYLINDER HEAD ASSEMBLY

1. Bolt
2. Washer
3. Rubber mount
4. Air scoop
5. Valve cover
6. Gasket
7. Bracket
8. Rear cam chain guide
9. Washer
10. Bolt
11. Cam sprocket bolt
12. Cam chain
13. Cam sprocket
14. Exhaust camshaft
15. Intake camshaft
16. Front cam chain guide
17. Bolt
18. Screw
19. Cam chain tensioner
20. Gasket
21. Screw
22. Dowel
23. Circlip
24. Valve guide
25. Bolt
26. Oil plug
27. Spark plug
28. Oil check bolt
29. Washer
30. Bolt
31. Washer
32. Decompression lever
33. Spring
34. Oil seal
35. Bolt
36. Cable clamp
37. Cylinder head
38. Washer
39. Nut

12

Removal

1. Place a milk crate or wood block(s) under the engine to support the bike securely.
2. Remove the side covers and seat.
3. Remove the fuel tank.
4. Remove the exhaust pipes and carburetor as described in the Chapter Six section of this supplement.
5. Remove the bolts securing the left-hand crankcase cover (**Figure 20**) and remove it.
6. Remove the decompression cable bracket at the cylinder head (**Figure 24**). Then disconnect the decompression cable.
7. Remove the valve cover (**Figure 51**).
8. Remove the oil plug from each camshaft cap. See **Figure 52**.

9. Turn the rotor counterclockwise to align the "T" mark on the rotor with the crankcase stationary pointer (**Figure 53**).

10. Loosen each cam sprocket bolt (**Figure 54**) but do not remove them at this time.

NOTE
If the camshafts turn when loosening the sprocket bolts, hold the rotor with a suitable tool.

11. Loosen the cam chain tensioner bolts and remove the tensioner assembly (**Figure 55**) from the cylinder.

12. Tie a wire to the cam chain and attach it to the upper frame tube.

13. Remove the cam sprocket bolts and remove both sprockets. See **Figure 54**.

14. Lift the front cam chain guide out of the engine (**Figure 56**).

15. Check the camshaft caps for alignment marks. If none are visible, make your own marks with a punch. The original camshaft cap alignment and positioning must be maintained during reassembly. **Figure 57** shows the camshaft caps removed with their alignment marks aligned for clarity.

16. Loosen the camshaft cap bolts (A, **Figure 58**) in a crisscross pattern and remove them. Remove the chain guide (B, **Figure 58**) from the right-hand side.

17. Remove the camshafts (**Figure 59**).

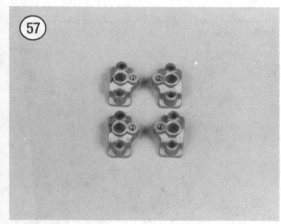

12

18. Remove the 8 dowel pins (**Figure 60**).

19. Loosen and remove the cylinder head fasteners in the order shown in **Figure 61**. An 8 mm Allen socket must be used to remove the top four bolts (**Figure 62**). Don't forget to remove the front and rear lower cylinder head-to-cylinder nuts (**Figure 63**) and the 6 mm Allen bolts in the cam chain cavity (**Figure 64**).

20. Loosen the head by tapping around the perimeter with a rubber or plastic mallet.

CAUTION
Remember, the cooling fins are fragile and may be damaged if tapped or pried on too hard. Never use a metal hammer.

21. Remove the cylinder head by pulling it straight up and off the cylinder.

22. Remove the cylinder head gasket and discard it.

NOTE
Don't lose the locating dowels in the top of the cylinder.

23. Place a clean shop rag into the cam chain opening in the cylinder to prevent the entry of foreign matter.

Cylinder Head Inspection

1. Inspect the cylinder head as described in Chapter Four of the main book, noting the following.

2. Remove the valve lifters and adjustment shims to prevent an accidental mixup. See **Figure 65**. Remove them one at a time and place them into a

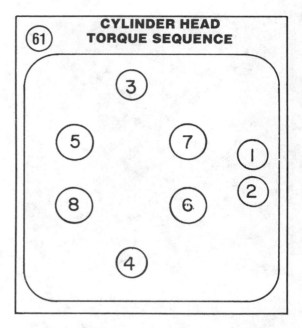

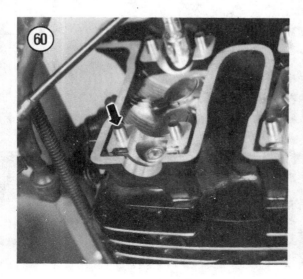

container such as an egg carton marked with their specific position.

CAUTION
The lifters and shims must be installed into their original position upon reassembly.

3. Check for cracks in the combustion chamber (A, **Figure 66**) and exhaust port. A cracked head must be replaced.

4. Check the 2 cylinder head-to-cylinder studs (B, **Figure 66**) for damaged threads or looseness. Replace the studs if necessary. Apply Loctite to the new studs during reassembly.

5. Check the cylinder head studs (**Figure 67**) for damaged threads. Replace if necessary.

6. Check the cylinder head oil plugs (**Figure 68**) for wear or damage; replace if necessary.

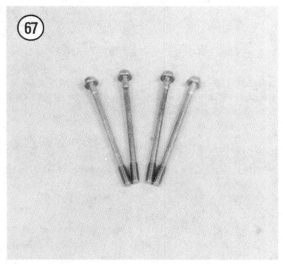

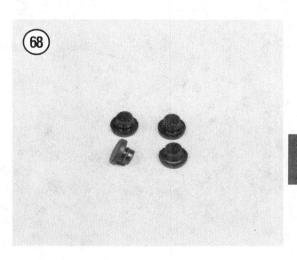

12

7. Remove the decompression lever nut (A, **Figure 69**) and withdraw the lever (B, **Figure 69**) and spring. Check the lever oil seal in the cylinder head and remove it, if necessary, by carefully prying it out. Install a new seal by tapping it into position with a suitable size drift. Install the lever assembly by reversing these steps.

8. Check the valves and valve guides as described in this supplement.

Camshaft Inspection

1. Check the bearing bores in the cylinder head (**Figure 70**) and bearing caps (**Figure 71**). They should not be scored or excessively worn. If necessary, replace the cylinder head and all bearing caps as a set.

2. Check the cam lobes for wear (**Figure 72**). The lobes should show no signs of scoring and the edges should be square. Slight damage may be removed with a silicone carbide oilstone. Use No. 100-120 grit stone initially, then polish with a No. 280-320 grit stone.

3. Even if the cam journals appear to be satisfactory, the bearing journals should be measured with a micrometer. Compare to dimensions given in **Table 1**. If worn to the service limit the cam must be replaced.

> *NOTE*
> *Measuring the cam lobes with a micrometer is important in maintaining engine performance. If the cam lobe wear exceeds factory wear limits, valve lift and timing will be affected.*

4. If the camshaft is within specifications in Steps 1-3, place it on a set of V-blocks and check its runout with a dial indicator. Replace the camshaft if runout exceeds specifications (**Table 1**).

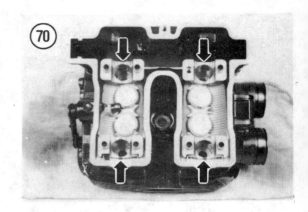

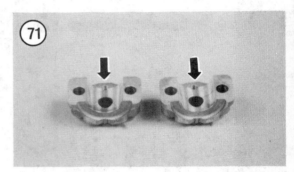

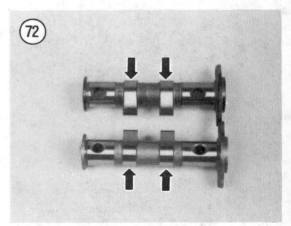

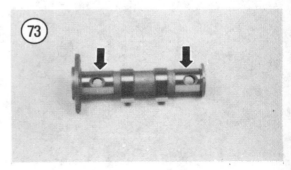

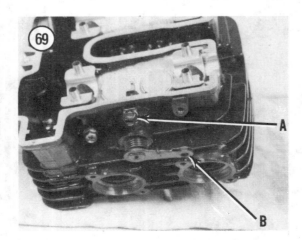

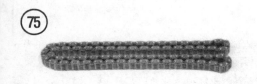

5. Check the bearing journals (**Figure 73**) for wear and scoring. Then measure the journals with a micrometer and compare to specifications (**Table 1**). Replace the camshaft if the bearing journals are worn beyond specifications.

6. Inspect the cam sprockets (**Figure 74**) and cam chain (**Figure 75**) for wear. If these parts are worn, check the crankshaft drive gear (A, **Figure 76**) for wear also. Replace all 3 parts as a set if any one part is worn excessively. Replace the drive gear as described under *Primary Drive and Balancer Gears* in this supplement and in Chapter Four of the main book.

**Camshaft Bearing
Clearance Measurement**

This procedure requires the use of a Plastigage set. The camshafts must be installed in the head. Before performing this procedure, wipe all oil residue from each cam bearing journal and bearing surface in the head and all camshaft holders.

1. If the engine has been turned, rotate the engine counterclockwise to align the "T" mark on the rotor with the crankcase pointer (**Figure 53**) to bring the piston to top dead center (TDC).

2. Install both camshafts into position in the head without the sprockets. Position the camshafts with the dot on the boss (next to the bearing cap) straight up. See **Figure 77**.

NOTE
*The camshafts are marked with an "E" (exhaust) or "I" (intake). See **Figure 78**. Install the exhaust camshaft at the front of the engine.*

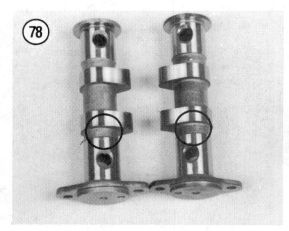

12

3. Place a strip of Plastigage on each camshaft journal lengthwise with the camshaft, as shown in **Figure 79**.

4. Install the bearing caps (**Figure 80**) in their original positions.

5. Install the bearing cap bolts and tighten them, working from the center toward the outside in a crisscross pattern. Tighten the bolts to 7.2 ft.-lb. (10 N•m).

> *NOTE*
> *Do not rotate either camshaft with the Plastigage material in place.*

6. Remove the bearing caps in the reverse order of installation.

7. Measure the width of the flattened Plastigage according to manufacturer's instructions (**Figure 81**).

8. If the clearance exceeds the wear limit in **Table 7**, measure the cam bearing journals (**Figure 71**) with a micrometer and compare to the wear limits in **Table 7**. If the journal is less than the dimension specified, replace the camshaft. If the camshaft is within specifications, the cylinder head and bearing caps must be replaced as a set.

Cam Chain Guide Inspection

Check the top surface of each guide. If it is worn or disintegrating it must be replaced. This may indicate a worn chain or improper chain adjustment. To remove the rear cam chain guide, remove the balancer and primary drive gears as described in this supplement. Remove the bolts (B, **Figure 76**) and remove the cam chain guide.

Cylinder Head Installation

1. Clean the mating surfaces of the head and cylinder block of any gasket material.

2. Install the locating dowels in the cylinder (A, **Figure 82**). Install a new O-ring on the center dowel (B, **Figure 82**).

3. Install a new cylinder head gasket.

4. Align the cylinder head over the cylinder. Then guide the cam chain (holding on to the wire) up through the cylinder head. Lower the cylinder head onto the cylinder. Secure it with the 4 long stud bolts (**Figure 83**) and the shorter bolts (**Figure 64**). Tighten all cylinder head fasteners in the sequence shown in **Figure 61** to the specifications listed in **Table 8**.

> *CAUTION*
> *Very expensive damage could result from improper cam and chain alignment. Recheck your work several times to be sure alignment is correct.*

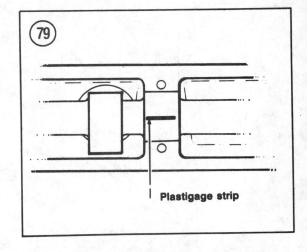

Plastigage strip

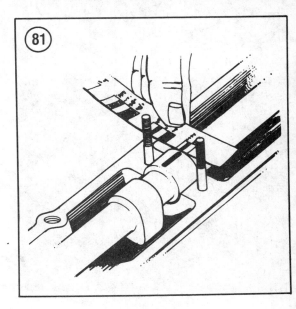

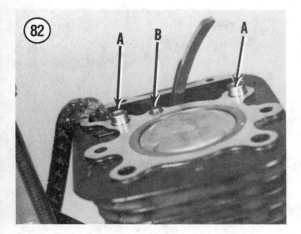

5. Turn the engine counterclockwise until the "T" mark on the rotor aligns with the stationary pointer on the crankcase (**Figure 53**). The piston is now at top dead center (TDC).

NOTE
When performing Step 5, pull the cam chain up to prevent it from binding in the lower crankcase.

6. Install the valve lifters and adjustment shims into their original position as noted during disassembly.

7. Lubricate all bearing surfaces in the cylinder head and bearing caps with assembly oil.

8. Install the camshafts through the cam chain and place into the cylinder head (**Figure 77**). Refer to identification marks cast into the camshafts: "E" (exhaust) or "I" (intake). The sprocket mount on each camshaft should face toward the right-hand side of the engine.

CAUTION
The bearing caps must be installed in their original position because they were machined with the cylinder head during manufacturing.

9. Install the bearing caps over the camshafts (**Figure 80**). Install the cam chain guide on the right-hand side (**Figure 84**). Install the bolts and tighten in a crisscross pattern to the specifications in **Table 8**.

10. Install the front cam chain guide through the cylinder head (**Figure 56**). Engage the lower end of the guide into the slot in the crankcase and the top end in the cylinder head (**Figure 85**).

NOTE
Push down on the cam chain guide to make sure it has engaged the slot.

12

11. Rotate each camshaft by hand until the cam lobes face outward and the punch marks on the end of each camshaft align with the index marks on the bearing caps. See **Figure 86**.

12. Align the exhaust sprocket with the cam chain and install the sprocket onto the exhaust camshaft. Install the sprocket bolts finger-tight. See **Figure 87**.

13. Align the intake sprocket with the cam chain and install the sprocket onto the intake camshaft. Put your finger through the cam chain tensioner hole to push the rear cam chain guide against the cam chain. Check that the camshaft-to-bearing cap marks are still aligned. If not, reposition the intake sprocket and repeat. When the marks align, install the intake sprocket bolts finger-tight. See **Figure 88**.

> *CAUTION*
> *The sprocket bolts are hardened shoulder bolts. Substitution of lesser quality bolts may cause severe engine damage if they break or work loose.*

14. Install the cam chain tensioner as follows:

   a. Replace the tensioner gasket if it is worn or damaged.

   b. Remove the bolt from the tensioner body (**Figure 89**).

   c. Insert a screwdriver into the bolt hole (**Figure 90**).

   d. Turn the screwdriver clockwise until it bottoms and keep it in this position. Do not remove the screwdriver at this point.

e. Install the tensioner (with the screwdriver still in position) onto the cylinder (**Figure 91**). Have an assistant install the tensioner bolts (**Figure 92**) and tighten them to 7.2 ft.-lb. (10 N•m).

f. Pull the screwdriver out of the tensioner body to release the tension rod. Install the center bolt and tighten it securely.

15. Rotate the crankshaft counterclockwise 2 complete revolutions and align the "T" mark on the rotor with the fixed pointer on the crankcase (**Figure 53**).

16. Check that the dot on each camshaft is aligned with the bearing cap index mark (**Figure 86**).

> *CAUTION*
> *If there is any binding while rotating the crankshaft, **stop**. Determine the cause before proceeding. If one or both cams are misaligned in Step 16, disassemble and repeat Steps 11-16 until all marks are correctly aligned. This alignment provides correct valve timing; any mistake will cause expensive damage to the piston and valve train.*

17. Tighten all sprocket bolts to 14 ft.-lb. (20 N•m).

> *NOTE*
> *If necessary, hold the rotor with a holder to prevent the cams from turning when tightening the bolts.*

18. Check the valve clearance as described in the Chapter Three section of this supplement.

19. Install the oil plugs (**Figure 52**) into each bearing cap.

20. Install the decompression cable and bracket. Adjust the decompression cable as described in the Chapter Three section of this supplement.

21. Install the cylinder head cover with a new gasket. Tighten the bolts securely.

22. Install all parts previously removed.

12

VALVES AND VALVE COMPONENTS

Refer to the procedures in Chapter Four of the main book for valve guide replacement, valve seat reconditioning and valve lapping.

Removal/Installation

Refer to **Figure 93** for this procedure.

> *CAUTION*
> *All component parts of each valve assembly must be kept together; do not mix with like components from the opposite valve or excessive wear may result.*

1. Remove the cylinder head as described in this supplement.

2. Remove the valve lifters and adjustment shims (**Figure 65**) from the cylinder head. Place them in a container with each marked to their installed position.

3. Install a valve spring compressor squarely over the valve retainer with other end of tool placed against the valve head (**Figure 94**).

4. Tighten the valve spring compressor until the split valve keeper separates. Lift out split keeper with a magnet (**Figure 95**).

5. Gradually loosen valve spring compressor and remove from head. Lift off valve retainer (**Figure 96**).

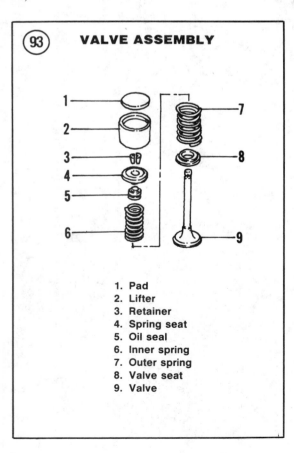

93 **VALVE ASSEMBLY**

1. Pad
2. Lifter
3. Retainer
4. Spring seat
5. Oil seal
6. Inner spring
7. Outer spring
8. Valve seat
9. Valve

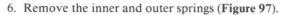

6. Remove the inner and outer springs (**Figure 97**).

> *CAUTION*
> *Remove any burrs from the valve stem grooves before removing the valve (**Figure 98**). Otherwise the valve guides will be damaged.*

7. Remove the valve (**Figure 99**).
8. Remove the lower valve seat (**Figure 100**).
9. Remove the seal (**Figure 101**).
10. Repeat Steps 3-9 to remove the remaining valves.

Inspection

Refer to the procedures in Chapter Four of the main book for valve inspection, noting the following.

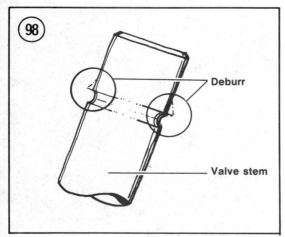

Deburr

Valve stem

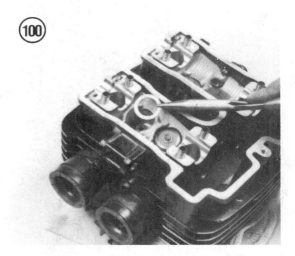

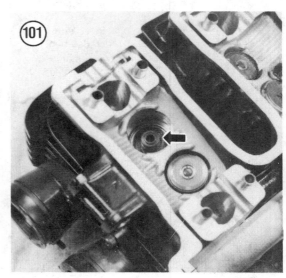

12

INTAKE AND EXHAUST VALVE SPECIFICATIONS

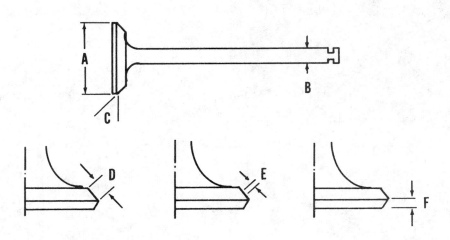

INTAKE

A. 1.098-1.106 in.
   (27.90-28.10 mm)
B. 0.2156-0.2161 in.
   (5.475-5.490 mm)
C. 45°
D. 0.09 in. (2.26 mm)
E. 0.08 in. (2.0 mm)
F. 0.024 in. (0.60 mm)

EXHAUST

A. 0.980-0.988 in.
   (24.90-25.10 mm)
B. 0.2150-0.2156 in.
   (5.460-5.475 mm)
C. 45°
D. 0.09 in. (2.26 mm)
E. 0.08 in. (2.0 mm)
F. 0.031 in. (0.080 mm)

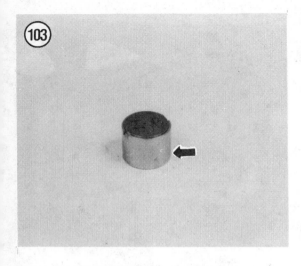

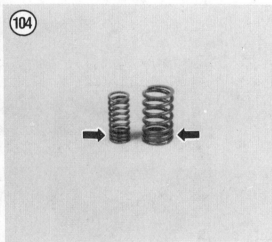

1. Refer to **Figure 102** for new valve specifications.
2. Check the valve lifters (**Figure 103**) for wear or damage. Replace if necessary.

Installation

1. Install new seals onto the guides (**Figure 101**).

NOTE
Oil seals should be replaced whenever a valve is removed or replaced.

2. Coat the valve stems with molybdenum disulfide paste and insert into cylinder head.
3. Install the bottom spring seat (**Figure 100**).
4. Install valve springs with the narrow pitch end (end with coils closest together) facing the head (**Figure 104**).
5. Install the upper valve spring retainer (**Figure 96**).
6. Push down on upper valve spring retainers with the valve spring compressor and install valve keepers. After releasing tension from compressor, examine valve keepers to make sure they are seated correctly. See **Figure 105**.

CYLINDER

Removal

1. Remove the cylinder head as described in this supplement.
2. Loosen the cylinder by tapping around the perimeter with a rubber or plastic mallet.
3. Pull the cylinder straight up and off the crankcase studs.
4. Remove the cylinder base gasket and discard it. Remove the dowel pins from the bottom of the cylinder (**Figure 106**).

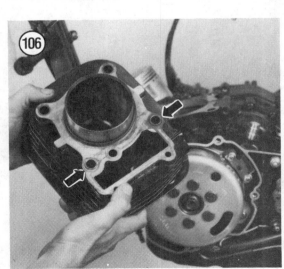

12

5. Install a piston holding fixture under the piston to protect the piston skirt from damage. This fixture may be purchased or may be a homemade unit of wood.

6. Stuff clean shop rags into the crankcase opening to prevent objects from falling into the crankcase.

Inspection

Inspect the cylinder as described in Chapter Four of the main book, noting the following.

1. Refer to **Table 7** for new cylinder specifications.
2. Replace the bottom cylinder O-ring (**Figure 107**) if worn or damaged.
3. Replace the oil dowel O-ring (**Figure 108**) if worn or damaged.

Installation

1. If the base gasket is stuck to the bottom of the cylinder it should be removed and the cylinder surface cleaned thoroughly.
2. Check that the top cylinder surface is clean of all old gasket material.
3. Install the 2 lower dowel pins (**Figure 106**).
4. Install the 3 upper dowel pins as shown in **Figure 109**.

> *CAUTION*
> *Make sure the center dowel (**Figure 109**) is installed with an O-ring. Failure to install the O-ring can cause loss of oil pressure and engine damage.*

5. Install a new cylinder base gasket. Make sure all holes align.

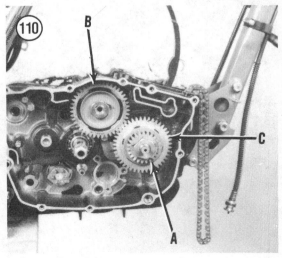

6. Carefully install the cylinder over the piston. Slowly work the cylinder past each piston ring.

7. Continue to slide the cylinder down until it bottoms on the piston holding fixture.

8. Remove the piston holding fixture and push the cylinder down until it bottoms on the crankcase.

9. Install the cylinder head as described in this supplement.

PRIMARY DRIVE AND BALANCER GEARS

The primary drive and balancer gears may be removed with the engine in the frame.

Removal/Installation

NOTE
*The gears are identified in **Figure 110**: A, primary drive gear; B, balancer driven gear; C, balancer drive gear.*

1. Remove the clutch assembly as described in Chapter Five of the main book.

2. Flatten the primary drive gear lockwasher (**Figure 111**). Place a folded rag between the balancer drive gear and balancer driven gear at the point shown in **Figure 112** and loosen the primary drive gear locknut.

3. Flatten the balancer driven gear lockwasher (**Figure 113**). Place a folded rag between the balancer gears at the point shown in **Figure 114** and loosen the locknut.

4. Remove the following balancer driven gear parts (**Figure 115**) in order:

12

a. Locknut and lockwasher (**Figure 116**).
b. Washer (**Figure 117**).
c. Balancer driven gear (**Figure 118**).
d. Woodruff key (**Figure 119**).
e. Washer (**Figure 120**).

5. Remove the following primary drive gear parts (**Figure 121**) in order:

a. Primary drive nut (**Figure 122**).
b. Lockwasher (**Figure 123**).
c. Washer (**Figure 124**).
d. Primary drive gear (**Figure 125**).
e. Pin (**Figure 126**).
f. Spring (**Figure 127**).
g. Washer (**Figure 128**).
h. Balancer drive gear (**Figure 129**).
i. Washer (**Figure 130**).
j. Washer (**Figure 131**).
k. Woodruff key (**Figure 132**).
l. Cam chain (**Figure 133**).
m. Cam chain drive gear (**Figure 134**).

6. Inspect the drive and balancer gears as described in Chapter Four of the main book, noting the following:

    a. The balancer driven gear is an assembly composed of a gear, boss, 3 pins and 6 springs (**Figure 135**).

    b. Disassemble the balancer driven gear by pushing the boss out of the gear and removing the pins and springs.

    c. Check all parts for wear or damage; replace all parts as necessary.

    d. To assemble the balancer, insert the boss into the gear, making sure to align the punch marks on the boss and gear. See **Figure 136**.

12

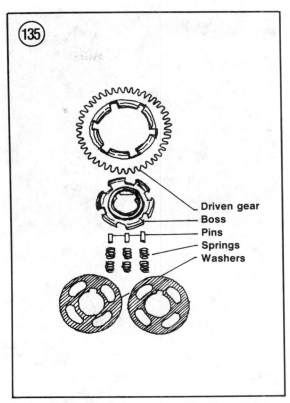

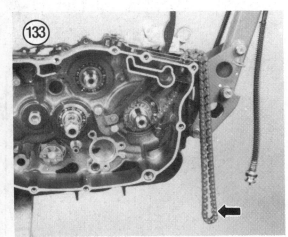

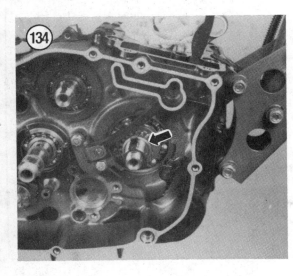

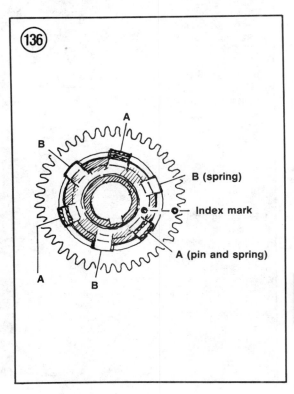

e. Install a damper spring. Then install a damper spring with a pin in it. Repeat this sequence to install the remaining springs and pins. See **Figure 136**.

7. Installation is the reverse of these steps, noting the following.

8. When installing the balancer drive gear, push on the boss instead of the gear to prevent the springs and pins from coming out.

9. When installing the balancer drive and driven gears, align the timing mark on each gear as shown in **Figure 137**.

10. Tighten the balancer driven gear and primary drive locknuts to the specifications in **Table 8**.

11. After tightening the locknuts, bend the lockwasher tabs over the locknuts.

Table 7 ENGINE SPECIFICATIONS (XT250)

Item	Specification in. (mm)	Wear limit in. (mm)
General		
Type	4-stroke, air-cooled, DOHC	
Number of cylinders	1	
Bore and stroke	2.87×2.35	
	(73×59.6)	
Displacement	249 cc	
Compression ratio	9.5:1	
Lubrication	Wet sump	
Cylinder		
Bore	2.875-2.876	—
	(73.025-73.040)	—
Taper	—	0.0002 (0.005)
Cylinder head		
Warp limit	—	0.0012 (0.03)
Piston		
Clearance	0.0015-0.0024	—
	(0.040-0.060)	—
Measuring point	0.120 (3)	—
Piston rings		
Nuber of rings		
Compression	2	—
Oil control	1	—
End gap		
Top/second	0.008-0.014 (0.20-0.35)	—
Oil	0.012-0.035 (0.3-0.9)	—
Side clearance		
Top	0.002-0.003 (0.04-0.08)	—
Second	0.001-0.003 (0.03-0.07)	—

(continued)

Table 7 ENGINE SPECIFICATIONS (continued)

Item	Specification in. (mm)	Wear limit in. (mm)
Camshaft		
Runout	—	0.001 (0.03)
Lobe height		
Intake	1.427-1.431	1.421
	(36.25-36.35)	(36.10)
Exhaust	1.427-1.431	1.421
	(36.25-36.35)	(36.10)
Diameter		
Intake	1.113-1.117	1.107
	(28.269-28.369)	(28.12)
Exhaust	1.113-1.117	1.107
	(28.269-28.369)	(28.12)
Valve		
Stem runout	—	0.0004 (0.01)
Valve dimensions	See text	—
Valve spring free length		
Inner	1.500 (38.1)	—
Outer	1.622 (41.2)	—
Crankshaft		
Runout	—	0.0012 (0.03)
Clearance	0.014-0.033 (0.35-0.85)	—
Oil pump		
Rotor to rotor clearance		
	0.0012-0.0035	0.006
	(0.03-0.09)	(0.15)
Side clearance	0.001-0.004 (0.03-0.09)	—

Table 8 ENGINE TIGHTENING TORQUES

Item	ft.-lb.	N•m
Cylinder head		
Flange bolt (M10)	29	40
Nut (M8)	14	20
Bolt (M6)	7	10
Cylinder head cover	14	20
Camshaft cap	7.2	10
Cylinder head cover bolt	7.2	10
Primary drive gear	50	70
Balancer shaft driven gear	43	60
Camshaft sprocket	14	20
Chain tensioner	8.7	12
Rear cam chain guide bolt	5.8	8
Oil pump assembly	5.1	7
Oil pump cover	5.1	7
Oil strainer plug	23	32
Drain plug	31	43
Crankcase screws	5.1	7
Neutral switch	14	20

12

CHAPTER FIVE

CLUTCH AND TRANSMISSION

CLUTCH

New clutch specifications are listed in **Table 9** and **Table 10**.

TRANSMISSION

The crankcase must be disassembled as described in Chapter Four of the main book to gain access to the transmission components. The transmission is shown in **Figure 138**.

Removal/Installation

1. Remove the engine and split the crankcase as described in Chapter Four of the main book.
2. Lift up and remove the transmission components in the following order:
    a. Shift fork shafts (**Figure 139**).
    b. Shift drum (**Figure 140**).
    c. Shift forks (**Figure 141**).
    d. Transmission shafts (**Figure 142**).
    e. Balancer shaft (**Figure 143**).

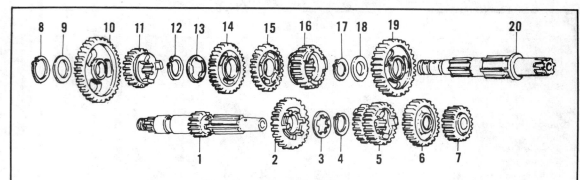

TRANSMISSION

1. Main shaft
2. Main shaft 6th gear
3. Spacer
4. Circlip
5. Main shaft 3rd/4th gear combination
6. Main shaft 5th gear
7. Main shaft 2nd gear
8. Circlip
9. Washer
10. Countershaft 1st gear

11. Countershaft 6th gear
12. Circlip
13. Spacer
14. Countershaft 3rd gear
15. Countershaft 4th gear
16. Countershaft 5th gear
17. Circlip
18. Washer
19. Countershaft 2nd gear
20. Countershaft

3. Installation is the reverse of these steps, noting the following:

a. If the transmission assemblies were disassembled, make sure all circlips are seated completely in their respective grooves.

b. Prior to installation coat all bearings and sliding surfaces of the shift forks, shafts, shift drum and transmission shafts with assembly oil.

c. Make sure all cam pin followers are in mesh with the shift drum grooves.

d. Spin the transmission shafts and shift through the gears using the shift drum. See

12

Figure 144. Make sure you can shift into all gears. This is the time to find that something may be installed incorrectly—not after the crankcase is completely assembled.

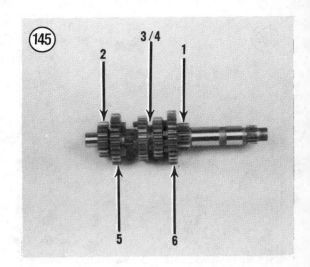

NOTE
This procedure is best done with the aid of a helper as the assemblies are loose and do not want to spin very easily. Have the helper spin the transmission shaft while you turn the shift drum through all the gears.

5. Assemble the crankcase as described in Chapter Four of the main book.

Main Shaft Disassembly/Assembly

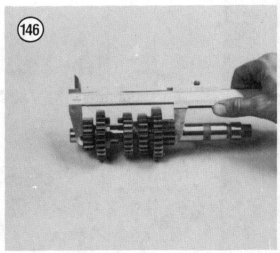

Refer to **Figure 138** and **Figure 145** for this procedure.

NOTE
A helpful "tool" that should be used for transmission disassembly is a large egg carton. As you remove a part from the shaft, identify it and then set it in one of the depressions in the same order in which it was removed. This is an easy way to remember the correct relationship of all parts.

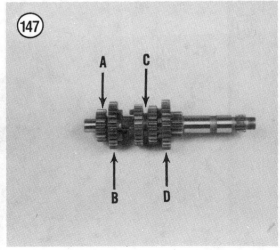

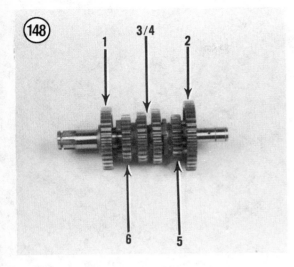

1. Place the assembled shaft into a large can or plastic bucket and thoroughly clean with solvent and a stiff brush. Dry with compressed air or let it sit on rags to drip dry.

NOTE
A hydraulic press is required to remove some gears from the main shaft. Before disassembly, measure the gear assembly with a vernier caliper (Figure 146). The correct length is 4.031 in. (102.4 mm). This length must be maintained during reassembly.

2. Press off 2nd gear (A, **Figure 147**).
3. Slide off 5th gear (B, **Figure 147**).
4. Slide off 3rd/4th gear combination (C, **Figure 147**).
5. Remove the circlip and splined washer.
6. Slide off 6th gear (D, **Figure 147**).
7. Inspect the main shaft assembly as described in Chapter Five of the main book.
8. Make sure that all splined gears slide smoothly on the main shaft splines.
9. Slide on 6th gear (D, **Figure 147**) and install the thrust washer and circlip.
10. Slide on 3rd/4th gear combination (C, **Figure 147**).
11. Slide on 5th gear (B, **Figure 147**).
12. Press on 2nd gear (C, **Figure 147**) to that the installed length is 4.031 in. (102.4 mm). See **Figure 146**.
13. Make sure all circlips are seated correctly in the main shaft grooves.

Countershaft Disassembly/Assembly

Refer to **Figure 138** and **Figure 148** for this procedure.

NOTE
A helpful "tool" that should be used for transmission disassembly is a large egg carton. As you remove a part from the shaft, identify it and then set it in one of the depressions in the same order in which it was removed. This is an easy way to remember the correct relationship of all parts.

1. Remove the circlip and washer (**Figure 149**) and slide off 1st gear (**Figure 150**) and 6th gear (**Figure 151**).

12

2. Remove the circlip and the splined washer (**Figure 152**) and slide off 3rd gear (**Figure 153**).

3. Remove 4th gear (**Figure 154**) and 5th gear (**Figure 155**).

4. Remove the circlip and washer (**Figure 156**) and slide off 2nd gear (**Figure 157**).

5. Inspect the countershaft assembly as described in Chapter Five of the main book.

6. Make sure that all splined gears slide smoothly on the countershaft splines.

7. Slide on 2nd gear (**Figure 157**) so that it rests against the countershaft stop.

8. Slide on the washer and install the circlip. Then install 5th gear (**Figure 155**) and 4th gear (**Figure 154**).

9. Install 3rd gear (**Figure 153**).

10. Install the splined washer and circlip. Then install 6th gear (**Figure 151**) and 1st gear (**Figure 150**).

11. Install the washer and circlip.

12. Make sure all circlips are seated correctly in the countershaft grooves.

Internal Shift Mechanism Inspection

Refer to **Figure 158**. Inspect the internal shaft mechanism as described in Chapter Five of the main book.

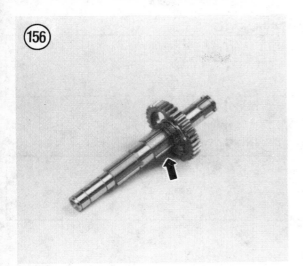

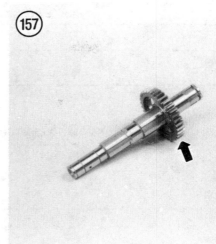

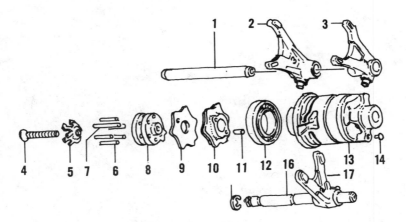

SHIFT FORKS AND DRUM

1. Shift fork shaft No. 2
2. Shift fork No. 3
3. Shift fork No. 1
4. Screw
5. Side plate
6. Dowel pin (5 short)
7. Dowel pin (1 long)
8. Segment
9. Guide

10. Plate
11. Pin
12. Bearing
13. Shift drum
14. Neutral detent
15. Circlip
16. Shift fork shaft No. 1
17. Shift fork No. 2

12

Table 9 CLUTCH SPECIFICATIONS

Item	Standard	Wear limit
Clutch springs	1.374 in. (34.9 mm)	1.339 in. (34.0 mm)

Table 10 CLUTCH TIGHTENING TORQUES

Item	ft.-lb.	N·m
Clutch boss	43	60
Clutch spring	5.8	8

CHAPTER SIX

FUEL, EXHAUST AND EMISSION CONTROL SYSTEMS

CARBURETOR

New carburetor specifications are listed in **Table 11**.

Removal/Installation

1. Place a milk crate or wood block(s) under the engine to support it securely.
2. Remove both side covers and the seat.
3. Turn the fuel shutoff valve (**Figure 159**) to the OFF position and disconnect the fuel line at the carburetor.
4. Remove the fuel tank as described in Chapter Six of the main book.
5. Remove the carburetor-to-air filter hoses (**Figure 160**).
6. Loosen and remove the 2 throttle cables at the carburetor. See **Figure 161**.

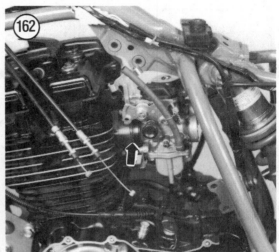

7. Remove the front intake manifold clamp (**Figure 162**).

8. Label and disconnect all hoses from the carburetor.

9. Carefully work the carburetor free from the rubber boots and remove it.

10. Take the carburetor to a workbench for disassembly and cleaning.

11. Install by reversing these removal steps. Make sure the carburetor-to-air filter hose seats in the air box completely. See **Figure 163**.

Disassembly/Cleaning/ Inspection/Assembly

Refer to **Figure 164** for this procedure.

1. Remove the fuel, drain and overflow hoses.

NOTE
Steps 2-11 describe disassembly of the secondary carburetor.

12

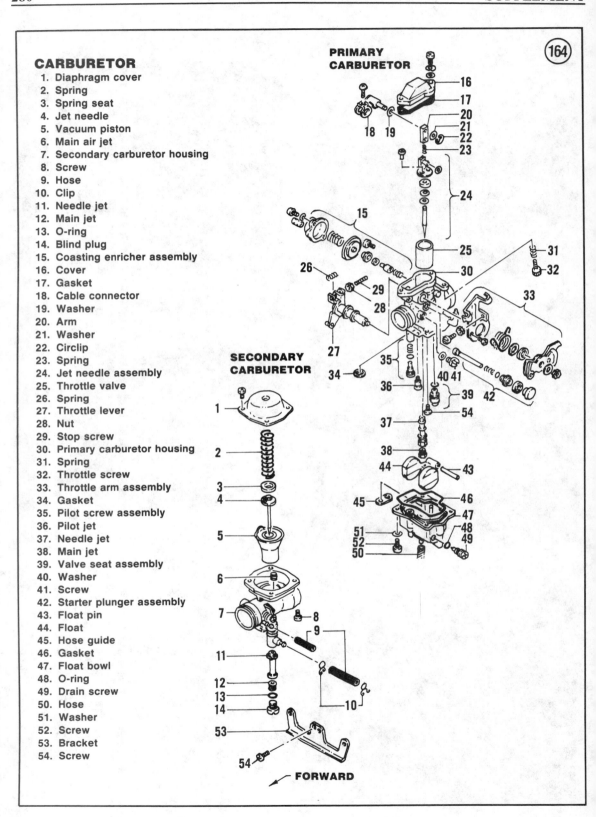

CARBURETOR

1. Diaphragm cover
2. Spring
3. Spring seat
4. Jet needle
5. Vacuum piston
6. Main air jet
7. Secondary carburetor housing
8. Screw
9. Hose
10. Clip
11. Needle jet
12. Main jet
13. O-ring
14. Blind plug
15. Coasting enricher assembly
16. Cover
17. Gasket
18. Cable connector
19. Washer
20. Arm
21. Washer
22. Circlip
23. Spring
24. Jet needle assembly
25. Throttle valve
26. Spring
27. Throttle lever
28. Nut
29. Stop screw
30. Primary carburetor housing
31. Spring
32. Throttle screw
33. Throttle arm assembly
34. Gasket
35. Pilot screw assembly
36. Pilot jet
37. Needle jet
38. Main jet
39. Valve seat assembly
40. Washer
41. Screw
42. Starter plunger assembly
43. Float pin
44. Float
45. Hose guide
46. Gasket
47. Float bowl
48. O-ring
49. Drain screw
50. Hose
51. Washer
52. Screw
53. Bracket
54. Screw

PRIMARY CARBURETOR

SECONDARY CARBURETOR

FORWARD

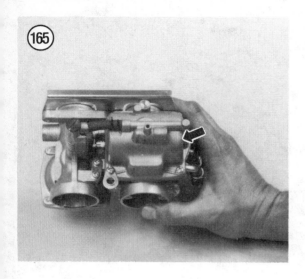

2. Remove the screws securing the float bowl (**Figure 165**) and remove it from the carburetor housing.

3. Unscrew the main jet (**Figure 166**) and remove it.

4. Unscrew the needle jet (**Figure 167**) and remove it.

5. Remove the pilot jet (**Figure 168**).

6. Remove the float pin and float (**Figure 169**).

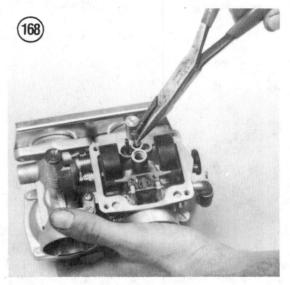

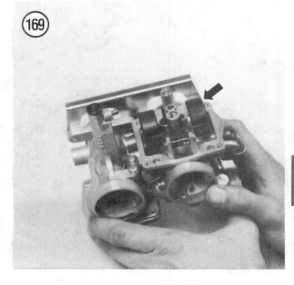

12

7. Remove the needle valve (**Figure 170**).

8. Remove the screw (**Figure 171**) and remove the needle valve seat (**Figure 172**).

9. Turn the carburetor over and remove the diaphram cover (**Figure 173**), spring (**Figure 174**) and diaphragm (**Figure 175**).

10. Disassemble the diaphragm as follows:

   a. Remove the screw inside the diaphragm piston.

   b. Remove the jet needle (**Figure 176**).

   c. **Figure 177** shows the diaphragm assembly removed.

11. Remove the main air jet (**Figure 178**).

NOTE
. Steps 12-15 describe disassembly of the primary carburetor.

12. Remove the primary carburetor cover (**Figure 179**).

13. Remove the screw (**Figure 180**) and withdraw the piston assembly (**Figure 181**).

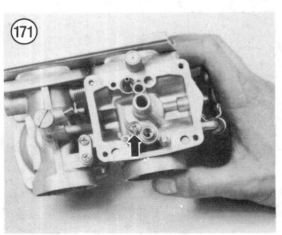

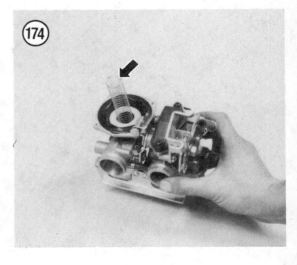

(175)

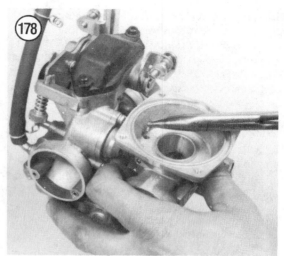

(178)

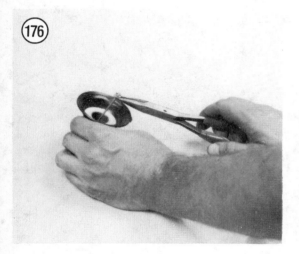

(176)

(179)

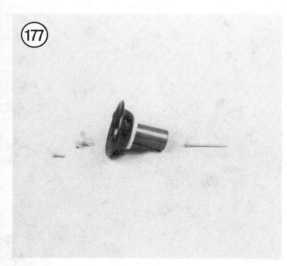

(177)

(180)

12

14. Remove the screw from inside the piston assembly and remove the jet needle (**Figure 182**).

15. Remove the blind plug (**Figure 183**) and remove the main jet (**Figure 184**) and needle jet (**Figure 185**).

16. Clean and inspect all parts as described in Chapter Six of the main book.

17. Assembly is the reverse of these steps, noting the following.

18. Install a new float bowl O-ring if the old one is damaged.

19. Align the secondary carburetor diaphragm tang with the cutout in the carburetor and install the diaphram (**Figure 186**). Make sure the diaphragm is seated completely around the carburetor cutout.

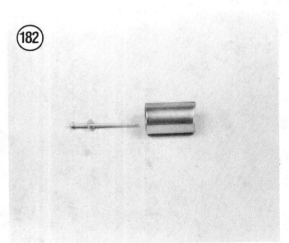

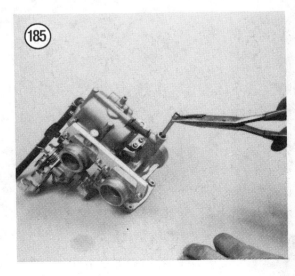

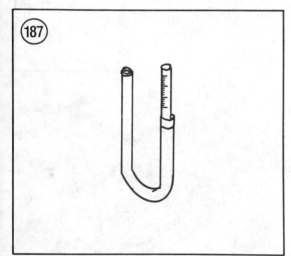

20. Adjust the carburetor as described in this supplement.

21. After the carburetor has been assembled, adjust the idle speed. Refer to the Chapter Three section of this supplement.

CARBURETOR ADJUSTMENTS

Fuel Level Adjustment

Procedures used to adjust the fuel level remain the same as for 1983 models, noting the following.

1. A fuel level gauge with an inside diameter of 0.24 in. (6 mm) must be used. See **Figure 187**.

2. Attach the fuel gauge to the nozzle shown in **Figure 188**.

3. The correct fuel level specification is listed in **Table 11**.

Primary Carburetor
Full-open Adjustment

Refer to **Figure 189**.

1. Move the cable holder (**Figure 190**) to the full-throttle position to lift the primary throttle valve all the way up.

2. Measure the height of the primary throttle valve at the point shown in **Figure 189**. The correct height is 0-0.04 in. (0-1.0 mm).

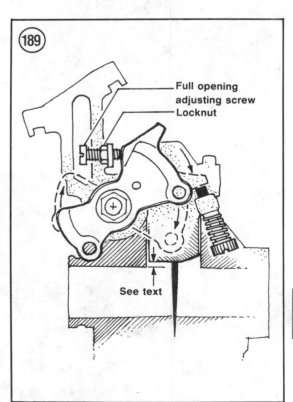

Full opening adjusting screw

Locknut

See text

12

3. To adjust the height, loosen the adjusting screw locknut and turn the adjusting screw (**Figure 191**) in or out as necessary. Tighten the locknut and recheck.

Secondary Carburetor Synchronization

Refer to **Figure 192**.

1. Move the throttle cable holder (**Figure 190**) to raise the primary throttle valve 0.24 in. (6 mm) as indicated in **Figure 192**.

2. Check that the secondary throttle shaft just begins to contact the secondary throttle push lever. If not, turn the synchronizing screw (**Figure 193**).

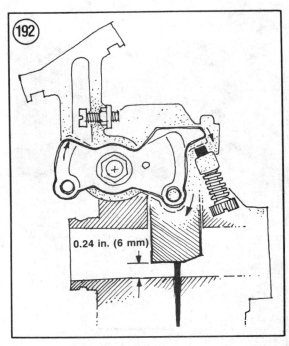

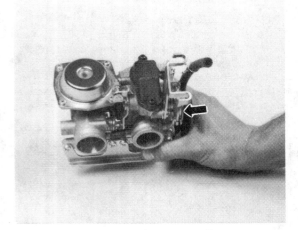

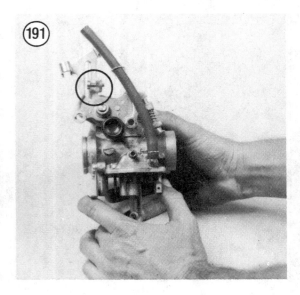

EXHAUST SYSTEM

Refer to Chapter Six in the main book for general exhaust system information.

Removal/Installation

1. Place a milk crate or wood block(s) under the engine to support the bike securely. Remove the right-hand side cover.

2. Remove the front (**Figure 194**) and rear (**Figure 195**) muffler bolts. Then slide the muffler back and remove it.

3. Remove the bolts securing the header pipes to the cylinder (**Figure 196**) and remove them.
4. Inspect the gaskets at all joints; replace as necessary.

5. Install the head pipe gaskets or seals and install the exhaust pipe assembly into position. Install the complete exhaust assembly before tightening any fastener to minimize an exhaust leak at the cylinder.

6. Tighten all fasteners securely.
7. Make sure the head pipes are correctly seated in the exhaust ports.

8. Install the seat and fenders.
9. After installation is complete, start the engine and make sure there are no exhaust leaks.

Tale 11 CARBURETOR SPECIFICATIONS

Item	Primary	Secondary
Type	Y22PV	Y22PV
Manufacturer	TK-Kikaki	TK-Kikaki
Main jet	130	125
Main air jet	1.6	0.6
Jet needle/clip position	4C98-1/1	4X71/1
Needle jet	2.595	2.600
Pilot jet	38	38
Pilot air jet	1.0	1.0
Pilot screw	Pre-set	Pre-set
Valve seat	2.5	2.5
Starter jet	GS1 #74	GS1 #74
	GS2 #78	GS2 #78
Fuel level	0.28 in.	0.28 in.
	(7.0 mm)	(7.0 mm)
Float height	1.02 in.	1.02 in.
	(26.0 mm)	(26.0 mm)
Idle speed	1,350 rpm	1,350 rpm

12

CHAPTER SEVEN

ELECTRICAL SYSTEM

New electrical system specifications are listed in **Table 12**.

ALTERNATOR

Removal/Installation

Rotor

1. Place a milk crate or wood block(s) under the engine to support the bike securely.
2. Disconnect the negative battery cable.
3. Remove the left-hand side cover and disconnect the alternator connector.
4. Remove the screws securing the alternator cover and remove it.
5. Hold the rotor with a holding tool (**Figure 197**) and remove the nut and washer securing the alternator rotor.

> *NOTE*
> *Because of the depth of the rotor on this model, a spacer must be used with the puller (**Figure 198**). A spacer can be made by cutting an 8mm bolt to the specifications in **Figure 199**.*

6. Install the spacer in front of the puller's pressure screw (**Figure 198**) and screw in the puller until it stops. Use a wrench on the puller and hold the rotor as in the previous step to keep it from turning. Gradually tighten the puller until the rotor disengages from the crankshaft.

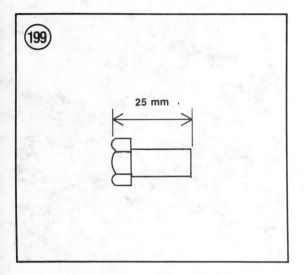

NOTE
If the rotor is difficult to remove, strike the end of the puller with a hammer a few times. This will usually break it loose. Do not hit the rotor.

CAUTION
If normal rotor removal attempts fail, do not force the puller as the threads may be stripped out of the rotor, causing expensive damage. Take it to a dealer and have it removed.

7. Remove the puller and rotor. Don't lose the Woodruff key on the crankshaft.

CAUTION
Carefully inspect the inside of the rotor for small bolts, washers or other metal debris that may have been picked up by the magnets. These small metal bits can cause severe damage to the magneto stator plate components.

8. Install by reversing these removal steps, noting the following.
9. Make sure the Woodruff key (**Figure 200**) is in place on the crankshaft and align the keyway in the rotor with the key when installing the rotor.
10. Be sure to install the washer prior to installing the rotor nut. Install the rotor nut.
11. To keep the rotor from turning, hold it with the same tool setup used in Step 5.
12. Tighten the rotor bolt to 43 ft.-lb. (60 N•m).

Stator assembly

1. Remove the rotor as described in this supplement.
2. Disconnect the stator coil electrical connectors and the neutral switch connector (**Figure 201**).
3. Remove the 2 stator plate mounting screws (**Figure 202**) and remove the stator assembly.

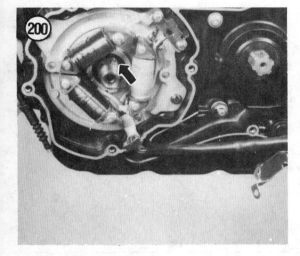

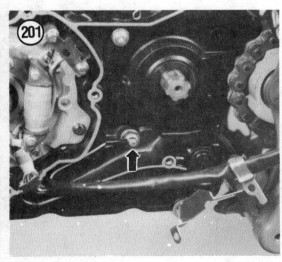

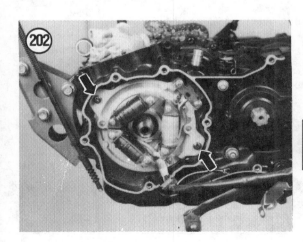

12

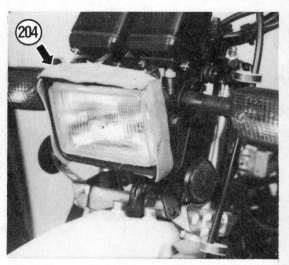

4. Install by reversing these removal steps. Clean all electrical connectors before reassembly.

LIGHTING SYSTEM

Table 13 lists new replacement bulbs.

Headlight Replacement

1. Remove the front cover screw (**Figure 203**) and remove the cover.

2. Remove the socket cover (**Figure 204**).

> *WARNING*
> *If the headlight has just burned out or turned off it will be **Hot**. Don't touch the bulb until it cools off.*

3. Remove the sealed beam unit from the bezel.
4. Install by reversing these steps.
5. Adjust the headlight as described in Chapter Seven of the main book.

Table 12 ELECTRICAL SYSTEM SPECIFICATIONS

Magneto system	
Pickup coil resistance	221 ohms ±10%*
Pickup coil test wires	Black to white/red
Charging coil resistance	440 ohms ±10%*
Charging coil test wires	Black to brown
Ignition coil	
Primary winding resistance	0.79 ±20%*
Secondary winding resistance	5.9 K ohms ±15%*
Charging/lighting system specifications	
Charging current	
Lights off	1.6 A @ 3,000 rpm
Lights on	3.9 A @ 3,000 rpm
Charging coil resistance	0.46 ohms ±10%*
Charging coil test wires	Black to white
Lighting coil resistance	0.39 ohms ±20%*
Lighting coil test wires	Black to yellow/red
Lighting voltage	12 volts or more @ 1,600 rpm

* Measurements made @ 68° F (20° C).

Table 13 REPLACEMENT BULBS

Item	Voltage/wattage
Headlight	12V 45/45W
Tail/brake light	12V 8W/27W
Flasher light	12V 27W
Indicator lights	
Meter light	12V 3W
Neutral light	12V 3W
High beam light	12V 3W
Turn light	12V 3W

CHAPTER EIGHT

FRONT SUSPENSION AND STEERING

Suspension specifications that differ from 1983 models are in **Table 14** and **Table 15**.

STEERING HEAD

Bearing race replacement and steering head adjustment are described in Chapter Eight of the main book.

Disassembly

Refer to **Figure 205** for this procedure.
1. Remove the fuel tank.
2. Remove the front wheel as described in Chapter Eight of the main book.
3. Disconnect the wiring connectors at the headlight.
4. Disconnect the speedometer and tachometer cables.
5. Remove the headlight cowling (**Figure 204**) and headlight.
6. Remove the headlight body bracket and meter assembly.
7. Remove the handlebar clamps (**Figure 206**) and lay the handlebar assembly over the front of the bike. It is not necessary to disconnect any cables.
8. Remove the bolts securing the front fender and remove the fender.
9. Remove the front forks as described in this supplement.

12

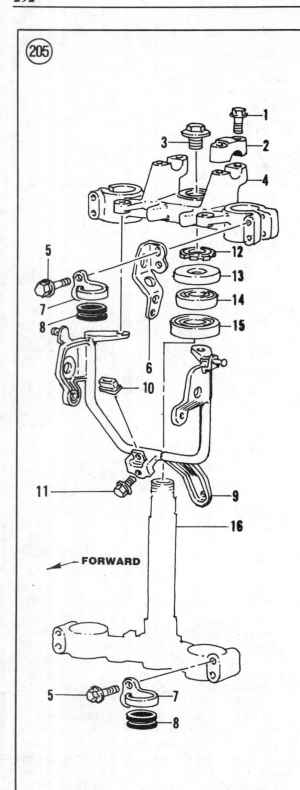

STEERING HEAD

1. Bolt
2. Clamp
3. Bolt
4. Upper fork bridge
5. Bolt
6. Bracket
7. Guide
8. Rubber collar
9. Bracket
10. Damper
11. Bolt
12. Locknut
13. Cover
14. Bearing
15. Bearing
16. Steering stem

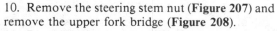

10. Remove the steering stem nut (**Figure 207**) and remove the upper fork bridge (**Figure 208**).

11. Remove the upper adjusting nut with a spanner wrench (**Figure 209**).

12. While holding onto the steering stem, remove the bearing cover (**Figure 210**) and lower the steering stem out of the frame with the lower bearing.

13. Remove the upper bearing from the frame.

Inspection

1. Clean the bearing races in the steering head and all bearings with solvent.

2. Check for broken welds on the frame around the steering head. If any are found, have them repaired by a competent frame shop or welding service familar with motorcycle frame repair.

12

3. Check the bearings for pitting, scratches or discoloration indicating wear or corrosion. Replace each bearing as a set if necessary.

4. Check the upper and lower races in the steering head. See Chapter Eight of the main book if races are pitted, scratched or badly worn.

5. Check the steering stem for cracks.

Assembly

Refer to **Figure 205** for this procedure.

1. Make sure the steering head bearing races are properly seated.

2. Coat both bearings with a good grade of wheel bearing grease.

3. Slide the lower bearing onto the steering stem.

4. Insert the steering stem into the head tube. Hold it firmly in place.

5. Install the upper bearing and upper bearing cover (**Figure 210**).

6. Install the lower adjusting nut (**Figure 211**) and tighten it securely to seat the bearings. Then loosen it enough so that the steering assembly will turn to both lock positions under its own weight after an initial assist.

> *NOTE*
> *The adjusting nut should be tight enough to remove play, both horizontal and vertical (**Figure 212**).*

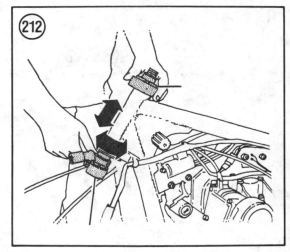

7. Continue assembly by reversing *Removal* Steps 1-10. Torque the bolts as follows:
   a. Front fork pinch bolts: 17 ft.-lb. (23 N•m).
   b. Steering stem bolt: 39 ft.-lb. (54 N•m).
   c. Handlebar clamp bolts: 14.5 ft.-lb. (20 N•m).

8. After the total assembly is installed, check the stem for looseness or binding—readjust if necessary.

FRONT FORKS

Removal/Installation

Procedures used to remove the front forks remain the same as for 1983 models, except for the following initial steps.

1. Remove the air valve cap and depress the air valve to release all air pressure. See **Figure 213**.

> *CAUTION*
> *Release the air pressure gradually. If released too fast, oil may spurt out with the air. Protect your eyes and clothing accordingly.*

2. After installing the fork caps, make sure the air valves face in the direction shown in **Figure 213**. If not, loosen the fork tube upper and lower pinch bolts and rotate the fork tubes as required.

3. Refill the front fork air pressure as described in the Chapter Three section of this supplement.

Disassembly

The fork tubes (**Figure 214**) on the XT250L and LC requires a press and special tools for complete disassembly and reassembly. Thus it is recommended that all service be referred to a Yamaha dealer. Fork oil replacement and suspension adjustment is described in the Chapter Three section of this supplement.

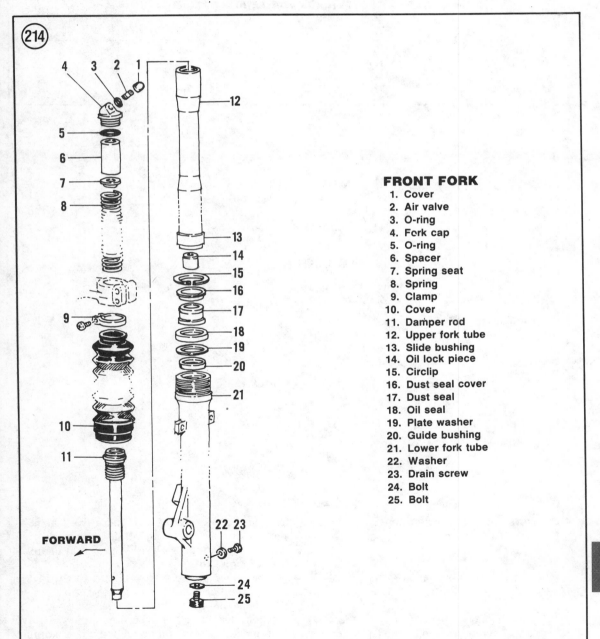

FRONT FORK

1. Cover
2. Air valve
3. O-ring
4. Fork cap
5. O-ring
6. Spacer
7. Spring seat
8. Spring
9. Clamp
10. Cover
11. Damper rod
12. Upper fork tube
13. Slide bushing
14. Oil lock piece
15. Circlip
16. Dust seal cover
17. Dust seal
18. Oil seal
19. Plate washer
20. Guide bushing
21. Lower fork tube
22. Washer
23. Drain screw
24. Bolt
25. Bolt

FORWARD

12

Table 14 FRONT SUSPENSION SPECIFICATIONS

Front fork travel	10.04 in. (255 mm)
Fork spring free length	22.835 in. (580 mm)
Front fork oil capacity	10.09 oz. (323 cc)
Oil viscosity	SAE 10

Table 15 FRONT SUSPENSION TIGHTENING SPECIFICATIONS

Item	ft.-lb.	N·m
Front axle nut	75	105
Fork bridge bolts	17	23
Fork cap	17	23
Steering stem nut	39	54

CHAPTER NINE

REAR SUSPENSION

New rear suspension specifications are listed in **Table 16** and **Table 17**.

SWING ARM

Refer to **Figure 215** when servicing the swing arm.

Removal

1. Place a milk crate or wood block(s) under the frame so the rear wheel is off the ground.

2. Remove the rear wheel and drive chain as described in Chapter Nine of the basic book.

3. Remove the shock absorber mount at the relay arm (**Figure 216**).

4. Disconnect the relay arm pivot bolt (A, **Figure 217**) at the frame.

5. When the upper end of the swing arm is disconnected, grasp the swing arm and try to move it from side-to-side in a horizontal arc. Maximum allowable side play is 0-0.04 in. (0-1.0 mm). If play

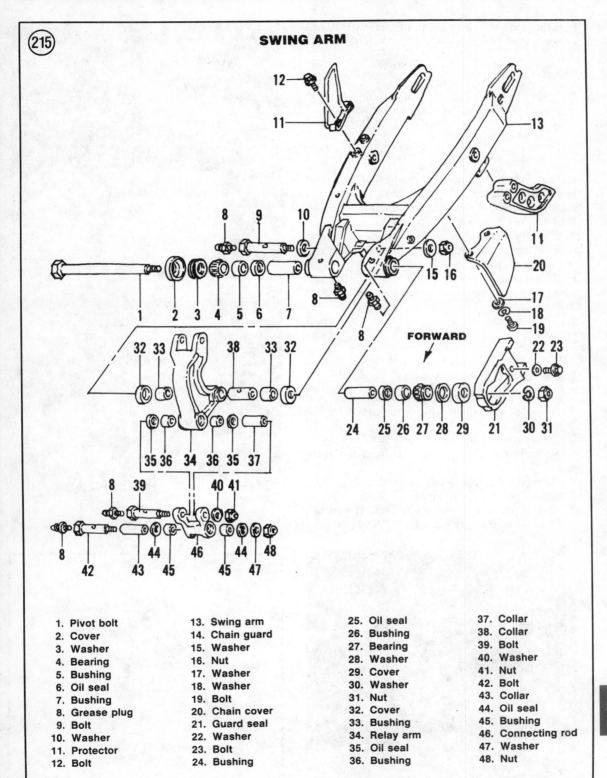

SWING ARM

FORWARD

1. Pivot bolt	13. Swing arm	25. Oil seal	37. Collar
2. Cover	14. Chain guard	26. Bushing	38. Collar
3. Washer	15. Washer	27. Bearing	39. Bolt
4. Bearing	16. Nut	28. Washer	40. Washer
5. Bushing	17. Washer	29. Cover	41. Nut
6. Oil seal	18. Washer	30. Washer	42. Bolt
7. Bushing	19. Bolt	31. Nut	43. Collar
8. Grease plug	20. Chain cover	32. Cover	44. Oil seal
9. Bolt	21. Guard seal	33. Bushing	45. Bushing
10. Washer	22. Washer	34. Relay arm	46. Connecting rod
11. Protector	23. Bolt	35. Oil seal	47. Washer
12. Bolt	24. Bushing	36. Bushing	48. Nut

12

is greater than this, and the pivot shaft is tightened correctly, the bushings should be replaced.

NOTE
When completing swing arm removal, keep track of all bushings and spacers. These must be reinstalled in their original position.

6. Remove the swing arm pivot shaft nut and lockwasher (**Figure 218**). Then remove the pivot shaft by tapping it out with a long brass rod from the left-hand side. See B, **Figure 217**.
7. Slide the swing arm back out of the frame and remove the swing arm, relay arm and connecting rod as an assembly.
8. If necessary, remove the relay arm and connecting rod from the swing arm. See **Figure 219**.
9. Remove the chain guide from the swing arm, if necessary.

Disassembly/Inspection/Assembly

Refer to **Figure 215** for this procedure.
1. Remove the swing arm as described in this supplement.
2. Secure the swing arm in a vise with soft jaws.
3. Remove the chain guard seal from the swing arm.
4. Remove the thrust covers, seals, shims and bearings from the swing arm.
5. Inspect inner and outer bushings. If they are worn or damaged they must be replaced.

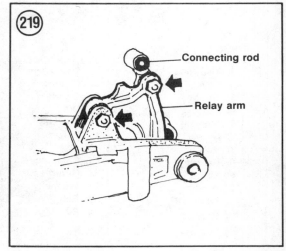

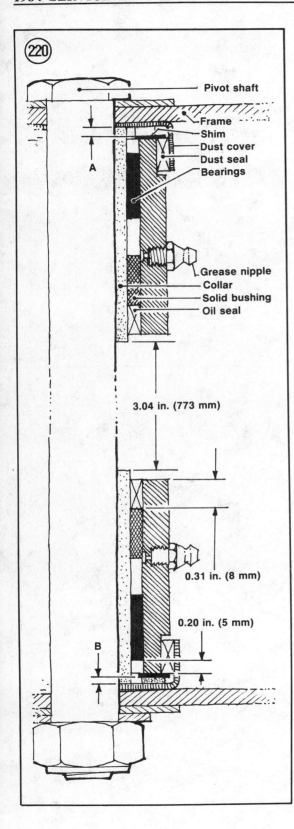

Figure 220

- Pivot shaft
- Frame
- Shim
- Dust cover
- Dust seal
- Bearings
- A
- Grease nipple
- Collar
- Solid bushing
- Oil seal
- 3.04 in. (773 mm)
- 0.31 in. (8 mm)
- 0.20 in. (5 mm)
- B

6. If necessary, tap out the bushings. Use a suitable size drift or socket and extension and drive them out with a hammer.

CAUTION
Do not remove the bushings just for inspection as they are damaged during removal

7. Wash all parts, including the inside of the swing arm pivot area, in solvent and thoroughly dry.
8. Apply a light coat of waterproof grease to all parts prior to installation.
9. Install all parts in the reverse order of disassembly. Tap the new bushings into place slowly and *squarely* with a block of wood and hammer. If the bushings seem to be cocked sideways, stop and realign them before installing any further. Make sure they are completely seated.

WARNING
Never install a bushing that has been removed. During removal it becomes slightly damaged and is no longer true to alignment. If installed, it will create an unsafe riding condition.

10. When installing new bearings and bushings, observe the following assembly specifications:
   a. Bearings should be installed at a distance of 0.20 in. (5 mm) from each end of the swing arm. See **Figure 220**.
   b. Solid bushings should be installed at a distance of 0.31 in. (8 mm) from each end of the swing arm. See **Figure 220**.
11. After installing the bearings and bushings, measure the swing arm side clearance at points A and B, **Figure 220**. The specified side clearance should be 0.016-0.028 in. (0.4-0.7 mm). If the side clearance is incorrect, adjust with 1 or 2 shims.

NOTE
If 2 shims are used, they should be installed with one on each side of the swing arm. If only 1 shim is required, it should be installed on the right-hand side.

Installation

1. Install the chain guard if removed.
2. Install the thrust covers, washers and oil seals in the correct position on the swing arm. See **Figure 215**.

12

3. Lubricate the following parts with wheel bearing grease:
   a. Swing arm pivot bolt.
   b. All bushing inside surfaces.
   c. All oil seal lips.
   d. Dust seal outside and inside surfaces.
   e. Thrust cover inner surfaces.

4. Install the relay arm and connecting rod onto the frame. Tighten the bolts to the specifications in **Table 17**.

5. Position the swing arm into the lower mounting area. Align the holes in the swing arm with the hole in the frame. Insert a drift in from the side opposite where the bolt is to be inserted to align the holes.

6. Install the pivot bolt. Install the washer and nut. Tighten the nut to the specifications in **Table 17**.

7. Install the lower shock absorber mount at the swing arm. Tighten the nut to specifications in **Table 17**.

8. Install the rear wheel as described in Chapter Nine of the basic book.

REAR SUSPENSION (DECARBON MONOCROSS SYSTEM)

WARNING
The monoshock unit contains highly compressed nitrogen gas. Do not tamper with or attempt to open the damper/cylinder assembly. See the warning label on your monoshock. Do not place it near an open flame or other extreme heat. Do not weld on the frame near it. Do not dispose of the damper subassembly yourself. Take it to a Yamaha dealer where it can be deactivated and disposed of properly.

Removal/Installation

Refer to **Figure 221**.

1. Place a milk crate or wood block(s) under the frame to lift the rear wheel off the ground at least 10-12 inches.

2. Remove the side panels and seat.

3. Remove the fuel tank as described in Chapter Six of the main book.

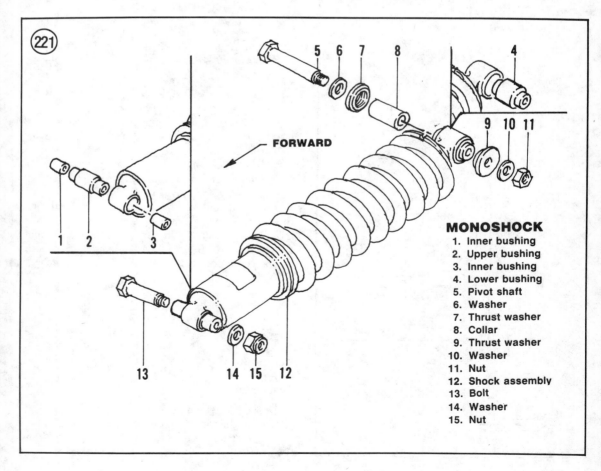

FORWARD

MONOSHOCK
1. Inner bushing
2. Upper bushing
3. Inner bushing
4. Lower bushing
5. Pivot shaft
6. Washer
7. Thrust washer
8. Collar
9. Thrust washer
10. Washer
11. Nut
12. Shock assembly
13. Bolt
14. Washer
15. Nut

4. Remove the lower monoshock bolt at the swing arm and allow the swing arm to pivot down. See **Figure 216**.
5. Remove the top shock mount bolt (**Figure 222**).
6. Carefully withdraw the monoshock assembly through the rear of the frame and over the rear wheel.
7. Install by reversing these removal steps, noting the following.

8. Lubricate the following components with a lithium base grease before installation:
   a. Upper bolt.
   b. Lower pivot bolt and spacers.
   c. Oil seal lips.
9. Tighten the upper and lower monoshock mounting bolts to the specifications in **Table 17**.

Inspection

Refer to **Figure 221** for this procedure.
1. Remove the monoshock as described in this supplement.
2. Inspect the upper and lower mounting bushings. Have a Yamaha dealer replace them if necessary.
3. Check the housing for leakage and make sure the damper rod is straight. Replace the shock absorber if necessary.

> *WARNING*
> *The monoshock unit contains highly compressed nitrogen gas. Do not tamper with or attempt to open the damper/cylinder assembly. Do not place it near an open flame or other extreme heat. Do not dispose of the damper subassembly yourself. Take it to a Yamaha dealer where it can be deactivated and disposed of properly.*

Tables are on the following page.

12

Table 16 REAR SUSPENSION SPECIFICATIONS

Shock absorber travel	2.874 in. (73 mm)
Shock absorber spring	
Free length	9.390 in. (238.5 mm)
Installed length	
Standard	8.878 in. (225.5 mm)
Minimum	8.41 in. (213.5 mm)
Maximum	9.23 in. (234.5 mm)

Table 17 REAR SUSPENSION TIGHTENING TORQUES

Item	ft.-lb.	N·m
Rear axle nut	75	105
Swing arm pivot shaft	61	85
Rear shock absorber and relay arm	19	27

CHAPTER TEN

BRAKES

Brake specifications that differ from 1983 are listed in **Table 18**.

Table 18 BRAKE SPECIFICATIONS

Item	Standard	Wear limit
Front/rear drum inside diameter	5.12 in. (130 mm)	5.16 in. (131 mm)
Brake lining thickness (front and rear)	—	0.08 in. (2 mm)

INDEX

13

NOTES

NOTES